FIFTH EDITION

The Humanistic Tradition

Book 4

Faith, Reason, and Power
in the Early Modern World

FIFTH EDITION

The Humanistic Tradition

Book 4

Faith, Reason, and Power
in the Early Modern World

Gloria K. Fiero

Boston   Burr Ridge, IL   Dubuque, IA   Madison, WI   New York
San Francisco   St. Louis   Bangkok   Bogotá   Caracas   Kuala Lumpur
Lisbon   London   Madrid   Mexico City   Milan   Montreal   New Delhi
Santiago   Seoul   Singapore   Sydney   Taipei   Toronto

Higher Education

THE HUMANISTIC TRADITION, BOOK 4
FAITH, REASON, AND POWER IN THE EARLY MODERN WORLD

Published by McGraw-Hill, a business unit of The McGraw-Hill Companies, Inc.
1221 Avenue of the Americas, New York, NY, 10020.

This book is printed on acid-free paper.

1 2 3 4 5 6 7 8 9 0 DOW/DOW 0 9 8 7 6 5

Library of Congress Cataloging-in-Publication Data

Fiero, Gloria K.
    The humanistic tradition / Gloria K. Fiero.– 5th ed.
        p. cm.
    Includes bibliographical references and indexes.
    ISBN 0-07-291007-0 – ISBN 0-07-291009-7
    1. Civlization, Western–History–Textbooks. 2. Humanism–History–Textbooks. I.
Title.

CB245.F47 2006
909'.09821–dc22

2005052239

ISBN 0-07-291010-0

Permissions Acknowledgments appear on page 169,
and on this page by reference.

Publisher: *Lyn Uhl*
Director of Development: *Lisa Pinto*
Marketing manager: *Zina Craft*
Media technology producer: *Shannon Gattens*
Editorial Assistant: *Elizabeth Sigal*
Managing Editor: *Jean Dal Porto*
Production supervisor: *Randy Hurst*
Typeface: *10/12 Goudy*
Printer: *RR Donnelley, Willard*

http://www.mhhe.com

This book was designed and produced by
Laurence King Publishing Ltd., London
www.laurenceking.co.uk

Commissioning Editor: *Melanie White*
Picture researcher: *Fiona Kinnear*
Designer: *Ian Hunt*

Front cover
Main image: Jules Hardouin-Mansart and
Charles Le Brun, Galerie des Glaces (Hall of
Mirrors), Versailles, ca. 1680. Length 240 ft.
Musée de Versailles. © Paul M. R. Maeyaert,
El Tossal, Spain.

Inset: Taj Mahal, Agra, India, 1623–1643.
AKG Images, London/Jean-Louis Nou.

Frontispiece: Antoine Watteau, *Departure
from the Island of Cythera,* 1717. Oil on
canvas, 4 ft. 3 in. x 6 ft. 4 in. Louvre, Paris.
© Gérard Blot.

Series Contents

Book 4 Contents

26 Eighteenth-Century Art, Music, and Society   139

MAPS

MUSIC LISTENING SELECTIONS

CD Two Selections 1 to 11

Preface

"It's the most curious thing I ever saw in all my life!" exclaimed Lewis Carroll's Alice in Wonderland, as she watched the Cheshire Cat slowly disappear, leaving only the outline of a broad smile. "I've often seen a cat without a grin, but a grin without a cat!" A student who encounters an ancient Greek epic, a Yoruba mask, or a Mozart opera—lacking any context for these works—might be equally baffled. It may be helpful, therefore, to begin by explaining how the artifacts (the "grin") of the humanistic tradition relate to the larger and more elusive phenomenon (the "cat") of human culture.

The Humanistic Tradition and the Humanities

In its broadest sense, the term *humanistic tradition* refers to humankind's cultural legacy—the sum total of the significant ideas and achievements handed down from generation to generation. This tradition is the product of responses to conditions that have confronted all people throughout history. Since the beginnings of life on earth, human beings have tried to ensure their own survival by achieving harmony with nature. They have attempted to come to terms with the inevitable realities of disease and death. They have endeavored to establish ways of living collectively and communally. And they have persisted in the desire to understand themselves and their place in the universe. In response to these ever-present and universal challenges—*survival*, *communality*, and *self-knowledge*—human beings have created and transmitted the tools of science and technology, social and cultural institutions, religious and philosophic systems, and various forms of personal expression, the sum total of which we call *culture*.

Even the most ambitious survey cannot assess all manifestations of the humanistic tradition. This book therefore focuses on the creative legacy referred to collectively as *the humanities*: literature, philosophy, history (in its literary dimension), architecture, the visual arts (including photography and film), music, and dance. Selected examples from each of these disciplines constitute our *primary sources*. Primary sources (that is, works original to the age that produced them) provide first-hand evidence of human inventiveness and ingenuity. The primary sources in this text have been chosen on the basis of their authority, their beauty, and their enduring value. They are, simply stated, the great works of their time and, in some cases, of all time. Universal in their appeal, they have been transmitted from generation to generation.

Such works are, as well, the landmark examples of a specific time and place: they offer insight into the ideas and values of the society in which they were produced. *The Humanistic Tradition* joins "the grin" to "the cat" by examining them within their political, economic, and social contexts.

The humanities are the legacy of a given culture's values, ambitions, and beliefs. Poetry, painting, philosophy, and music are not, generally speaking, products of unstructured leisure or indulgent individuality; rather, they are tangible expressions of the human quest for the good (one might even say the "complete") life. Throughout history, these forms of expression have served the domains of the sacred, the ceremonial, and the communal. And even in the early days of the twenty-first century, as many time-honored traditions come under assault, the arts retain their power to awaken our imagination in the quest for survival, communality, and self-knowledge.

The Scope of the Humanistic Tradition

The humanistic tradition is not the exclusive achievement of any one geographic region, race, or class. For that reason, this text assumes a global and multicultural rather than exclusively Western perspective. At the same time, Western contributions are emphasized, first, because the audience for these books is predominantly Western, but also because in recent centuries the West has exercised a dominant influence on the course and character of global history. Since, the humanistic tradition belongs to all of humankind, the best way to understand the Western contribution to that tradition is to examine it in the arena of world culture.

As a survey, *The Humanistic Tradition* cannot provide an exhaustive analysis of our creative legacy. The critical reader will discover many gaps. Some aspects of culture that receive extended examination in traditional Western humanities surveys have been pared down to make room for the too often neglected contributions of Islam, Africa, and Asia. This book is necessarily selective—it omits many major figures and treats others only briefly. Primary sources are arranged, for the most part, chronologically, but they are presented as manifestations of the informing ideas of the age in which they were produced. The intent is to examine the evidence of the humanistic tradition thematically and topically, rather than to compile a series of mini-histories of the individual arts.

Studying the Humanistic Tradition

To study the creative record is to engage in a dialogue with the past, one that brings us face to face with the values of our ancestors, and, ultimately, with our own. This dialogue is (or should be) a source of personal revelation and delight; like Alice in Wonderland, our strange, new encounters will be enriched according to the degree of curiosity and patience we bring to them. Just as lasting friendships with special people are cultivated by extended familiarity, so our appreciation of a painting, a play, or a symphony depends on close attention and repeated contact. There are no shortcuts to the study of the humanistic tradition, but there are some techniques that may be helpful. It is useful, for instance, to approach each primary source from the triple perspective of its text, its context, and its subtext.

TEXT

The *text* of any primary source refers to its *medium* (that is, what it is made of), its *form* (its outward shape), and its *content* (the subject it describes).

LITERATURE Whether intended to be spoken or lead, literature depends on the medium of words—the American poet Robert Frost once defined literature as "performance in words." Literary form varies according to the manner in which words are arranged. So poetry, which shares with music and dance rhythmic organization, may be distinguished from prose, which normally lacks regular rhythmic pattern. The main purpose of prose is to convey information, to narrate, and to describe; poetry, by its freedom from conventional patterns of grammar, provides unique opportunities for the expression of intense emotions. Philosophy (the search for truth through reasoned analysis) and history (the record of the past) make use of prose to analyze and communicate ideas and information. In literature, as in most kinds of expression, content and form are usually interrelated. The subject matter or the form of a literary work determines its *genre*. For instance, a long narrative poem recounting the adventures of a hero constitutes an *epic*, while a formal, dignified speech in praise of a person or thing constitutes a *eulogy*.

THE VISUAL ARTS The *visual arts*—painting, sculpture, architecture, and photography—employ a wide variety of media, such as wood, clay, colored pigments, marble, granite, steel, and (more recently) plastic, neon, film, and computers. The form or outward shape of a work of art depends on the manner in which the artist manipulates the formal elements of color, line, texture, and space. Unlike words, these formal elements lack denotative meaning. The artist may manipulate form to describe and interpret the visible world (as in such genres as portraiture and landscape painting); to generate fantastic and imaginative kinds of imagery; or to create imagery that is nonrepresentational—without identifiable subject matter. In general, however, the visual arts are spatial; that is, they operate and are apprehended in space.

MUSIC AND DANCE The medium of *music* is sound. Like literature, music is durational: it unfolds over the period of time in which it occurs. The formal elements of music are melody, rhythm, harmony, and tone color—elements that also characterize the oral life of literature. As with the visual arts, the formal elements of music are without symbolic content: literature, painting, and sculpture may imitate or describe nature, but music is almost always nonrepresentational—it rarely has meaning beyond the sound itself. For that reason, music is the most difficult of the arts to describe in words. It is also (in the view of some) the most affective of the arts. Dance, the artform that makes the human body itself a medium of expression, resembles music in that it is temporal and performance-oriented. Like music, dance exploits rhythm as a formal tool, but, like painting and sculpture, it unfolds in space as well as time.

In analyzing the text of a work of literature, art, or music, we ask how its formal elements contribute to its meaning and affective power. We examine the ways in which the artist manipulates medium and form to achieve a characteristic manner of execution and expression that we call *style*. And we try to determine the extent to which a style reflects the personal vision of the artist and the spirit of his or her time and place. Comparing the styles of various artworks from a single era, we may discover that they share certain defining features and characteristics. Similarities (both formal and stylistic) between, for instance, golden age Greek temples and Greek tragedies, between Chinese lyric poems and landscape paintings, and between postmodern fiction and pop sculpture, prompt us to seek the unifying moral and aesthetic values of the cultures in which they were produced.

CONTEXT

We use the word *context* to describe the historical and cultural environment. To determine the context, we ask: in what time and place did the artifact originate? How did it function within the society in which it was created? Was the purpose of the piece decorative, didactic, magical, propagandistic? Did it serve the religious or political needs of the community? Sometimes our answers to these questions are mere guesses. Nevertheless, understanding the function of an artifact often serves to clarify the nature of its form (and vice versa). For instance, much of the literature produced prior to the fifteenth century was spoken or sung rather than read; for that reason, such literature tends to feature repetition and rhyme, devices that facilitate memorization. We can assume that literary works embellished with frequent repetitions, such as the *Epic of Gilgamesh* and the Hebrew Bible, were products of an oral tradition. Determining the original function of an artwork also permits us to assess its significance in its own time and place: the paintings on the walls of Paleolithic caves, which are among the most compelling animal illustrations in the history of world art, are not "artworks" in the modern sense of the term but, rather, magical signs that accompanied hunting rituals, the performance of which was essential to the survival of the community. Understanding the relationship between text and context is one of the principal concerns of any inquiry into the humanistic tradition.

SUBTEXT

The *subtext* of the literary or artistic object refers to its secondary and implied meanings. The subtext embraces the emotional or intellectual messages embedded in, or implied by, a work of art. The epic poems of the ancient Greeks, for instance, which glorify prowess and physical courage in battle, suggest that such virtues are exclusively male. The state portraits of the seventeenth-century French ruler Louis XIV carry the subtext of unassailable and absolute power. In our own century, Andy Warhol's serial adaptations of soup cans and Coca-Cola bottles offer wry commentary on the supermarket mentality of postmodern American culture. Identifying the implicit message of an artwork helps us to determine the values and customs of the age in which it was produced and to assess those values against others.

Beyond *The Humanistic Tradition*

This book offers only small, enticing samples from an enormous cultural buffet. To dine more fully, students are encouraged to go beyond the sampling presented at this table; and for the most sumptuous feasting, nothing can substitute for first-hand experience. Students, therefore, should make every effort to supplement this book with visits to art museums and galleries, concert halls, theaters, and libraries. *The Humanistic Tradition* is designed for students who may or may not be able to read music, but who surely are able to cultivate an appreciation of music in performance. The music logos ♪ that appear in the margins of the text refer to the Music Listening Selections found on two accompanying compact discs, available from the publishers. Lists of suggestions for further reading are included at the end of each book, while a selected general bibliography of electronic humanities resources appears in the Online Learning Center at http://www.mhhe.com/fierotht5.

The Fifth Edition

In the fifth edition of *The Humanistic Tradition*, Study Questions follow each primary source readings; thse are desinged to provoke thought and discussion. Chapter 37 has been reorganized and expanded to explore a number of important global themes, such as ethnic identity and ecology. There is a reading selection from the Book of Psalms, a new modern translation of the *Quran*, and excerpts from the writings of Annie Dillard, E.O Wilson, Sandra Cisneros, Mahmoud Darwish, and Yehuda Amichai. Content has been expanded to a number of topics, including the life of Muhammad (Chapter 10), the Columbian Exchange (Chapter 18), artists' optical aids (Chapters 17 and 23), Islam since 1500 (Chapters 21, 35, 37), the training of female artists (Chapters 20 and 23, and the Middle Passage (Chapter 25). Among the new color illustrations for the fifth edition are Zoser's Pyramid, Nok sculpture, London's new Globe Theater, Bernini's *David*, Steen's *Drawing Lesson*, Hick's *Peaceable Kingdom*, Monet's Japanese Bridge, and Beardon's Empress of the Blues. This edition also updates the contemporary scene to include significant developments in architecture, photography, and film (Chapter 38). Two new Sony Music Listening CDs illustrate the muscial works discussed in the text, and new Music Listening Guides provide helpful analyses of these selections. Revised and expanded Timelines and Glossaries, along with Science and Technology boxes, locator maps, and pedagogical resources provide useful study aids (see the "Guided Tour" on page xii). Updated suggestions for additional reading appear at the end of each book, rather than by chapter.

A Note to Instructors

The key to successful classroom use of *The Humanistic Tradition* is *selectivity*. Although students may be assigned to read whole chapters that focus on a topic or theme, as well as complete works that supplement the abridged readings, the classroom should be the stage for a selective treatment of a single example or a set of examples. The organization of this textbook is designed to emphasize themes that cut across geographic boundaries—themes whose universal significance prompts students to evaluate and compare rather than simply memorize and repeat lists of names and places. To assist readers in achieving global cultural literacy, every effort has been made to resist isolating (or "ghettoizing") individual cultures and to avoid the inevitable biases we bring to our evaluation of relatively unfamiliar cultures.

Key Map Indicating Areas Shown as White Highlights on the Locator Maps

Acknowledgments

Writing *The Humanistic Tradition* has been an exercise in humility. Without the assistance of learned friends and colleagues, assembling a book of this breadth would have been an impossible task. James H. Dormon read all parts of the manuscript and made extensive and substantive editorial suggestions; as his colleague, best friend, and wife, I am most deeply indebted to him.

The following colleagues generously shared their knowledge and training in matters of content: in the sciences, Barbara J. Reeves (Virginia Tech); literature, Robert W. Butler, Darrell Bourque (University of Louisiana, Lafayette), and John Lowe (Louisiana State University); in the visual arts, Roy Barineau (Tallahassee Community College); music, Richard Harrison, Stephen Husarik (University of Arkansas), and Jack Jacobs; film, Joseph Warfield (New York University).

In the preparation of the fifth edition, I have also benefited from the suggestions and comments generously offered by Linda A. Austin (Glendale Community College), Edward Bonahue (Santa Fe Community College), Diane Boze (Northeastern State University), Peggy Brown (Collin County Community College), Michael Coste (Front Range Community College), Harry Coverston (University of Central Florida), Jaymes Dudding (Albuquerque Technical Vocational Institute), Scott Earle (Tacoma Community College), Joshua Fausty (New Jersey City University), Luis Samuel Gonzalez (Sinclair Community College), Jeanne McGlinn (University of North Carolina—Asheville), Khadijah O. Miller (Norfolk State University), Yvonne Milspaw (Harrisburg Area Community College), Thomas R. Moore (Maine Maritime Academy), Rachel M. Rumberger (Valencia Community College), Jerome P. Soneson (University of Northern Iowa), Sonia Sorrell (Pepperdine University), Nancy A. Taylor (California State University—Northridge), Mary Tripp (University of Central Florida), and Naomi Yavneh (University of South Florida).

The burden of preparing the fifth edition has been lightened by the assistance of Kristen N. Mellit (McGraw-Hill) and the editors at Laurence King Publishing. I am also indebted to Lyn Uhl, Lisa Pinto, and Elizabeth Sigal (McGraw-Hill) for their support and encouragement, and to Fiona Kinnear for discerning photographic research.

A Guided Tour of *The Humanistic Tradition*, FIFTH EDITION

Illustrated part-opening **TIMELINES** provide a chronological overview of major historical events, as well as key works of literature, art, and music featured in each part.

Science and Technology

2650 B.C.E.	Pharaoh Khufu (or Cheops) orders construction of the Great Pyramid of Gizeh¹
1500 B.C.E.	Egyptians employ a simple form of the sundial
1450 B.C.E.	the water clock is devised in Egypt
1400 B.C.E.	glass in produced in Egypt and Mesopotamia

¹All dates in this chapter are approximate

SCIENCE AND TECHNOLOGY BOXES offer a chronology of key scientific and technological developments.

READING 4.7 From Donne's *Meditation 17* (1623)

All mankind is of one author, and is one volume; when one man   1
dies, one chapter is not torn out of the book, but translated into
a better language; and every chapter must be so translated. God
employs several translators; some pieces are translated by age,
some by sickness, some by war, some by justice; but God's hand   5
is in every translation, and his hand shall bind up all our
scattered leaves again for that library where every book shall lie
open to one another. As therefore the bell that rings to a
sermon calls not upon the preacher only but upon the
congregation to come, so this bell calls us all. . . . No man is an   10
island entire of itself; every man is a piece of the continent, a
part of the main. If a clod be washed away by the sea, Europe is
the less, as well as if a promontory were, as well as if a manor
of thy friend's or of thine own were. Any man's death diminishes
me, because I am involved in mankind, and therefore never send   15
to know for whom the bell tolls; it tolls for thee.

 Q What three metaphors are invoked in *Meditation 17*?

PRIMARY SOURCE READINGS from a variety of genres provide a wealth of important and influential writings. New to the fifth edition, study questions designed to provoke thought and discussion follow each primary source reading.

GLOSSARY

asceticism strict self-denial and self-discipline

bodhisattva (Sanskrit, "one whose essence is enlightenment") a being who has postponed his or her own entry into *nirvana* in order to assist others in reaching that goal; worshiped as a deity in Mahayana Buddhism

Messiah Anointed One, or Savior; in Greek, *Christos*

rabbi a teacher and master trained in the Jewish law

sutra (Sanskrit, "thread") an instructional chapter or discourse in any of the sacred books of Buddhism

Terms marked in bold are defined in a **GLOSSARY** at the end of each chapter.

 MUSICAL LOGOS in the margins refer to the Music Listening Selections found on accompanying compact disks, available separately from the publisher.

LOCATOR MAPS give readers their geographical bearings, alerting them to where events discussed in the section to follow took place.

EXPERIMENTAL FILM

Léger produced one of the earliest and most influential abstract films in the history of motion pictures. Developed in collaboration with the American journalist Dudley Murphy, *Ballet mécanique* (Mechanical Ballet, 1923–1924) puts into motion a series of abstract shapes and mundane objects (such as bottles and kitchen utensils), which, interspersed with human elements, convey a playful but dehumanized sense of everyday experience. The rhythms and juxtapositions of the images suggest—without any narrative—the notion of modern life as mechanized, routine, standardized, and impersonal. The repeated image of a laundry woman, for instance, alternating with that of a rotating machine part, plays on the associative qualities of visual motifs in ways that would influence film-makers for decades.

FILM ESSAYS explore various aspects of this important, relatively new medium.

Supplements for the Instructor and the Student

A number of useful supplements are available to instructors and students using *The Humanistic Tradition*. Please contact your sales representative to obtain these resources, or to ask for further details.

ONLINE LEARNING CENTER A complete set of web-based resources for *The Humanistic Tradition* can be found at www.mhhe.com/fierotht5.com. Materials for students include an audio pronunciation guide, self-tests, interactive maps, links to relevant images and complete primary source readings. Instructors will benefit from discussion and lecture suggestions, chapter summaries, music listening guides, and other resources. All resources from the Online Learning Center are also available in cartridges for WebCT and Blackboard course management systems.

INSTRUCTOR'S RESOURCE CD-ROM The Instructor's Resource CD-ROM (IRCD) is designed to assist instructors as they plan and prepare for classes. Chapter summaries emphasize key themes and topics that give focus to the primary source readings. Music listening guides provide instructors with ideas for integrating selections on the Music Listening CDs into their courses. Study questions for each chapter can be used for student discussion or written assignments. A list of suggested videos, DVDs, and recordings is also included. The CD-ROM also offers a Test Bank containing a comprehensive bank of multiple-choice questions for use in constructing student exams.

EZ TEST McGraw-Hill's EZ Test, also included on the IRCD, is a flexible and easy-to-use electronic testing program that allows instructors to create book-specific tests, drawing from a ready-made database and/or designing their own questions. Tests can be exported for use with course management systems such as WebCT, BlackBoard or PageOut. The program is available for use with Windows and Macintosh.

CORE CONCEPTS A groundbreaking *Core Concepts in the Humanities* DVD-ROM may be packaged free with every new copy of *The Humanistic Tradition* (ISBN 0073136433). The DVD-ROM augments students' understanding of the humanities through multimedia presentations on visual art, dance, theater, film, literature, and music. With over eighty interactive exercises, timelines, and extensive video clips, the DVD-ROM allows students to explore these disciplines in an exciting way. Study materials such as outlines,

summaries, and self-correcting quizzes are provided for every chapter of the text. Contact your McGraw-Hill representative at www.mhhe.com/rep for information about packaging this program with the textbook.

MUSIC LISTENING COMPACT DISCS Two audio compact discs have been designed exclusively for use with *The Humanistic Tradition*. CD One corresponds to the music listening selections discussed in Books 1-3 (Volume I), and CD Two contains the music in Books 4-6 (Volume II). Instructors may obtain copies of the recordings for classroom use, and the CDs are also available for individual purchase by students. They can be packaged with any or all of the six books or two-volume versions of the text. Consult your local sales representative for details.

SLIDE SETS A set of book-specific slides is available to qualified adopters of *The Humanistic Tradition*. These slides have been especially selected to include many of the key images in the books. Additional slides are available for purchase directly from Universal Color Slides. For further information, consult our web site at www.mhhe.com/fierotht5.com.

IMAGE VAULT Selected images from *The Humanistic Tradition*'s illustration program are available to adopting instructors in digital format in *The Image Vault*, McGraw-Hill's new web-based program. Instructors can incorporate images from *The Image Vault* in digital presentations that can be used in class offline, burned to CD-ROM, or embedded in course Web pages. See www.mhhe.com/theimage-vault for more details.

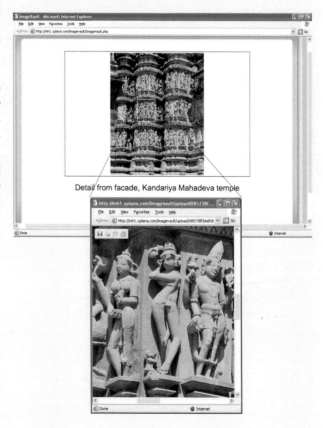

Detail from facade, Kandariya Mahadeva temple

Summary of the Renaissance and the Reformation

The following paragraphs provide an overview of the Renaissance and Reformation, the two movements that ushered in the modern era in the West. This summary of fifteenth- and sixteenth-century culture (dealt with in detail in Book 3) offers some background to the materials contained in Books 4, 5, and 6, which deal with the modern era in a global context.

Classical Humanism

The effort to recover, edit, and study ancient Greek and Latin manuscripts, a movement known as classical humanism, first occurred in fourteenth-century Italy, where it marked the beginnings of the Renaissance. This revival of Greco-Roman culture was to spread throughout Western Europe over the following three hundred years. Petrarch, known as the father of humanism, provided the model for Renaissance scholarship and education. He promoted the study of the classic Greek and Latin writers, especially Cicero, encouraged textual criticism, and wrote introspective and passionate sonnets that were revered and imitated for centuries to come.

The city of Florence was the unrivaled center of classical humanism in the first 150 years of the Renaissance. A thriving commercial and financial center dominated by a well-to-do middle class, Florence found political and cultural leadership in such wealthy and sophisticated families as the Medici. Classical humanism helped to cultivate a sense of civic pride, a new respect for oral and written eloquence, and a set of personal values that sustained the ambitions of the rising merchant class.

Fifteenth-century humanists carried on Petrarch's quest to recover the classical past. Ficino translated the entire body of Plato's writings, while Pico's investigations in Hebrew and Arabic led him to believe that the world's great minds shared a single, universal truth. Pico's *Oration on the Dignity of Man* proclaimed the centrality of humankind and defended the unlimited freedom of the individual within the universal scheme.

Renaissance humanists cultivated the idea of the good life. Following Alberti's maxim, "A man can do anything he wants," they applied the moral precepts of the classical past to such contemporary pursuits as diplomacy, politics, and the arts. While Petrarch and his peers were concerned primarily with the recovery of classical manuscripts and the production of critical editions, Alberti, Castiglione, and Machiavelli eagerly infused scholarship with action. Allying their scrutiny of the past with an empirical study of the present, they fostered a heroic ideal of the individual that surpassed all classical models. For Alberti, wealth and authority proceeded from the exercise of *virtù*;

for Castiglione, the superior breed of human being was identical with *l'uomo universale*, the well-rounded person; for Machiavelli, only a ruthless master of power politics could ensure the survival of the state. Alberti, Castiglione, and Machiavelli were representative of the larger group of Renaissance humanists who asserted the human capacity for self-knowledge and exalted the role of the individual in the secular world. Their views shaped the modern character of the humanistic tradition in the European West.

Renaissance Artists

Most significant about the artists of the Renaissance is that they were disciples of nature: they brought a scientific curiosity to the study of the natural world and untiringly investigated its operations. Such Early Renaissance artists as Donatello, Pollaiuolo, Masaccio, and Brunelleschi studied the mechanics of the human body, the effects of light on material substances, and the physical appearance of objects in three-dimensional space. At the same time, Renaissance artists were masters of invention: they perfected the technique of oil painting, formulated the laws of perspective, and applied the principles of classical art to the representation of Christian and contemporary subjects. Patronized by a wealthy European middle class, they revived such this-worldly genres as portraiture and gave new attention to the nude body as an object of natural beauty.

The art of the High Renaissance marks the culmination of a hundred-year effort to wed the techniques of naturalistic representation to classical ideals of proportion and order. Leonardo da Vinci, the quintessential artist–scientist, tried to reconcile empirical experience with abstract principles of design. The compositions of Raphael, with their monumental scale and unity of design, became standards by which Western paintings would be judged for centuries. The multitalented Michelangelo brought a heroic idealism to the treatment of traditional Christian and classical themes. In Venice, Titian's painterly handling of the reclining female nude represented a new and more sensuous naturalism. In architecture, the centrally planned buildings of Bramante and Palladio fulfilled the quest of such Early Renaissance architects as Brunelleschi and Alberti for an architecture of harmony, balance, and clarity.

The Renaissance produced an equally splendid flowering in music, especially among Franco-Flemish composers. Secular compositions began to outnumber religious ones. The techniques of imitation and word painting infused both religious and secular music with homogeneity and increased expressiveness. Printed sheet music helped to popularize the madrigal and other secular, vernacular song forms. Instrumental music and dance now emerged as independent genres. Like their classical predecessors, Renaissance artists placed human concerns and feelings at the center of a harmonious universe. Such optimism, combined with intellectual curiosity and increasing worldliness, fueled the early modern era in the West.

Shattering the Old Order: Protest and Reform

The sixteenth century was a time of rapid change marked by growing secularism, advancing technology, and European overseas expansion. It was also an age of profound religious and social upheaval. Northern humanists led by Erasmus of Rotterdam made critical studies of early Christian literature and urged a return to the teachings of Jesus and the early church fathers. Demands for church reform went hand in hand with the revival of early Christian writings to culminate in the Protestant Reformation.

Aided by Gutenberg's printing press, Martin Luther contested the authority of the Church of Rome. He held that Scripture was the sole basis for religious interpretation and emphasized the idea of salvation through faith in God's grace rather than through good works. As Lutheranism and other Protestant sects proliferated throughout Europe, the unity of medieval Christendom was shattered.

The music and the art of the Northern Renaissance reflect the mood of religious reform. In music, the Lutheran chorale became the vehicle of Protestant piety. In art, the increasing demand for illustrated devotional literature and private devotional art stimulated the production of woodcuts and metal engravings. The works of Dürer and Grünewald exhibit the Northern Renaissance passion for realistic detail and graphic expression, while the fantastic imagery of Hieronymus Bosch suggests a pessimistic and typically Northern concern with sin and death. Bosch's preoccupation with the palpable forces of evil found its counterpart in the witch-hunts of the sixteenth century. In painting, too, such secular subjects as portraiture, landscapes, and scenes of everyday life mirrored the tastes of a growing middle-class audience for an unidealized record of the visual world.

Northern Renaissance writers took a generally skeptical and pessimistic view of human nature. Erasmus, More, and Rabelais lampooned individual and societal failings and described the ruling influence of folly in all aspects of human conduct. In France, Montaigne devised the essay as an intimate form of rational reflection. In Spain, Cervantes' novel, *Don Quijote*, wittily attacked outmoded feudal values and ideals. The most powerful form of literary expression to evolve in the late sixteenth century, however, was secular drama. In the hands of William Shakespeare, drama became the ultimate expression of the sixteenth-century quest to examine the human personality in its secular and spiritual dimensions. Shakespeare's tragedies (as opposed, for instance, to Montaigne's essays) reveal the human condition through overt action, rather than through private reflection.

By the end of the sixteenth century, national loyalties, religious fanaticism, and commercial rivalries for control of trade with Africa, Asia, and the Americas had splintered the European community. These conditions rendered ever more complex the society of the West. And yet, on the threshold of modernity, the challenges to the human condition—economic survival, communality, self-knowledge, and the inevitability of death—were no less pressing than they had been two thousand years earlier. If the technology of the sixteenth century offered greater control over nature than ever before, it also provided more devastating weapons of war and mass destruction. In the centuries to come, the humanistic tradition would be shaped and reshaped by changing historical circumstances and the creative imagination of indomitable humankind.

PART 1

The Age of the Baroque

The period between approximately 1600 and 1800 was an age of contradictions. In Western Europe, deeply felt, even mystical, religious sentiment vied with the rise of science and rational methods of scientific investigation. Newly developed theories of constitutional government contended with firmly entrenched claims to divine right among "absolute" rulers—monarchs who recognized no legal limitations to their authority. The rising wealth of a small segment of the population failed to offset widespread poverty and old aristocratic privilege.

The early modern era witnessed the beginnings of the European state system and the establishment of the fundamental political, economic, and cultural norms of European and, by extension, American life. Rival religious claims following the Protestant Reformation complicated the scramble for land and power among European states. The first half of the seventeenth century witnessed the Thirty Years' War and other devastating conflicts between Catholics and Protestants. In 1648, however, by the terms of the Treaty of Westphalia, which ended the Thirty Years' War, the principle of national sovereignty was firmly established in the West: by that principle, each European state would exercise independent and supreme authority over its own territories and inhabitants.

In the economic arena, the prosperity of the sixteenth century was followed by marked decline in the seventeenth. Nevertheless, after 1660, commercial capitalism and the production of manufactured goods flourished in the West, where economic growth was tied to a pattern of global commerce. Asia, Africa, and the Americas—lucrative markets for European goods—were frontiers for European traders. And as global perceptions widened, Europeans realized that the "Old World" would never again live in isolation.

In Asia, as well, the seventeenth and eighteenth centuries brought major changes: Muslim rulers united the primarily Hindu peoples of India and proceeded to establish the glorious Mogul dynasty. The Ming emperors of China, who governed an empire larger than any other in the world, fell to Mongol (Manchu) tribes in the early seventeenth century. These foreign rulers secured internal stability through rigid control of Chinese culture.

In the West, the years between 1600 and 1750 were closely associated with a style known as "the baroque." Characterized by dramatic expression, theatrical spectacle, and spatial grandeur, the baroque became the hallmark of an age of exuberant expansion. The style also reflected the new, dynamic view of the universe as set forth by proponents of the Scientific Revolution. The baroque encompassed various phases: in Italy, it mirrored the intensely religious mood of the Catholic Reformation; in Northern Europe, it reflected the intimate spirit of Protestant devotionalism as well as the reliance on sensory experience associated with the New Science; and among authoritarian regimes throughout Europe and Asia, it worked to glorify secular power and wealth.

The age of the baroque was fueled by the human ambition to master nature on a colossal scale. This ambition—inspired perhaps by a more detached and objective view of the self in relation to the world—is as evident in Galileo's efforts to understand and explain the operations of nature as it is in Louis XIV's attempts to exert unlimited power over vast territories and peoples. A similar kind of energy is apparent in the complexities of a Bach fugue, the cosmic scope of Milton's *Paradise Lost*, the spectacle of early Italian opera, the panoramic sweep of Dutch landscape paintings, the splendor of the royal palaces at Versailles, Delhi, and Beijing, and the efforts of Ming and Manchu emperors to collect and copy all of China's literary classics. Under King Louis XIV of France, as among the Safavid Persians, the Moguls of India, the Ming and Manchu emperors of China, and the Tokugawa shoguns in Japan, there emerged an aristocratic style that aimed to glorify the majesty and authority of the ruler.

(opposite) **ARTEMISIA GENTILESCHI**, detail of *Judith Slaying Holofernes*, ca. 1614–1620. Oil on canvas, 6 ft. 6¼ in. × 5 ft. 4 in. Uffizi Gallery, Florence.

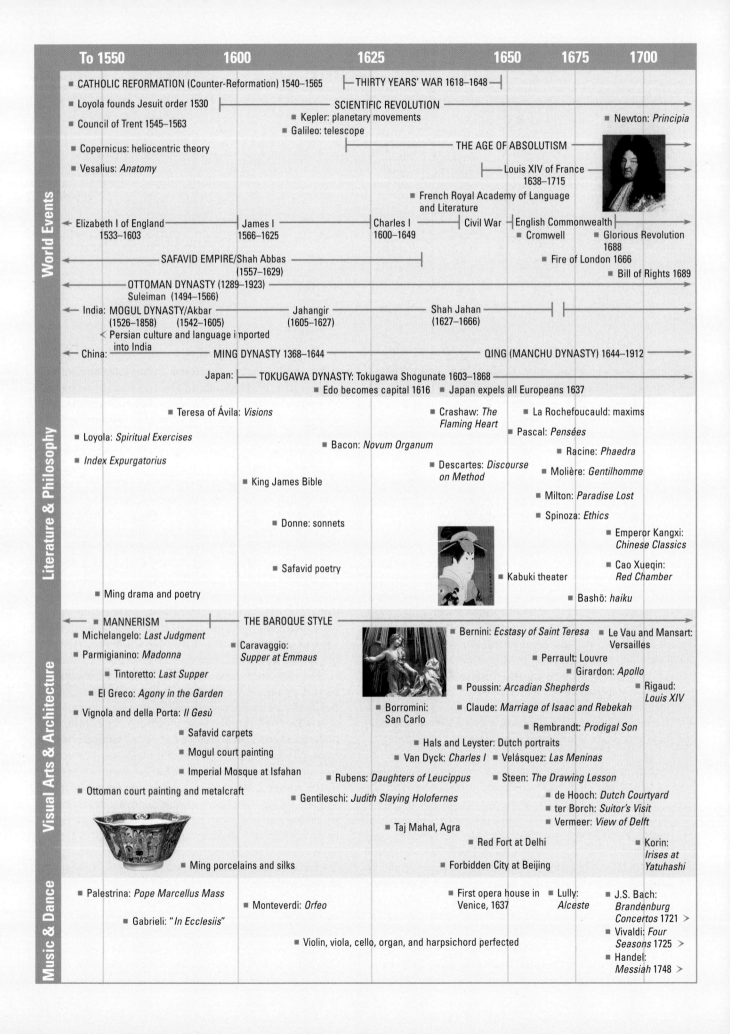

	To 1550	1600	1625	1650	1675	1700

World Events

- CATHOLIC REFORMATION (Counter-Reformation) 1540–1565 ⊢ THIRTY YEARS' WAR 1618–1648 ⊣
- Loyola founds Jesuit order 1530 ⊢ SCIENTIFIC REVOLUTION
  - Kepler: planetary movements
  - Galileo: telescope
  - Newton: *Principia*
- Council of Trent 1545–1563
- Copernicus: heliocentric theory — THE AGE OF ABSOLUTISM →
- Vesalius: *Anatomy*
  - Louis XIV of France 1638–1715
  - French Royal Academy of Language and Literature
- ← Elizabeth I of England 1533–1603 — James I 1566–1625 — Charles I 1600–1649 — Civil War — English Commonwealth
  - Cromwell
  - Glorious Revolution 1688
- ← SAFAVID EMPIRE/Shah Abbas (1557–1629)
  - Fire of London 1666
  - Bill of Rights 1689
- ← OTTOMAN DYNASTY (1289–1923) — Suleiman (1494–1566)
- ← India: MOGUL DYNASTY/Akbar (1526–1858) (1542–1605) — Jahangir (1605–1627) — Shah Jahan (1627–1666)
  - ‹ Persian culture and language imported into India
- ← China: MING DYNASTY 1368–1644 — QING (MANCHU DYNASTY) 1644–1912
- Japan: ⊢ TOKUGAWA DYNASTY: Tokugawa Shogunate 1603–1868 →
  - Edo becomes capital 1616 • Japan expels all Europeans 1637

Literature & Philosophy

- Teresa of Ávila: *Visions*
- Crashaw: *The Flaming Heart*
- La Rochefoucauld: maxims
- Loyola: *Spiritual Exercises*
- Pascal: *Pensées*
- Bacon: *Novum Organum*
- *Index Expurgatorius*
- Racine: *Phaedra*
- Descartes: *Discourse on Method*
- Molière: *Gentilhomme*
- King James Bible
- Milton: *Paradise Lost*
- Spinoza: *Ethics*
- Donne: sonnets
- Emperor Kangxi: *Chinese Classics*
- Cao Xueqin: *Red Chamber*
- Safavid poetry
- Kabuki theater
- Ming drama and poetry
- Bashō: *haiku*

Visual Arts & Architecture

- ← MANNERISM — THE BAROQUE STYLE →
- Michelangelo: *Last Judgment*
- Bernini: *Ecstasy of Saint Teresa*
- Le Vau and Mansart: Versailles
- Parmigianino: *Madonna*
- Caravaggio: *Supper at Emmaus*
- Perrault: Louvre
- Tintoretto: *Last Supper*
- Girardon: *Apollo*
- El Greco: *Agony in the Garden*
- Poussin: *Arcadian Shepherds*
- Rigaud: *Louis XIV*
- Vignola and della Porta: *Il Gesù*
- Borromini: San Carlo
- Claude: *Marriage of Isaac and Rebekah*
- Rembrandt: *Prodigal Son*
- Safavid carpets
- Hals and Leyster: Dutch portraits
- Mogul court painting
- Van Dyck: *Charles I* • Velásquez: *Las Meninas*
- Imperial Mosque at Isfahan
- Rubens: *Daughters of Leucippus*
- Steen: *The Drawing Lesson*
- Ottoman court painting and metalcraft
- Gentileschi: *Judith Slaying Holofernes*
- de Hooch: *Dutch Courtyard*
- ter Borch: *Suitor's Visit*
- Vermeer: *View of Delft*
- Taj Mahal, Agra
- Red Fort at Delhi
- Korin: *Irises at Yatuhashi*
- Ming porcelains and silks
- Forbidden City at Beijing

Music & Dance

- Palestrina: *Pope Marcellus Mass*
- First opera house in Venice, 1637
- Lully: *Alceste*
- J.S. Bach: *Brandenburg Concertos* 1721 ›
- Monteverdi: *Orfeo*
- Gabrieli: "*In Ecclesiis*"
- Vivaldi: *Four Seasons* 1725 ›
- Violin, viola, cello, organ, and harpsichord perfected
- Handel: *Messiah* 1748 ›

CHAPTER 20

The Catholic Reformation and the Baroque Style

"So sweet are the colloquies of love which pass between the soul and God ..."
Saint Teresa of Avila

The Protestant Reformation created a religious upheaval unlike any other in the history of Western Christianity. Luther's criticism of the Roman Catholic Church had encouraged religious devotion free of papal authority and had prepared the way for the rise of other Protestant sects (see chapter 19). The rival religious beliefs that fragmented Western Europe quickly accelerated into armed combat. The Thirty Years' War (1618–1648), which ended with the establishment of Protestantism throughout most of Northern Europe, caused the death of some five million Christians. During the sixteenth century, as Protestant sects began to lure increasing numbers of Christians away from Roman Catholicism, the Church undertook a program of internal reform and reorganization known as the Catholic Reformation, or Counter Reformation. Further, by the 1540s, the Church launched an evangelical campaign to win back to Catholicism those who had strayed to Protestantism. These two interdependent movements gradually introduced a more militant form of Catholicism that encouraged intensely personalized religious expressions. Initiated in Spain, Italy, and Latin America, a vigorous new style—the baroque—became the vehicle for this new, more dynamic, outpouring of religious fervor.

The Catholic Reformation

Confronting Protestant challenge, the Roman Catholic Church pursued a path that ensured its survival in the modern world. Between 1540 and 1565 churchmen undertook papal and monastic reforms that eliminated corruption and restored Catholicism to many parts of Europe. The impetus for renewal came largely from fervent Spanish Catholics, the most notable of whom was Ignatius Loyola (1491–1556). A soldier in the army of King Charles I of Spain (the Holy Roman emperor Charles V; 1500–1558), Loyola brought to Catholicism the same iron will he had exercised on the battlefield. After his right leg was fractured by a French cannonball at the siege of Pamplona, Loyola became a religious teacher and a hermit, traveling lame and barefoot to Jerusalem in an effort to convert Muslims to Christianity. In the 1530s he founded the Society of Jesus, the most important of the many new monastic orders associated with the Catholic Reformation. The Society of Jesus, or Jesuits, followed Loyola in calling for a militant return to fundamental Catholic dogma and the strict enforcement of traditional Church teachings. In addition to the monastic vows of celibacy, poverty, and obedience, the Jesuits took an oath of allegiance to the pope, whom they served as soldiers of Christ.

Under Loyola's leadership, the Jesuit order became the most influential missionary society of early modern times. Rigorously trained, its members acted as preachers, confessors, and teachers—leaders in educational reform and moral discipline. Throughout Europe, members of the newly formed order worked as missionaries to win back those who had strayed from "Mother Church." The Jesuits were fairly successful in stamping out Protestantism in much of France, Southern Germany, and other parts of Europe. But their reach extended further: as pioneers in learning the languages and customs of India, China, and Japan, the Jesuits were the prime intermediaries between Europe and Asia from the sixteenth through the nineteenth century. In the Americas, which became prime targets for Jesuit activity, missionaries mastered Native American tribal languages and proceeded to convert thousands to Roman Catholicism. Their success in Mexico and Central and South America has stamped these parts of the world with a distinctive cultural character.

The Jesuit order was a fascinating amalgam of two elements: mysticism and militant religious zeal. The first emphasized the personal and intuitive experience of God, while the second involved an attitude of unquestioned submission to the Church as the absolute source of truth. These two aspects of Jesuit training—mysticism and militancy—are reflected in Loyola's influential handbook, the *Spiritual Exercises*. In his introductory observations, Loyola explains that the spiritual exercises should do for the soul what such physical exercises as running and walking do for the body. As aids to the development of perfect spiritual discipline, these devotional exercises—each of which should occupy a full hour's time—engage the body in perfecting the soul. For example, in the Fifth Exercise, a meditation on Hell, each of the five senses is summoned to heighten the mystical experience:

> FIRST POINT: This will be to *see* in imagination the vast fires, and the souls enclosed, as it were, in bodies of fire.
> SECOND POINT: To *hear* the wailing, the howling, cries, and blasphemies against Christ our Lord and against His saints.
> THIRD POINT: With the sense of *smell* to perceive the smoke, the sulphur, the filth, and corruption.
> FOURTH POINT: To *taste* the bitterness of tears, sadness, and remorse of conscience.
> FIFTH POINT: With the sense of *touch* to feel the flames which envelop and burn the souls.

Loyola also insists on an unswerving commitment to traditional Church teachings. Among the "rules for thinking with the Church" is Loyola's advice that Christians put aside all judgments of their own and remain obedient to the "holy Mother, the hierarchical Church."

READING 4.1 From Loyola's *Spiritual Exercises* (1548)

The following rules should be observed to foster the true attitude of mind we ought to have in the church militant.

1 We must put aside all judgment of our own, and keep the mind ever ready and prompt to obey in all things the true Spouse of Christ our Lord, our holy Mother, the hierarchical Church.

2 We should praise sacramental confession, the yearly reception of the Most Blessed Sacrament, and praise more highly monthly reception, and still more weekly Communion, provided requisite and proper dispositions are present.

3 We ought to praise the frequent hearing of Mass, the singing of hymns, psalmody, and long prayers whether in the church or outside; likewise, the hours arranged at fixed times for the whole Divine Office, for every kind of prayer, and for the canonical hours.[1]

4 We must praise highly religious life, virginity, and continency; and matrimony ought not be praised as much as any of these.

5 We should praise vows of religion, obedience, poverty, chastity, and vows to perform other works . . . conducive to perfection. . . .

6 We should show our esteem for the relics of the saints by venerating them and praying to the saints. We should praise visits to the Station Churches,[2] pilgrimages, indulgences, jubilees,[3] crusade indults,[4] and the lighting of candles in churches.

7 We must praise the regulations of the Church with regard to fast and abstinence. . . . We should praise works of penance, not only those that are interior but also those that are exterior.

8 We ought to praise not only the building and adornment of churches, but also images and veneration of them according to the subject they represent.

9 Finally, we must praise all the commandments of the Church, and be on the alert to find reasons to defend them, and by no means in order to criticize them. . . .

13 If we wish to proceed securely in all things, we must hold fast to the following principle: What seems to me white, I will believe black if the hierarchical Church so defines. For I must be convinced that in Christ our Lord, the bridegroom, and in His spouse the Church, only one Spirit holds sway, which governs and rules for the salvation of souls. For it is by the same Spirit and Lord who gave the Ten Commandments that our holy Mother Church is ruled and governed.

 Q What is meant by "the true attitude of mind?" What by "the church militant?"

Loyola's affirmation of Roman Catholic doctrine anticipated the actions of the Council of Trent, the general church council that met between 1545 and 1563 to make reforms. The Council of Trent reconfirmed all seven of the sacraments and reasserted the traditional Catholic position on all theological matters that had been challenged by the Protestants. It also set clear guidelines for the elimination of abuses among members of the clergy, emphasized preaching to the uneducated laity, and encouraged the regeneration of intellectual life within Catholic monasteries. Church leaders revived the activities of the Inquisition (see chapter 12) and established the *Index Expurgatorius*, a list of books judged heretical and therefore forbidden to Catholic readers. The Catholic Reformation supported a broadly based Catholicism that emphasized the direct and intuitive—hence, mystical—experience of God. Although the Church of Rome would never again reassume the universal authority it had enjoyed during the Middle Ages, both its internal reforms and its efforts to rekindle the faith restored its dignity in the minds and hearts of its followers.

---

[1] The eight times of the day appointed for special devotions; see chapters 9 and 15.

[2] Churches with images representing the stages of Christ's Passion.
[3] A time of special solemnity, ordinarily every twenty-five years, proclaimed by the pope; also, special indulgences granted during that time. The jubilee principle is based on a biblical injunction to free slaves, return land to its original owners, and leave fields untilled once every fifty years (Leviticus 25).
[4] Church indulgences granted to Christian Crusaders.

Catholicism's Global Reach

The evangelical activities of the Jesuits and other religious orders were widespread, but not uniformly successful. In China, where European traders were regarded as "ocean devils," the Catholic missionaries assumed a cordial relationship with the intellectual classes and succeeded in converting a number of Chinese scholars. By the eighteenth century, however, disputes between the Jesuits and the Dominicans over the veneration of Confucius (aggravated by papal condemnation of Confucian rites in 1744) weakened Catholic influence. In Japan, the first Jesuit missionaries, admirers of Tokugawa culture (see chapter 21), diligently mastered the Japanese language and culture. While the Jesuits introduced the Japanese to European styles of painting and music, the Portuguese (and thereafter, Dutch and English) merchants brought imperialistic commercial interests to Japan, thus clouding the evangelical aims of the Jesuits with European material ambitions. The Jesuit efforts at conversion were also frustrated by rival Franciscan missionaries. Over time, the Jesuits fell into disfavor with Japanese Buddhists, who came to view all Christians as potentially subversive to the traditional social order. By 1606, following decades of disruption caused by European efforts to win trading privileges in Japan, the Japanese outlawed Christianity.

Figure 20.1 *The Virgin of Guadalupe*, 1746. Oil on wood. National Palace, Mexico City, Dagli Orti. The Art Archive.

The country expelled almost all Western foreigners from Japanese soil by 1624, after a wave of brutal persecutions of both European Christians and Japanese converts to Catholicism.

Christian evangelism in the Americas proved to be far more successful. In sixteenth-century Latin America, where Spanish political authority went largely unchallenged, Catholicism went hand in hand with colonization. The arrival of the Jesuits in Mexico in 1571 followed that of the Augustinians, the Dominicans, and the Franciscans in a vast program of Christianization. Just as the convergence of Europeans and Indians came to produce a unique new "Latin American" population, so the blend of European Catholic and native religious traditions produced a unique synthesis in the culture of Mexico. A formidable example of this creolizing phenomenon, and one that testifies to the powerful religious impact of Catholicism, is the Miracle of the Virgin of Guadalupe. In 1531, ten years after the conquest of Mexico by Cortés, on the site of a former shrine to the Aztec mother-goddess, a dark-skinned Virgin Mary appeared in a vision before a simple Mexican peasant. The legend of this miraculous apparition of the Mother of God, commemorated in hundreds of carved and painted images (Figure **20.1**), became the basis for the most important religious cult in Mexican history: the cult of the Virgin of Guadalupe. The colonial cult of Guadalupe worships the Virgin in the traditional medieval guise of mother, intercessor, and protector, but it also exalts her as the symbol of Mexican national consciousness. At her shrine—the goal of thousands of pilgrims each year—and at hundreds of chapels throughout Mexico, the faithful pay homage to the Black Madonna, who is shown standing on a crescent moon, surrounded by a corona of sunrays and angels bearing the colors of the Mexican flag. The significance of the Virgin of Guadalupe as a Christian devotional image, enthusiastically promoted by the Jesuits beginning in the late sixteenth century, and her widespread popularity as protectress of Mexico have persisted even into modern times: in 1910, she was made an honorary general of the Mexican Revolution.

Literature and the Catholic Reformation

The passionate mysticism of the Catholic Reformation infused the arts of the sixteenth and seventeenth centuries. In literature, there appeared a new emphasis on heightened spirituality and on personal visionary experience acquired by way of the senses. One of the most colorful personalities to emerge in forging the new language of mysticism was the Spanish Carmelite nun Teresa of Avila (1515–1582), who was canonized in 1622. Teresa's activities in founding religious houses and in defending groups of Carmelites, who symbolized their humility by going without shoes, took her all over Spain and earned her the nickname "the roving nun." It was not until she was almost forty years old that her life as a visionary began. Teresa's

Figure 20.2 GIANLORENZO BERNINI, *The Ecstasy of Saint Teresa*, 1645–1652. Marble, height of group 11 ft. 6 in. Altar of Cornaro Chapel, Santa Maria della Vittoria, Rome. © 1990 Scala – Ministero Beni e Att. Culturali.

visions, including the one described in the following autobiographical excerpt, marry sensory experience to spiritual contemplation. They address the intriguing kinship between physical suffering and psychic bliss and between divine and erotic fulfillment. For Saint Teresa, love is the desire for oneness with God. The language by which the saint describes that union is charged with passion, for instance, when she relates how God's flaming arrow leaves her "completely afire."

READING 4.2 From Saint Teresa's *Visions* (1611)

It pleased the Lord that I should sometimes see the following   1
vision. I would see beside me, on my left hand, an angel in
bodily form—a type of vision which I am not in the habit of
seeing, except very rarely. Though I often see representations
of angels, my visions of them are of the type which I first
mentioned. It pleased the Lord that I should see this angel in
the following way. He was not tall, but short, and very
beautiful, his face so aflame that he appeared to be one of the
highest types of angel who seem to be all afire. They must be
those who are called cherubim: they do not tell me their names   10
but I am well aware that there is a great difference between
certain angels and others, and between these and others still,
of a kind that I could not possibly explain. In his hands I saw a
long golden spear and at the end of the iron tip I seemed to
see a point of fire. With this he seemed to pierce my heart
several times so that it penetrated to my entrails. When he
drew it out, I thought he was drawing them out with it and he
left me completely afire with a great love for God. The pain
was so sharp that it made me utter several moans; and so
excessive was the sweetness caused me by this intense pain   20
that one can never wish to lose it, nor will one's soul be
content with anything less than God. It is not bodily pain, but
spiritual, though the body has a share in it—indeed, a great
share. So sweet are the colloquies of love which pass between
the soul and God that if anyone thinks I am lying I beseech
God, in His goodness, to give him the same experience. ...

Q Which strikes you as more affective: the written or the visual version of Saint Teresa's vision? Why so?

The sensuous tone of Teresa's visions enriched the religious verse of the age, including that of her Spanish contemporaries, Saint John of the Cross (1542–1591), also a Carmelite, and Luis de Góngora y Argote (1561–1637). Similarly, in the poetry of devout English Catholics such as Richard Crashaw (1613–1649), the language of religious ecstasy swells with brooding desire.

Born into a Protestant family, Crashaw converted to Catholicism early in life. His religious poems, written in Latin and English, reflect the dual influence of Loyola's meditations and Teresa's visions. At least two of his most lyrical pieces are dedicated to Saint Teresa: *A Hymn to the Name and Honor of the Admirable Saint Teresa* and *The*

Flaming Heart, upon the Book and Picture of the Seraphical Saint Teresa, as She Is Usually Expressed with a Seraphim beside Her. The latter poem suggests that Crashaw was familiar with Bernini's sculpted version of Teresa's vision before it was publicly unveiled in Rome (Figure **20.2**). Representative of this visionary sensibility, the last sixteen lines of *The Flaming Heart*, reproduced in Reading 4.3, are rhapsodic in their intense expression of personal emotion. Erasing boundaries between erotic and spiritual love, Crashaw pleads that Teresa ravish his soul, even as she has been ravished by God.

READING 4.3 From Crashaw's *The Flaming Heart* (1652)

O thou undaunted daughter of desires!
By all thou dower of lights and fires;
By all the eagle in thee, all the dove;
By all thy lives and deaths of love;
By thy large draughts of intellectual day,
And by thy thirsts of love more large than they;
By all thy brim-filled bowls of fierce desire,
By thy last morning's draught of liquid fire;
By the full kingdom of that final kiss
That seized thy parting soul, and sealed thee His;
By all the heavens thou hast in Him,
Fair sister of the seraphim,
By all of Him we have in thee;
Leave nothing of myself in me!
Let me so read thy life that I
Unto all life of mine may die.

Q What is the nature of the love that Crashaw describes?
Q Which images in this poem contribute to its erotic undertone?

The Visual Arts and the Catholic Reformation

Mannerist Painting

The religious zeal of the Catholic reformers inspired a tremendous surge of artistic activity, especially in Italy and Spain. In Venice and Rome, the centers of Italian cultural life, the art of the High Renaissance underwent radical transformation. The clearly defined, symmetrical compositions of High Renaissance painters gave way to *mannerism*, a style marked by spatial complexity, artificiality, and affectation. Mannerist artists brought a new psychological intensity to visual expression. Their paintings mirrored the self-conscious spirituality and the profound insecurities of an age of religious wars and political rivalry.

The mannerist style is already evident in *The Last Judgment* that the sixty-year-old Michelangelo painted on the east wall of the Sistine Chapel (Figure **20.3**). Between 1534 and 1541, only a few years after the armies of the Holy

Figure 20.3 MICHELANGELO BUONARROTI, *The Last Judgment* (after restoration), 1536–1540. Fresco, 48 × 44 ft. Altar wall, Sistine Chapel, Vatican Museums, Rome. Nippon Television, Tokyo.

Figure 20.4
PARMIGIANINO, *Madonna of the Long Neck*, 1534–1540. Oil on panel, 7 ft. 1 in. × 4 ft. 4 in. Uffizi Gallery, Florence. © 1996 Scala – Ministero Beni e Att. Culturali.

Roman Empire had sacked the city of Rome, Michelangelo returned to the chapel whose ceiling he had painted some twenty years earlier with the optimistic vision of salvation. Now, in a mood of brooding pessimism, he filled the altar wall with agonized, writhing figures that press dramatically against one another. Surrounding the wrathful Christ are the Christian martyrs, who carry the instruments of their torture, and throngs of the resurrected—originally depicted nude but later, in the wake of Catholic reform, draped to hide their genitals. Reflecting the anxieties of his day, Michelangelo has replaced the classically proportioned figures, calm balance, and spatial clarity of High Renaissance painting with a more troubled vision of salvation.

The traits of the mannerist style can be seen best in the *Madonna of the Long Neck* (Figure **20.4**) by Parmigianino (1503–1540). In this work, the traditional subject of Madonna and Child is given a new mood of theatricality (compare Raphael's *Alba Madonna*; see chapter 17). Perched

Figure 20.5 JACOPO TINTORETTO, *The Last Supper*, 1592–1594. Oil on canvas, 12 ft. × 18 ft. 8 in. San Giorgio Maggiore, Venice. © 1990 Scala, Florence.

precariously above a courtyard adorned with a column that supports no superstructure, the unnaturally elongated Mother of God—her spidery fingers affectedly touching her chest—gazes at the oversized Christ child, who seems to slip lifelessly off her lap. Onlookers crowd into the space from the left, while a small figure (perhaps a prophet) at the bottom right corner of the canvas draws our eye into distant space. Cool coloring and an overall smoky hue make the painting seem even more contrived and artificial, yet, by its very contrivance, unforgettable.

The degree to which the mannerists rejected the guiding principles of High Renaissance painting is nowhere better illustrated than by a comparison of *The Last Supper* (Figure **20.5**) by the Venetian artist Jacopo Tintoretto (1518–1594) with the mural of the same subject by Leonardo da Vinci (see chapter 17) executed approximately a century earlier (Figure **20.6**). In his rendering of the sacred event, Tintoretto renounces the symmetry and geometric clarity of Leonardo's composition. The receding lines of the table and the floor in Tintoretto's painting place the viewer

Figure 20.6 LEONARDO DA VINCI, *The Last Supper*, ca. 1485–1498. Oil and tempera on plaster, 14 ft. 5 in. × 28 ft. Refectory, Santa Maria delle Grazie, Milan. © 2002 Scala, Florence.

above the scene and draw the eye toward a vanishing point that lies in a distant and uncertain space beyond the canvas. The even texture of Leonardo's fresco gives way in Tintoretto's canvas to vaporous contrasts of dark and light, produced by a smoking oil lamp. Clouds of angels flutter spectrally at the ceiling, and phosphorescent halos seem to electrify the agitated figures of the apostles. At the most concentrated burst of light, the Savior is pictured distributing bread and wine to his disciples. While Leonardo focuses on the human element of the Last Supper—the moment when Jesus acknowledges his impending betrayal—Tintoretto illustrates the miraculous moment when Jesus initiates the sacrament by which the bread and wine become his flesh and blood. Yet Tintoretto sets the miracle amidst the ordinary activities of household servants, who occupy the entire right-hand portion of the picture.

The mannerist passion for pictorial intensity was most vividly realized in the paintings of Domenikos Theotokopoulos, generally known (because of his Greek origins) as El Greco (1541–1614). A master painter who worked in Italy and Spain in the service of the Church and the devout Philip II (1527–1598), El Greco preferred the expressive grace of Tintoretto to the more muscular vitality of Michelangelo. With the inward eye of a mystic, he produced visionary canvases marked by bold distortions of form, dissonant colors, and a daring handling of space. His elongated and flamelike figures, often highlighted by ghostly whites and yellow-grays, seem to radiate halos of light—auras that symbolize the luminous power of divine revelation. In *The Agony in the Garden*, the moment of Jesus' final submission to the divine will, El Greco created a moonlit landscape in which clouds, rocks, and fabrics billow and swell with mysterious energy (Figure **20.7**). Below the tempestuous sky, Judas (the small pointing figure on the lower right) leads the arresting officers to the Garden of Gethsemane. The sleeping apostles, tucked away in a cocoonlike envelope, violate rational space: they are too small in relation to the oversized image of Jesus and

Figure 20.7 EL GRECO, *The Agony in the Garden*, ca. 1585–1586. Oil on canvas, 6 ft. 1 in. × 9 ft. 1 in. Courtesy of the Toledo Museum of Art, Ohio. Purchased with funds from the Libbey Endowment, Gift of Edward Drummond Libbey.

the angel who hovers above. El Greco's ambiguous spatial fields, which often include multiple vanishing points, his acrid greens and acid yellows, and his "painterly" techniques—his brushstrokes remain engagingly visible on the surface of the canvas—all contribute to the creation of a highly personal style that captured the mystical fervor of the new Catholicism.

Baroque Painting in Italy

If mannerism was the vehicle of the Counter-Reformation, the *baroque style* conveyed the dynamic spirit of an entire age. Derived from the Portuguese word *barocco*, which describes the irregularly shaped pearls often featured in ornamental European decoration, the term *baroque* is associated with such features as ornateness, spatial grandeur, and theatrical flamboyance. In painting, the baroque is characterized by asymmetric compositions, strong contrasts of light and dark, and bold, illusionistic effects.

The baroque style originated in Italy and came to dominate artistic production in the years between 1600 and 1750 throughout Europe and in those parts of the Americas colonized by Spain. Italian baroque artists worked to increase the dramatic expressiveness of religious subject matter in order to give viewers the sense that they were participating in the action of the scene. They copied nature faithfully and without idealization. Such was the ambition of the North Italian artist Michelangelo Merisi, better

known as Caravaggio (1571–1610). The leading Italian painter of the seventeenth century, Caravaggio flouted Renaissance artistic conventions, even as he flouted the law—he was arrested for violent acts that ranged from throwing a plate of artichokes in the face of a tavern keeper to armed assault and murder. Having killed a tennis opponent in 1606, he was forced to flee Rome. In his paintings, Caravaggio renounced the grand style of the High Renaissance, which called for dignity, decorum, and the idealization of figures and setting. Rather, he recreated the early Christian past as though its major events were occurring in the local taverns and streets of sixteenth-century Italy. Caravaggio dramatized these events with strong contrasts of light and dark that give his figures a sculptural presence. A golden light bathes Christ and his disciples in *The Supper at Emmaus* (Figure **20.8**); Caravaggio "spotlights" Jesus at the moment when, raising his hand to bless the bread, he is recognized as the Christ (Luke 24:30–31). Caravaggio underscores the moment of recognition by means of vigorous theatrical gestures and by the use of a perspective device known as **foreshortening**: Christ's right arm, painted at a right angle to the picture plane, seems to project sharply outward, as if to bless us as well as the bread. At the moment of recognition, the disciple at the right flings his arms outward along a diagonal axis that draws the viewer into the composition, while the figure at the left grips the arm of his chair as though

Figure 20.8 CARAVAGGIO, *The Supper at Emmaus*, ca. 1600. Oil on canvas, 4 ft. 7 in. × 6 ft. 5½ in. National Gallery, London.

Figure 20.9
CARAVAGGIO, *The
Crucifixion of Saint Peter*,
1601. Oil on canvas,
7 ft. 6 in. × 5 ft. 9 in.
Santa Maria del Popolo,
Rome. © 1990 Scala,
Florence.

to rise in astonishment. Unlike the visionary El Greco, Caravaggio brings sacred subjects down to earth with an almost cameralike naturalism. Where El Greco's saints and martyrs are ethereal, Caravaggio's are solid, substantive, and often quite ordinary. Their strong physical presence and frank homeliness transform biblical miracles into human narratives—a bold repudiation of Italian Renaissance conventions of beauty.

Caravaggio organized traditional religious compositions with unprecedented theatrical power and daring. In *The Crucifixion of Saint Peter* (Figure **20.9**), he arranged the figures in a tense, off-centered pinwheel that catches the eccentricity of Saint Peter's torment (he was crucified upside down). The saint's powerful physique is belied by the expression of vulnerability on his aging face. By placing the vigorously modeled figures close to the viewer, Caravaggio reduces the psychological distance between viewer and subject. By illuminating them against a darkened background, he "stages" the action so that it seems

to take place within the viewer's space—a space whose cruel light reveals such banal details as the executioner's dirty feet. True to the ideals of the Catholic Reformation, Caravaggio's paintings appealed to the senses rather than to the intellect. They also introduced into European art a new and vigorously lifelike realization of the natural world—one that daringly mingled the sacred and the profane.

Caravaggio's powerful style had considerable impact throughout Europe; however, his most talented follower was also Italian. Born in Rome, Artemisia Gentileschi (1593–1653) was the daughter of a highly esteemed painter, himself a follower of Caravaggio. Artemisia was trained by her father, but soon outstripped him in technical proficiency and imagination. Since women were not permitted to draw from nude male models, they rarely painted large-scale canvases with biblical, historical, or mythological themes that usually required nude figures; instead, their efforts were confined to the genres of portrait painting and

Figure 20.10 ARTEMISIA GENTILESCHI, *Judith Slaying Holofernes*, ca. 1614–1620. Oil on canvas, 6 ft. 6⅓ in. × 5 ft. 4 in. Uffizi Gallery, Florence.

Apocrypha, Book of Judith, 12:16–20; 13:1–10

¹⁶Holofernes' heart was ravished with [Judith] and his passion was aroused, for he had been waiting for an opportunity to seduce her from the day he first saw her. ¹⁷So Holofernes said to her, "Have a drink and be merry with us!" ¹⁸Judith said, "I will gladly drink, my lord, because today is the greatest day in my whole life." ¹⁹Then she took what her maid had prepared and ate and drank before him. ²⁰Holofernes was greatly pleased with her, and drank a great quantity of wine, much more than he had ever drunk in any one day since he was born.

¹When evening came, his slaves quickly withdrew. . . . They went to bed, for they all were weary because the banquet had lasted so long. ²But Judith was left alone in the tent, with Holofernes stretched out on his bed, for he was dead drunk. . . . ⁴Then Judith, standing beside his bed, said in her heart, "O Lord God of all might, look in this hour on the work of my hands for the exaltation of Jerusalem. ⁵Now indeed is the time to help your heritage and to carry out my design to destroy the enemies who have risen up against us." ⁶She went up to the bedpost near Holofernes' head, and took down his sword that hung there. ⁷She came close to his bed, took hold of the hair of his head, and said, "Give me strength today, O Lord God of Israel!" ⁸Then she struck his neck twice with all her might, and cut off his head. ⁹Next she rolled his body off the bed and pulled down the canopy from the posts. Soon afterward she went out and gave Holofernes' head to her maid, ¹⁰who placed it in her food bag.

still life (see chapter 23). Gentileschi's paintings, however, challenged tradition. Her powerful rendering of Judith slaying Holofernes (Figure **20.10**), which compares in size and impact with Caravaggio's *Crucifixion of Saint Peter* (see Figure 20.9), illustrates the decapitation of an Assyrian general and enemy of Israel at the hands of a clever Hebrew widow. A tale found in the Apocrypha (the noncanonical books of the Bible), the slaying of the tyrannical Holofernes was a favorite Renaissance allegory of liberty and religious defiance. Gentileschi brought to this representation the dramatic techniques of Caravaggio: realistically conceived figures, stark contrasts of light and dark, and a composition that brings the viewer painfully close to the event. She invested her subject with fierce intensity—the foreshortened body of the victim and the pinwheel arrangement of human limbs forces the eye to focus on the gruesome action of the swordblade as it severs head from neck in a shower of blood.

Gentileschi's favorite subjects were biblical heroines—she painted the Judith story some seven times. The violence she brought to these depictions may be said to reflect her profound sense of victimization: at the age of eighteen, she was raped by her drawing teacher and (during the sensational trial of her assailant) subjected to torture as a test of the truth of her testimony.

Baroque Sculpture in Italy

Gianlorenzo Bernini (1598–1680), Caravaggio's contemporary, brought the theatrical spirit of baroque painting to Italian architecture and sculpture. A man of remarkable technical virtuosity, Bernini was the chief architect of

Figure 20.11 GIANLORENZO BERNINI, *Fountain of the Four Rivers*, 1648–1651. Travertine and marble. Piazza Navona, Rome. © Vincenzo Pirozzi, Rome fotopirozzi@inwind.it.

seventeenth-century Rome, as well as one of its leading sculptors. Under Bernini's direction, Rome became the "city of fountains," a phenomenon facilitated by the early seventeenth-century revival of the old Roman aqueducts. Richly adorned with dolphins, mermaids, and tritons, the fountain—its waters dancing and sparkling in the shifting wind and light—was the favorite ornamental device of the baroque era (Figure 20.11).

Just as Caravaggio reshaped the tradition of Renaissance painting by way of pictorial illusionism, so Bernini challenged Renaissance sculptural tradition by investing it with a daring degree of dramatic theatricality. His life-sized marble sculpture of David (Figure 20.12) renders this favorite biblical personality in a manner that recreates the very action of his assault; and since the object of that assault, Goliath, lies outside the boundary of the sculpture itself, the viewer is drawn into the space "implied" by the explosive action. In contrast with the languid and effeminate David of Donatello (see Figure 17.1) or the classically poised hero of Michelangelo (see Figure 17.35), Bernini's David appears in mid-action, stretching the slingshot behind him as he prepares to launch the rock at his unseen adversary: his torso twists vigorously at the waist, his face contorts with fierce determination, and his muscles strain with tense energy. Determined to "render marble flexible" (as he himself stated), Bernini animates this figure with an unparalleled athletic vitality that directly engages the beholder.

Bernini's most important contribution to baroque religious sculpture was his multimedia masterpiece *The Ecstasy of Saint Teresa* (see Figure 20.2), executed between 1645 and 1652 for the Cornaro Chapel of Santa Maria della Vittoria in Rome (Figure 20.13). The visually compelling piece illustrates Bernini's dazzling skill in bringing to life Saint Teresa's autobiographical description of divine seduction (see Reading 4.2). Bernini depicts the swooning saint with head sunk back and eyes half closed. A smiling angel, resembling a teenage cupid, gently lifts Teresa's bodice to insert the flaming arrow of divine love. Bold illusionism heightens the sensuous effect: the angel's marble draperies flutter and billow with tense energy, while the slack and heavy gown of Teresa echoes the emotion of ecstatic surrender. The vision takes place on a marble cloud, which floats in heavenly space, while the uncertain juxtaposition of the saint and the cloud on which she reclines suggests the experience of levitation described in her vision. Sweetness and eroticism are the central features of this extraordinary image.

But Bernini's conception goes beyond the sculpture of the two figures to achieve a dramatic unity of figure and setting. To capture the theatrical intensity of Teresa's mystical experience, Bernini engages the tools of architecture,

sculpture, and painting: he situates Teresa beneath a colonnaded marble canopy from which gilded wooden rays appear to cast heaven's supernatural light. Real light entering through the glazed yellow panes of a concealed window above the chapel bathes the saint in a golden glow—an effect comparable to the spotlighting in a Caravaggio painting. From the ceiling of the chapel a host of angels both painted and sculpted in **stucco** (a light, pliable plaster) miraculously descends from the heavens. Agate and dark green marble walls provide a somber setting for the gleaming white and gold central image. On either side of the chapel, the members of the Cornaro family (executed in marble) behold Teresa's ecstasy from behind prayer desks that resemble theater boxes. These life-sized figures extend the supernatural space of the chapel and reinforce the viewer's role as witness to an actual event.

It is no coincidence that Bernini's illusionistic tour de force appeared contemporaneously with the birth of opera in Italy, for both share the baroque affection for dramatic expression on a monumental scale.

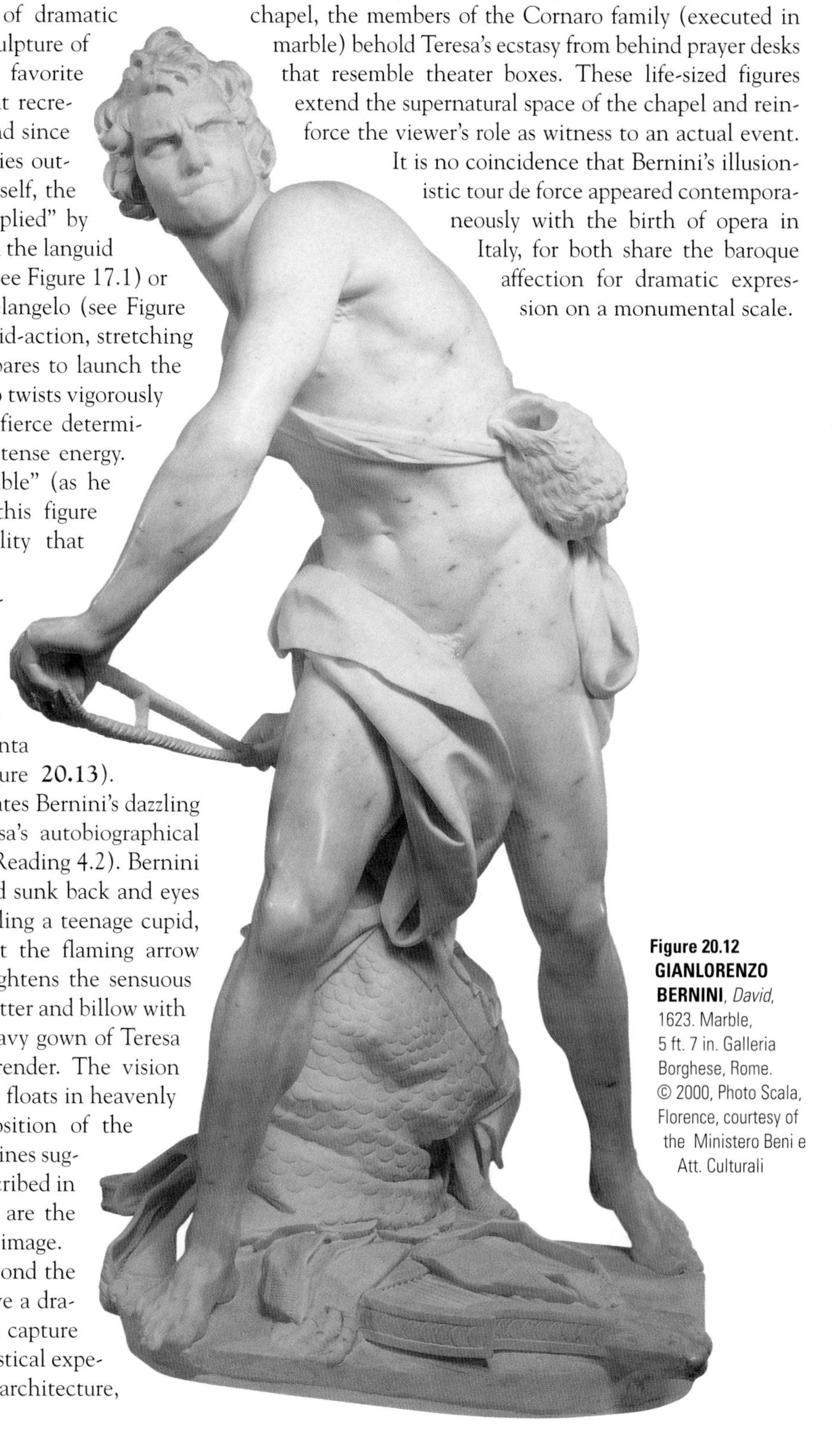

Figure 20.12
GIANLORENZO BERNINI, *David*, 1623. Marble, 5 ft. 7 in. Galleria Borghese, Rome. © 2000, Photo Scala, Florence, courtesy of the Ministero Beni e Att. Culturali

Figure 20.13 Anonymous, *Cornaro Chapel*, ca. 1644. Oil on canvas, 5 ft. 6¼ in. × 3 ft. 11¼ in. Staatliches Museum, Schwerin, Germany. © Vincenzo Pirozzi, Rome fotopirozzi@inwind.it.

Baroque Architecture in Italy

The city of Rome carries the stamp of Bernini's flamboyant style. Commissioned to complete the *piazza* (the broad public space in front of Saint Peter's Basilica), Bernini designed a trapezoidal space that opens out to a larger oval—the two shapes form, perhaps symbolically, a keyhole. Bernini's courtyard is bounded by a spectacular colonnade that incorporates 284 Doric columns (each 39 feet high) as well as 96 statues of saints (each 15 feet tall). In a manner consistent with the ecumenical breadth of Jesuit evangelism, the gigantic pincerlike arms of the colonnade reach out to embrace an area that can accommodate more than 250,000 people (Figure 20.14)—a vast proscenium on which devotional activities of the Church of Rome are staged to this day. The Saint Peter's of Bernini's time was the locus of papal authority; then, as now, popes used the central balcony of the basilica to impart the traditional blessing: "Urbi et Orbi" ("To the city and to the world"). The proportions of Bernini's colonnade are symbolic of the baroque preference for the grandiose, a preference equally apparent in the artist's spectacular setting for the Throne of Saint Peter and in the immense bronze canopy (*baldacchino*) he raised over the high altar of the basilica (Figure 20.15).

Figure 20.14 (below) **GIANLORENZO BERNINI**, Aerial view of colonnade and *piazza* of Saint Peter's, Rome, begun 1656. Travertine, longitudinal axis approx. 800 ft. Copper engraving by Giovanni Piranesi, 1750. Kunstbibliothek, Berlin. The enormous *piazza* in front of the east façade of Saint Peter's can accommodate more than 250,000 people.

Figure 20.15 (opposite) **GIANLORENZO BERNINI**, *Baldacchino* (canopy) ca. 1624–1633. Bronze with gilding, height 93 ft. 6 in. Saint Peter's, Rome. © 1990 Photo Scala, Florence.

Figure 20.16 GIACOMO DA VIGNOLA, interior of Il Gesù, Rome, 1568–1573. Length approx. 240 ft. Foto Marburg.

As with Saint Peter's, Italian baroque churches were designed to reflect the mystical and evangelical ideals of the Catholic Reformation. Il Gesù (the Church of Jesus) in Rome was the mother church of the Jesuit order and the model for hundreds of Counter-Reformation churches built throughout Europe and Latin America. Designed by Giacomo da Vignola (1507–1573), Il Gesù bears the typical features of the baroque church interior: a broad Latin cross nave with domed crossing and deeply recessed chapels (Figure 20.16). Lacking side-aisles, the 60-foot-wide nave allowed a large congregation to assemble close enough to the high altar and the pulpit to see the ceremony and hear the sermon. The wide nave also provided ample space for elaborate religious processions. Il Gesù's interior, with its magnificent altarpiece dedicated to Ignatius Loyola, exemplifies the baroque inclination to synthesize various media, such as painted stucco, bronze, and precious stones, in the interest of achieving sumptuous and ornate effects.

The exterior of Il Gesù, completed by Giacomo della Porta, is equally dramatic (Figure 20.17). Its design—especially the elegant buttressing scrolls—looks back to Alberti's two-storied façade of Santa Maria Novella (Figure 20.18). But in contrast to the linear sobriety of his Florentine model, della Porta's façade, with its deeply carved

Figure 20.17 GIACOMO DA VIGNOLA and **GIACOMO DELLA PORTA**, (right) façade of Il Gesù, Rome, ca. 1575–1584. Height 105 ft., width 115 ft. The Conway Library, Courtauld Institute of Art, London.

Figure 20.18 LEON BATTISTA ALBERTI, (below) façade of Santa Maria Novella, Florence, completed 1470. Width approx. 117 ft. Scala, Florence.

decorative elements, has a dynamic sculptural presence. For dramatic effect, the architect added structurally functionless engaged columns topped with Corinthian capitals. An ornate **cartouche** (oval tablet) and a double cornice add focus to the central doorway. While the Renaissance façade was conceived in two dimensions, according to an essentially geometric linear pattern, the baroque church-front is conceived in three. Like a Caravaggio painting, Il Gesù exploits dramatic contrasts of light and dark and of shallow and deep space.

The most daring of the Italian baroque architects was Francesco Borromini (1599–1667). Borromini designed the small monastic church of San Carlo alle Quattro Fontane (Saint Charles at the Four Fountains; Figure 20.19) to fit a narrow site at the intersection of two Roman streets. Rejecting the rules of

Figure 20.19 FRANCESCO BORROMINI, façade of San Carlo alle Quattro Fontane, Rome, 1667. Length 52 ft., width 34 ft., width of façade 38 ft. © Araldo de Luca, Rome.

**Figure 20.20
FRANCESCO
BORROMINI**, interior
of dome, San Carlo
alle Quattro Fontane,
Rome, ca. 1638. Width
approx. 52 ft. © 1990
Photo Scala, Florence.

classical design, he combined convex and concave units
to produce a sense of fluid, undulating movement. The
façade consists of an assortment of deeply cut decorative
elements: monumental Corinthian columns, a scrolled
gable over the doorway, and life-sized angels that support a
cartouche at the roofline. Borromini's aversion to the circle and the square—the "perfect" shapes of Renaissance
architecture—extends to the interior of San Carlo, which
is oval in plan. The dome, also oval, is lit by hidden windows that allow light to flood the interior. Carved with
geometric motifs that diminish in size toward the apex, the
shallow cupola appears to recede deep into space (Figure
20.20). Such inventive illusionism, accented by dynamic

spatial contrasts, characterized the Roman baroque style of
church architecture at its best.

But the theatricality of this architecture went further
still: by painting religious scenes on the walls and ceilings
of churches and chapels, baroque artists turned houses of
God into theaters for sacred drama. Such is the case with
the Church of Sant'Ignazio in Rome. Its barrel-vaulted
ceiling bears a breathtaking *trompe l'oeil* vision of Saint
Ignatius' apotheosis—his elevation to divine status (Figure
20.21). A master of the techniques of linear perspective

Figure 20.21 (opposite) **ANDREA POZZO**, *Apotheosis of Saint Ignatius*, 1691.
Fresco. Nave ceiling, Sant'Ignazio, Rome. Scala, Florence.

and dramatic foreshortening, the Jesuit architect and sculptor Andrea Pozzo (1642–1709) made the walls above Sant'Ignazio's clerestory appear to open up, so that the viewer gazes "through" the roof into the heavens that receive the levitating body of the saint. Pozzo's cosmic rendering—one of the first of numerous illusionistic ceilings found in seventeenth- and eighteenth-century European churches and palaces—may be taken to reflect a new perception of physical space inspired, in part, by European geographic exploration and discovery. Indeed, Pozzo underlines the global ambitions of Roman Catholic evangelism by adding at the four corners of the ceiling the allegorical figures of Asia, Africa, Europe, and America. The vast, illusionistic spatial fields of Italian baroque frescoes also may be seen as a response to the new astronomy of the Scientific Revolution, which presented a view of the universe as spatially infinite and dynamic rather than finite and static (see chapter 23). Whatever its inspiration, the spatial illusionism of baroque painting and architecture gave apocalyptic grandeur to Counter-Reformation ideals.

Baroque Music

In an effort to rid sacred music of secular influence, the Council of Trent condemned the borrowing of the popular tunes that had become common in religious music since the late Middle Ages. It also banned complex polyphony that tended to obscure the sacred text: the message of the words was to be primary. The Italian composer Giovanni di Palestrina (1525–1594) took these recommendations as strict guidelines: his more than one hundred polyphonic masses and 450 motets feature clarity of text, skillful counterpoint, and regular rhythms. The *a cappella* lines of Palestrina's Pope Marcellus Mass flow with the smooth grace of a mannerist painting. Called "the music of mystic serenity," Palestrina's compositions embody the conservative and contemplative side of the Catholic Reformation rather than its inventive, dramatic aspect. In the religious compositions of Palestrina's Spanish contemporary Tomás Luis de Victoria, there is a brooding but fervent mystical intensity. Like El Greco, his colleague at the court of Philip II, Victoria brought passion and drama to religious themes. And, recognizing that the Council of Trent had forbidden Palestrina to compose secular music, Victoria wrote not one note of secular song.

The Genius of Gabrieli

At the turn of the sixteenth century, the opulent city of Venice was the center of European religious musical activity. Giovanni Gabrieli (1555–1612), principal organist at Saint Mark's Cathedral in Venice and one of the greatest composers of his time, ushered in a new and dramatic style of choral and instrumental music. Gabrieli composed expansive **polychoral** religious pieces featuring up to five choruses. Abandoning the *a cappella* style favored in Rome, he included solo and ensemble groups of instruments—especially the trombones and cornets commonly used in Venice's ritual street processions. Gabrieli was the first composer to indicate a specific instrument for each voice part in the musical composition, earning him the name "the father of orchestration." Like baroque painters and sculptors, who sought sharp contrasts of light and shadow and dramatic spatial effects, Gabrieli created coloristic contrasts in sound. He was among the first composers to write into his scores the words *piano* (soft) and *forte* (loud) to govern the **dynamics** (the degree of loudness or softness) of the piece.

Gabrieli was also the first musician to make use of a divided choir employed in **concertato**, that is, in opposing or contrasting bodies of sound. At Saint Mark's, an organ was located on each side of the chancel, and four choirs were stationed on balconies high above the nave. The antiphonal play of chorus, instruments, and solo voices produced exhilarating sonorities (evident in the excerpt from Gabrieli's motet, *In Ecclesiis*) that met and mingled in the magical space above the heads of the congregation. In some of Gabrieli's compositions, echo effects produced by alternating voices and the use of unseen (offstage) voices achieve a degree of musical illusionism comparable to the visual illusionism of mannerist and baroque art. Like the extremes of light and dark in the paintings of El Greco and Caravaggio, Gabrieli's alternating bodies of sound (chorus versus chorus, solo voice versus chorus, chorus versus instruments) and contrasting musical dynamics (loud and soft) and pitches (high and low) produce strong harmonic textures and rich, dramatic effects. The *concertato* technique was the essence of early seventeenth-century baroque music and, in Gabrieli's hands, it was nothing less than majestic.

Gabrieli explored a type of musical organization that would come to dominate baroque music: *tonality* based on the melodic and harmonic vocabulary of the major–minor key system. **Tonality** refers to the arrangement of a musical composition around a central note, called the "tonic" or "home tone" (usually designated as the "key" of a given composition). A keynote or tonic can be built on any of the twelve tones of the **chromatic scale** (the seven white and five black keys of the piano keyboard). In baroque music—as in most music written to this day—all of the tones in the composition relate to the home tone. Tonality provided baroque composers with a way of achieving dramatic focus in a piece of music—much in the way that light served baroque painters to achieve dramatic focus in their compositions. By the mid-seventeenth century, the even progress of Renaissance polyphony, like the even lighting of Renaissance painting, had given way to the dynamic use of individual voices and the inventive combination of choral and instrumental textures.

Monteverdi and the Birth of Opera

The first master of baroque music-drama and the greatest Italian composer of the early seventeenth century was Claudio Monteverdi (1567–1643). Monteverdi served the court of Mantua until he became chapel master of Saint Mark's in Venice in 1621, a post he held for the rest of his life. During his long career, he wrote various kinds of

Figure 20.22 PIETRO DOMENICO OLIVIER, *The Teatro Regio, Turin*, painting of the opening night, December 26, 1740. Oil on canvas, 4 ft. 2 ⅛in. × 3 ft. 8 ⅞in. Courtesy of the Municipal Museum, Turin, Italy. Five tiers of boxes are fitted into the sides of the proscenium, one even perched over the semicircular pediment. Note the orchestra, without a conductor; the girls distributing refreshments; and the armed guard protecting against disorder.

with rich costumes and scenery. Baroque operas were more musically complex, however, and more dramatically cohesive than most Renaissance masques. The first opera house was built in Venice in 1637, and by 1700 Italy was home to seventeen more such houses, a measure of the vast popularity of the new genre. By the end of the seventeenth century, Italian courts and public theaters boasted all of the essential features of the modern theater: the picture-frame stage, the horseshoe-shaped auditorium, and tiers of galleries or boxes (Figure **20.22**). Interestingly enough, some of these opera houses, resplendent with life-sized sculptures and illusionistic frescoes, are aesthetically indistinguishable from Italian baroque church and chapel interiors (see Figures 20.13 and 20.16).

Orfeo, composed in 1607 for the duke of Mantua, was Monteverdi's first opera and one of the first full-length operas in music history. The **libretto** (literally, "little book") or text of the opera was written by Alessandro Striggio and based on a classical theme—the descent of Orpheus, the Greek poet-musician, to Hades. Orfeo required an orchestra of more than three dozen instruments, including keyboard instruments, ten viols, three trombones, and four trumpets. The instrumentalists performed the **overture**, an orchestral introduction to the opera. They also accompanied vocal music that consisted of **arias** (elaborate solo songs or duets) alternating with **recitatives** (passages spoken or recited to sparse chordal accompaniment). The aria tended to develop a character's feelings or state of mind, while the recitative served to narrate the action of the story or to heighten its dramatic effect.

Monteverdi believed that opera should convey the full range of human passions. To that end, he contrived inventive contrasts between singer and accompaniment, recitative and aria, soloist and chorus. He also employed abrupt changes of key to emphasize shifts in mood and action. And he introduced such novel and expressive instrumental effects as *pizzicato*, the technique of plucking rather than bowing a stringed instrument. Integrating music, drama, and visual display, Italian opera became the ideal expression of the baroque sensibility and the object of imitation throughout Western Europe.

SUMMARY

In the wake of the Protestant Reformation, the Roman Catholic Church launched a reform movement that took late sixteenth-century Europe by storm. Loyola's *Spiritual Exercises* and the autobiographical writings of Saint Teresa of Avila set the tone for a new, more mystical Catholicism.

religious music, as well as ballets, madrigals, and operas. Like Gabrieli, Monteverdi discarded the intimate dimensions of Renaissance chamber music and cultivated an expansive, dramatic style, marked by vivid contrasts of texture and color. His compositions reflect a typically baroque effort to imbue music with a vocal expressiveness that reflected the emotional charge of poetry. "The [written] text," declared Monteverdi, "should be the master of the music, not the servant." Monteverdi linked "affections" or specific emotional states with appropriate sounds: anger, for instance, with the high voice register, moderation with the middle voice register, and humility with the low voice register. With Monteverdi, the union of music and speech sought in the word painting techniques of Josquin (see chapter 17) blossomed into full-blown opera: that form of theater that combined all aspects of baroque artistic expression—music, drama, dance, and the visual arts.

Born in Italy, opera emerged out of Renaissance efforts to revive the music-drama of ancient Greek theater. While humanist composers had no idea what Greek music sounded like, they sought to imitate the ancient unity of music and poetry. The earliest performances of Western opera resembled the Renaissance masque, a form of musical entertainment that included dance and poetry, along

See Music Listening Selections at end of chapter.

In the spirit of Saint Teresa's ecstatic visions, such Catholic poets as Richard Crashaw wrote rhapsodic lyrics that fused sensual and spiritual yearnings. The arts of the seventeenth century reflect the religious intensity of the Catholic Reformation, even as they mirror the insecurities of the religiously divided and politically turbulent West.

The baroque style, which came to dominate Western Europe between 1600 and 1750, was born in Italy. The mannerist paintings of Parmigianino, Tintoretto, and El Greco anticipated the baroque style by their figural distortions, irrational space, bizarre colors, and general disregard for the "rules" of Renaissance painting. Italian baroque art, as typified by Caravaggio's paintings and Bernini's sculpture, featured dynamic contrasts of light and dark, an expanded sense of space, and the illusionistic staging of subject matter. Counter-Reformation churches, embellished with visionary paintings and sculptures, were ornate theaters for the performance of Catholic ritual. Bernini's *Ecstasy of Saint Teresa* and Pozzo's ceiling for the Church of Saint Ignatius in Rome achieved new heights of illusionistic theatricality. Addressing the passions rather than the intellect, baroque art broadcast the visionary message of Catholic reform to a vast audience that extended from Europe to the Americas.

Rome and Venice were fountainheads for Italian baroque art and music. Palestrina's polyphonic masses and motets emphasized clarity of text and calm sublimity, while Gabrieli's lofty polychoral compositions, performed at Saint Mark's Cathedral in Venice, featured dynamic contrasts between and among voices and musical instruments. The daring contrasts, rich color, and sheer volume of Gabrieli's music find their parallel in the canvases of Caravaggio.

The most important development in seventeenth-century European music was the birth of opera. Borrowing themes from classical mythology and history, Claudio Monteverdi integrated text and music to create the new and noble art of music-drama. In its synthesis of all forms of performance—music, literature, and the visual arts—Italian opera became the supreme expression of the theatrical exuberance and spiritual vitality of the baroque style.

MUSIC LISTENING SELECTIONS

CD Two Selection 1 Gabrieli, Motet, "In Ecclesiis," excerpt, 1615.
CD Two Selection 2 Monteverdi, *Orfeo*, Aria: "In questo prato adorno," 1607.

GLOSSARY

aria an elaborate solo song or duet, usually with instrumental accompaniment, performed as part of an opera or other dramatic musical composition

cartouche an oval tablet or medallion, usually containing an inscription or heraldic device

chromatic scale a series of twelve tones represented by the seven white and five black keys of the piano keyboard; see also Glossary, chapter 6, "scale"

concertato (Italian, concerto = "opposing" or "competing")

an early baroque style in which voices or instruments of different rather than similar natures are used in an opposing or contrasting manner

dynamics the degree of loudness or softness in music

foreshortening a perspective device by which figures or objects appear to recede or project into space

libretto (Italian, "little book") the words of an opera or other textual musical composition

overture an instrumental introduction to a longer musical piece, such as an opera

piazza (Italian) a broad, open public space

pizzicato (Italian) the technique of plucking (with the fingers) rather than bowing a stringed instrument

polychoral music written for two or more choruses, performed both in turn and together

recitative a textual passage recited to sparse chordal accompaniment; a rhythmically free vocal style popular in seventeenth-century opera

stucco a light, pliable plaster made of gypsum, sand, water, and ground marble

tonality the use of a central note, called the *tonic*, around which all other tonal material of a composition is organized, and to which the music returns for a sense of rest and finality

CHAPTER 21

Absolute Power and the Aristocratic Style

"Virtue would not go nearly so far if vanity did not keep her company."
La Rochefoucauld

The early modern era in the West is sometimes called the Age of Absolutism. Absolutism, a political theory asserting that unlimited power be vested in one or more rulers, confirmed longstanding theocratic tradition. During the seventeenth and well into the eighteenth century, divine right kings—rulers who were believed to hold their power directly from God—exercised unlimited power within their individual nation-states. But the term "Age of Absolutism" is equally appropriate to the period as it unfolded in the lands beyond Europe, for in China, India, and elsewhere, divine right monarchs also held unlimited control over their own vast states or empires (Map 21.1).

Absolute rulers maintained their authority by controlling a centralized bureaucracy and a standing army, and by pursuing economic policies designed to maximize the wealth of the state. In Western Europe, the mightiest of

Map 21.1 Empires in the Late Sixteenth and Early Seventeenth Centuries.

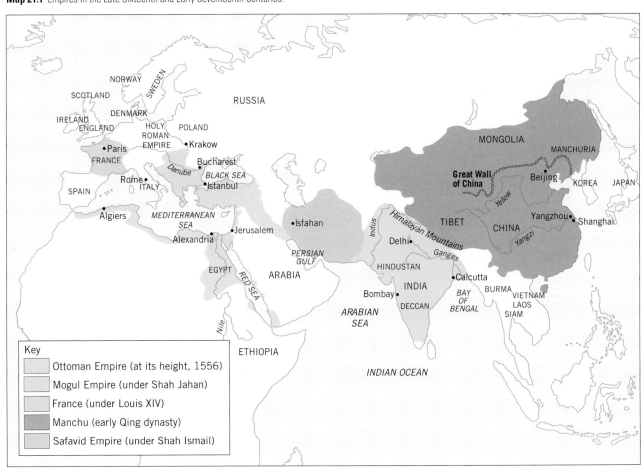

Key
- Ottoman Empire (at its height, 1556)
- Mogul Empire (under Shah Jahan)
- France (under Louis XIV)
- Manchu (early Qing dynasty)
- Safavid Empire (under Shah Ismail)

such potentates was King Louis XIV of France. During the nearly three-quarters of a century that Louis occupied the French throne (1643–1715), he dictated the political, economic, and cultural policies of the country. Under his guidance, France assumed a position of political and military leadership in Western Europe. As cultural arbiter, Louis helped to bring about a phase of the baroque called the *classical baroque*. This style pervaded the arts of seventeenth-century France and became one of the hallmarks of French absolutism. It also impressed its stamp on the rest of Europe and, somewhat later, on an emergent American culture.

Outside of Europe, absolute rulers also held sway: Suleiman the Magnificent (grand vizier of the Ottoman Empire), the Safavids of Persia in Southwest Asia, the Moguls in India, the Ming and Qing emperors in China, and the Tokugawa rulers in Japan. Within each of these territories, as within the European nation-states, the arts flourished as an expression of the majesty of the ruler and of the wealth and strength of his domain.

The Aristocratic Style in France

Louis XIV and French Absolutism

Like the pharaohs of ancient Egypt and in the tradition of his medieval ancestors, Louis XIV (1638–1715) governed France as the direct representative of God on earth (Figure **21.1**). Neither the Church, nor the nobility, nor the will of his subjects limited his power. During his seventy-two years on the throne, the Estates General, France's representative assembly, was never once called into session. As absolute monarch, Louis brought France to a position of political and military preeminence among the European nation-states. He challenged the power of the feudal nobility and placed the Church under the authority of the state, thus centralizing all authority in his own hands. By exempting the nobility and upper middle class from taxation and offering them important positions at court, he turned potential opponents into supporters. Even if Louis never uttered the famous words attributed to him, "I am the state," he surely operated according to that precept. Indeed, as an expression of his unrivaled authority, he took as his official insignia the image of the classical sun god Apollo and referred to himself as *le roi soleil* ("the Sun King").

As ruler of France, Louis was one of the world's most influential figures. Under his leadership, the center of artistic patronage and productivity shifted from Italy to France. French culture in all of its forms—from art and architecture to fashions and fine cuisine—came to dominate European tastes, a condition that prevailed until well into the early twentieth century. Although Louis was not an intellectual, he was both shrewd and ambitious.

He chose first-rate advisers to execute his policies and financed those policies with money from taxes that fell primarily upon the backs of French peasants. Vast amounts of money were spent to make France the undisputed military leader of Western Europe. But Louis, who instinctively recognized the propaganda value of the arts, also used the French treasury to glorify himself and his office. His extravagances left France in a woeful financial condition, a circumstance that contributed to the outbreak of the revolution at the end of the eighteenth century. Incapable of foreseeing these circumstances, Louis cultivated the arts as an adjunct to majesty.

Versailles: Symbol of Royal Absolutism

Architecture played a vital role in the vocabulary of royal power. The French royal family traditionally resided in Paris, at the palace known as the Louvre. But Louis, who detested Paris, moved his capital to a spot from which he might more directly control the nobility and keep them dependent upon him for honors and financial favors. Early in his career he commissioned a massive renovation of his father's hunting lodge at the village of Versailles, some 12 miles from Paris. It took 36,000 workers and nearly twenty years to build Versailles, but, in 1682, the French court finally established itself in the apartments of this magnificent unfortified *château* (castle). More than a royal residence, Versailles was—in its size and splendor—the symbol of Louis' absolute supremacy over the landed aristocracy, the provincial governments, the urban councils, and the Estates General.

The wooded site that constituted the village of Versailles, almost half the size of Paris, was connected to the old capital by a grand boulevard that (following the path of the sun) ran from the king's bedroom—where most state business was transacted—to the Avenue de Paris. Even a cursory examination of the plan of Versailles, laid out by the French architect Louis Le Vau (1612–1670), reveals esteem for the rules of symmetry, clarity, and geometric regularity (Figure **21.2**). These principles, in combination with a taste for spatial grandeur, dramatic contrast, and theatrical display, were the distinguishing features of the classical baroque style.

Shaped like a winged horseshoe, the almost 2,000-foot-long palace—best viewed in its entirety from the air—was the focus of an immense complex of parks, lakes, and forest (Figure **21.3**). Its central building was designed by Le Vau, while the two additional wings were added by Jules Hardouin-Mansart (1646–1708). Three levels of vertically aligned windows march across the palace façade like soldiers in a formal procession (Figure **21.4**). Porches bearing freestanding Corinthian columns accent the second level, and ornamental statues at the roofline help to relieve the monotonous horizontality of the structure. In its total effect, the palace is dignified and commanding, a baroque synthesis of classical and Palladian elements. Its calm nobility provides a striking contrast to the robust theatricality of most Italian baroque structures (see Figures 20.17 and 20.19).

The grandeur and majesty of Versailles made it the model for hundreds of palace-estates and city planning

Science and Technology

1657 the first fountain pens are manufactured in Paris

1688 the French army introduces bayonets attached to muskets

1698 champagne is invented in France

Figure 21.1 HYACINTHE RIGAUD, *Portrait of Louis XIV*, 1701. Oil on canvas, 9 ft. 1 in. × 6 ft. 4 in. Louvre, Paris. Photo R.M.N – © Gérard Blot.

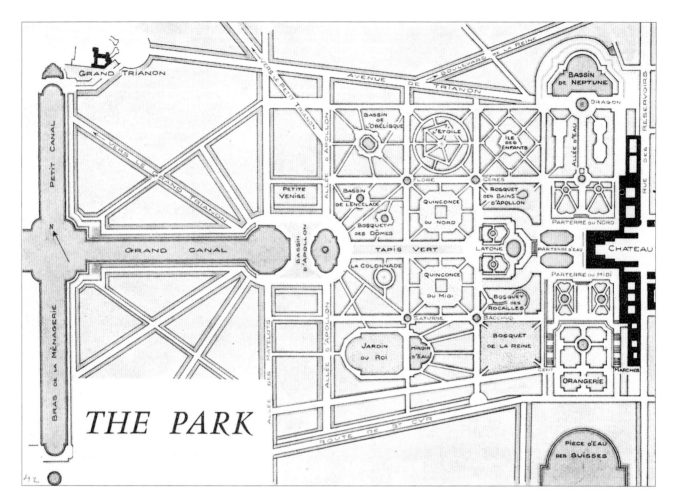

THE PARK

Figure 21.2 LOUIS LE VAU, plan of Versailles. Musée de Versailles.

Figure 21.3 ISIDORE-LAURENT DEROY, the park and palace of Versailles, France, nineteenth century. Chateau de Versailles et de Trianon. Photo RMN – © Gérard Blot

projects in both Europe and America for the following two centuries. Le Vau's façade became the prototype for the remodeled royal palace in Paris, the Louvre. Designed by Claude Perrault (1613–1688), the east façade of the Louvre echoes the basic classical baroque features of Louis' residence at Versailles: a strong rectilinear organization,

paired Corinthian columns, and a gabled entrance that provides dramatic focus (Figure **21.5**). Perrault's design was chosen over the plans of his competitor, Gianlorenzo Bernini (see chapter 20), whom Louis had invited to France to execute a number of royal commissions.

Figure 21.4 LOUIS LE VAU and **JULES HARDOUIN-MANSART**, Parterre du Midi, Palace of Versailles, 1669–1685. Chateau de Versailles et de Trianon.

Figure 21.5 CLAUDE PERRAULT, **LOUIS LE VAU**, and **CHARLES LE BRUN**, east façade of the Louvre, Paris, 1667–1670.
Photo: James Austin, Cambridge, U.K.

Figure 21.6 Ornamental Lake and Fountain of Latone, Versailles. Musée de Versailles. © Paul M. R. Maeyaert, El Tossal, Spain.

Figure 21.7 JEAN LE PAUTRE, *Marble Court, Versailles*. Engraving showing a performance of Lully's *Alceste*, 1674. The Metropolitan Museum of Art, New York. Harris Brisbane Dick Fund, 1930 (30–22.32[53]).

The palace at Versailles housed Louis' family, his royal mistresses (one of whom bore him nine children), and hundreds of members of the French nobility whose presence was politically useful to Louis. Life at the court of the Sun King was both formal and public—a small army of servants, courtiers, ministers, and pet animals constantly surrounded Louis. All forms of behavior were fixed by protocol. Rank at court determined where one sat at the dinner table and whether one or both panels of Versailles' "French doors" were to be opened upon entering.

Flanking the palace were barracks for honor guards, lodgings for more than fifteen hundred servants, kennels, greenhouses, and an orangery with over 2,000 orange trees. Over 7 square miles of gardens were designed by André Le Nôtre with the same compelling sense of order that Le Vau brought to the architecture. The great park featured an array of hedges clipped into geometric shapes, sparkling fountains (that favorite of all baroque mechanical devices), artificial lakes (Figure **21.6**), grottoes, a zoo, theaters, and outdoor "rooms" for private gatherings and clandestine meetings. When in bloom, the gardens—some planted with over 4 million tulip bulbs, which Louis imported annually from Holland—were a spectacular sight. They framed and embellished the long walkways that radiate from the central building. On the garden side of the palace, artificial pools reflected sculptures whose subject matter glorified the majesty of the king (see Figure 21.4). Itself a kind of outdoor theater, the royal palace provided the ideal backdrop for the ballets, operas, and plays that were regular features of court life (Figure **21.7**).

If the exterior of Versailles symbolized royal grandeur, the interior was a monument to princely self-indulgence (Figure **21.8**). Though now shorn of many of their original furnishings, Versailles' sumptuous *salons* (drawing rooms) still testify to Louis' success at cultivating French trades in such luxury items as crafted silver, clocks, lace, brocades, porcelain, and fine glass. During the seventeenth century, the silk industry reached its peak, French carpets competed with those of Turkey and Persia, the art of **marquetry** (inlaid wood) rivaled that of Italy, and the tapestries produced at the Gobelins factory in Paris outclassed those woven in Flanders. Versailles' *salons* were adorned with illusionistic frescoes, gilded stucco moldings, crystal chandeliers, and huge, ornate mirrors. The rooms housed some of the most lavish *objets d'art* (art objects) in Western history, all of which, it is sobering to recall, were enjoyed at a time when the peasant majority of the French population lived in one-room, thatch-roofed houses filled with coarse wooden furniture. Equally sobering is the fact that despite its splendor, the palace lacked any kind of indoor plumbing. Servants carried out the slops, but the unpleasant odor of human waste was difficult to mask, even with the finest French perfumes.

Figure 21.8 Apartment of the Queen/Salon of the Nobles, Versailles. Length 31 ft.; width 32 ft.; height 24 ft. 8 in. Musée de Versailles. Lauros/Giraudon/Bridgeman Art Library.

Each of Versailles' rooms illustrates a specific theme: the Salon de Venus was decorated by Charles Le Brun (1619–1690) with ceiling paintings portraying the influence of love on various kings in history. In the Salon de la Guerre (Drawing Room of War) an idealized, equestrian Louis, carved in low-relief marble, is shown receiving the victor's crown (Figure 21.9)—though, in fact, Louis himself rarely took part in combat. The most splendid interior space, however, is the 240-foot-long Galerie des Glaces (Hall of Mirrors), which once connected the royal apartments with the chapel (Figure 21.10). Embellished with glorious frescoes, marble pilasters, and gilded bronze capitals, and furnished with ornate candelabra and bejeweled trees (the latter have since disappeared), the hall features a wall of seventeen mirrored arcades that face an equal number of high-arched windows opening on to the garden. Framing this opulent royal passageway, mirrors and windows set up a brilliant counterpoint of image and reflection. Mirrors were to Versailles what fountains were to Rome: vehicles for the theatrical display of changing light in unbounded space.

Louis as Patron of the Arts

At the center of his court, Louis was the arbiter of fashion and manners. Within his dining *salons*, linen napkins came into use, forks replaced fingers for eating, and elaborate dishes were served to suit the royal palate. Graced with an eye for beauty and a passion for aggrandizement, Louis increased the number of paintings in the French royal collection from the two hundred he inherited upon his accession to the throne to the two thousand he left at his death. These paintings formed the basis of the permanent collection at the Louvre, now a world-renowned art museum.

On a grander scale, Louis dictated the standards for all forms of artistic production. Following in the tradition of his father, Louis XIII (1601–1643), who had instituted the French Royal Academy of Language and Literature in 1635, he created and subsidized government-sponsored institutions in the arts, appointing his personal favorites to oversee each. In 1648, at the age of ten, Louis founded the Academy of Painting and Sculpture; in 1661 he established the Academy of Dance; in 1666, the Academy of Sciences; in 1669, the Academy of Music; and in 1671,

Figure 21.9 JULES HARDOUIN-MANSART, Salon de la Guerre (Drawing Room of War), Versailles. Length and width 33 ft. 8 in; height 37 ft. 9 in. Musée de Versailles. Lauros/Giraudon/Bridgeman Art Library.

Figure 21.10 JULES HARDOUIN-MANSART and **CHARLES LE BRUN**, Galerie des Glaces (Hall of Mirrors), Versailles, ca. 1680. Length 240 ft. Musée de Versailles. © Paul M. R. Maeyaert, El Tossal, Spain.

the Academy of Architecture. The creation of the academies was a symptom of royal efforts to fix standards, but Louis also had something more personal in mind: he is said to have told a group of academicians, "Gentlemen, I entrust to you the most precious thing on earth—my fame." His trust was well placed, for the academies brought glory to the king and set standards that would govern the arts for at least two centuries. These standards were enshrined in "rules" inspired by the legacy of ancient Greece and Rome. Thus *neoclassicism*—the revival of classical style and subject matter—became the accepted style of academic art.

A typical example of the neoclassical style in sculpture is seen in the work of the French academician François Girardon (1628–1715). Girardon drew on Hellenistic models for the ideally proportioned statues that he arranged in graceful tableaux for the gardens of Versailles. In one such tableau, Girardon's neoclassical nymphs are seen entertaining the sun god Apollo—an obvious reference to Louis as *roi soleil* (Figure **21.11**).

Poussin and the Academic Style in Painting

Girardon's compositions owed much to the paintings of the leading exponent of French academic art, Nicolas Poussin (1594–1665). Poussin spent most of his life in Rome, absorbing the rich heritage of the classical and Renaissance past. He revered Raphael, master of the High Renaissance, as the leading proponent of the classical style, and, like many neoclassicists, he shared Raphael's esteem for lofty subjects drawn from Greco-Roman mythology and Christian legend. In an influential treatise on painting, Poussin formalized the rules that would govern academic art for centuries. These standards, enshrined in the works of Raphael (see chapter 17) and expounded in the aesthetic theories of seventeenth-century Italian painters, would come to characterize the Grand Manner in Western art: artists should choose only serious and elevated subjects (such as battles, heroic actions, and miraculous events) drawn from classical or Christian history, and reject crude, bizarre, and ordinary subject matter. As to the manner of representation, artists should make the physical action suit the mood of the narrative, avoiding, at all cost, the gross aspects of ordinary existence and any type of exaggeration. They should present their subjects clearly and evenly in harmonious compositions that were free of irrelevant and sordid details. Restraint, moderation, and decorum—that is, propriety and good taste—should govern all aspects of pictorial representation.

Figure 21.11 FRANÇOIS GIRARDON, *Apollo Attended by the Nymphs*, ca. 1666–1672. Marble, life-sized. Musée de Versailles. © Photo R.M.N., Paris.

Figure 21.12 NICOLAS POUSSIN, *Arcadian Shepherds*, 1638–1639. Oil on canvas, 33½ × 47⅝ in. Louvre, Paris. Photo R.M.N. – © René-Gabriel Ojéda.

Poussin faithfully practiced the rules of the academic or Grand Manner. His *Arcadian Shepherds*, completed in 1639, transports us to the idyllic region in ancient Greece known as Arcadia, a place where men and women were said to live in perfect harmony with nature (Figure **21.12**). Three shepherds have come upon an ancient tomb, a symbol of death; on the right, the stately Muse of History meditates upon the tomb's inscription, "*Et in Arcadia Ego*" ("I [death] also dwell in Arcadia")—that is, death reigns even in this most perfect of places. Poussin's moral allegory, at once a pastoral elegy and a *memento mori*, instructs us that death is universal. Cool, bright colors and even lighting enhance the elegiac mood, while sharp contours and the sure use of line provide absolute clarity of design. But the real power of the painting lies in its rigorous composition. Poussin arrived at this composition by arranging and rearranging miniature wax models of his figures within a small rectangular box. He then posed these figures—statuesque, heroically proportioned, and idealized—so that their every gesture served to narrate the story. Indeed, all of the elements in the painting, from the Muse's feet (which parallel the horizontal picture plane) to the trees in the landscape and at the right edge of the tomb (which parallel the vertical picture plane) contribute to the geometric order of the pictorial structure.

Despite the grand theatricality of Poussin's paintings, order dominates over spontaneity. Both in form and in content, Poussin's canvases are intellectual; that is, they appeal to the mind rather than to the senses. In contrast to Italian baroque painters such as Caravaggio, whose works he detested, Poussin soberly advanced the aesthetics of neoclassicism.

Poussin and his contemporary, Claude Gellée (1600–1682), known as Claude Lorrain, were responsible for creating the genre known as the "ideal landscape," a landscape painted in the high-minded, idealized style usually found in traditional moral subjects. For such paintings, academic artists made careful renderings of the countryside around Rome. They then deliberately assembled and combined the contents of their sketches according to the classical ideals of balance and clarity. Lorrain's landscapes, characterized by haunting qualities of light, were tranquil settings for lofty mythological or biblical subjects (Figure **21.13**). Unlike the Dutch landscape painters, who rendered nature with forthright realism (see Figure 23.10), academic artists imposed a preconceived, rationalized order upon the natural world.

Figure 21.13 CLAUDE LORRAIN (CLAUDE GELLÉE), *The Marriage of Isaac and Rebekah (The Mill)*, 1642. Oil on canvas, 4 ft. 11 in. × 6 ft. 5 in. National Gallery, London.

The Aristocratic Portrait

The baroque was the great period of aristocratic portraiture. Commissioned by the hundreds by Louis XIV and the members of his court, aristocratic portraits differ dramatically from the portraits of such artists as Hals, Leyster, and Rembrandt (see chapter 23). Whereas Dutch artists investigated the personalities of their sitters, bringing to their portraits a combination of psychological intimacy and forthrightness, French artists were concerned primarily with outward appearance. The classic example of French aristocratic portraiture is the image of Louis XIV shown at the beginning of this chapter (see Figure 21.1), painted in 1701 by Hyacinthe Rigaud (1659–1743). Rigaud shows the aging monarch in his coronation garments, with the royal paraphernalia: the scepter, the crown (on the cushion at the left), and the sword of state. He wears ermine-lined coronation robes, silk stockings, a lace cravat, high-heeled shoes, and a well-manicured wig—all but the first were fashionable hallmarks of upper-class wealth. Louis' mannered pose, which harks back to classical models, reflects self-conscious pride in status. Special devices enhance the themes of authority and regality: satin curtains theatrically frame the king, and a lone column compositionally and metaphorically underscores his rectitude. Such devices would become standard conventions in European and American portraits of the eighteenth century (see Figure 26.24).

The Aristocratic Style in Europe

Velázquez, Rubens, and van Dyck

While the aristocratic phase of the baroque style was initiated in France, it flourished in many other European courts. In Spain, Diego Velázquez (1599–1660), court painter to King Philip IV (1605–1665), became that country's most prestigious artist. Velázquez excelled at modeling forms so that they conveyed the powerful presence of real objects in atmospheric space. For the Spanish court, Velázquez painted a variety of classical and Christian subjects, but his greatest enterprise was the informal group portrait known as *Las Meninas* (*The Maids of Honor*; Figure **21.14**). In this painting, Velázquez depicted himself at his easel, alongside the members of the royal court: the *infanta*

Figure 21.14 DIEGO VELÁZQUEZ, *Las Meninas* (*The Maids of Honor*), 1656. Oil on canvas, 10 ft. 5 in. × 9 ft. Prado, Madrid.

Figure 21.15 PETER PAUL RUBENS, *Rape of the Daughters of Leucippus,* ca. 1618. Oil on canvas, 7 ft. 3 in. × 6 ft. 10 in. Alte Pinakothek, Munich.

(the five-year-old daughter of the king), her maids of honor, her dwarf, a mastiff hound, and the royal escorts. In the background is a mirror that reflects the images of the king and queen of Spain—presumably the subjects of the large canvas Velázquez shows himself painting in the left foreground. Superficially, this is a group portrait of the kind painted by the Dutch artist Rembrandt (see Figure 23.16), but it is far more complex in composition and in content—its "meaning" has been for decades the subject of extensive debate among art historians. Indisputably, however, *Las Meninas* comments intriguingly on the relationship between the perceived and the perceiver. Almost all of the characters in the painting, including the painter himself, are shown gazing at the royal couple, who must be standing outside of the picture space in the very spot occupied by the viewer. With baroque inventiveness, Velázquez expands the spatial field to invite the beholder to "enter" the space from a variety of vantage points. The painting becomes a "conceit" that provokes a visual dialogue between viewer and viewed and between patron and artist.

A contemporary of Velázquez, the internationally renowned Flemish painter Peter Paul Rubens (1577–1640) established his reputation in the courts of Europe.

Fluent in six languages, he traveled widely as a diplomat and art dealer for royal patrons in Italy, England, and France. He also headed a large studio workshop that trained scores of assistants to help fill his many commissions—a total lifetime production of some 1800 paintings. For the Luxembourg Palace of Paris, Rubens and his studio executed twenty-one monumental canvases that glorified Marie de' Medici, Louis XIV's grandmother, and her late husband, King Henry IV of France. Like Poussin, Rubens studied in Italy and was familiar with both classical and High Renaissance art. Rubens deeply admired the flamboyant colorists Titian and Tintoretto, and he developed a style that, by comparison with Poussin's, was painterly in technique and dynamic in composition.

One of Rubens' most memorable canvases, the *Rape of the Daughters of Leucippus* (Figure **21.15**), depicts the abduction of two mortal women by the Roman heroes Castor and Pollux. Rubens' portrayal of the classical story explodes with vigor: pressing against the picture plane are the fleshy bodies of the nude maidens, their limbs arranged in the pattern of a slowly revolving pinwheel. The masterful paintstrokes exploit sensuous contrasts of luminous pink flesh, burnished armor, gleaming satins, and dense horsehide. Probably commissioned to commemorate the double marriage of Louis XIII of France to a Spanish princess and Philip IV of Spain to a French princess (and, thus, to celebrate the diplomatic alliance of France and Spain), the painting carries a subtext of (male) power over (female) privilege—and, by extension, of political absolutism. Images of subjugation by force, whether in the form of lion hunts (as in ancient Assyrian reliefs; see chapter 2) or in paintings and sculptures depicting mythological stories of rape, were metaphors for the sovereign authority of the ruler over his subjects, hence a veiled expression of political absolutism.

In England, the most accomplished advocate of the aristocratic style was the Flemish master Anthony van Dyck (1599–1641). Born in Antwerp, van Dyck had been an assistant to Rubens and may have worked with him on the *Rape of the Daughters of Leucippus*. Unwilling to compete with Rubens, van Dyck moved to Genoa and then to London, where he became court painter to King Charles I of England (1600–1649). Van Dyck's many commissioned portraits of European aristocrats are striking for their polished elegance and idealized grandeur, features that are especially evident in his equestrian portrait of Charles I (see Figure 22.1). In this painting, which employs the traditional motif of ruler-on-horseback (see chapters 6, 11, and 17), van Dyck shows the king, who was actually short and undistinguished-looking, as handsome and regal. The combination of fluid composition and naturalistic detail, and the shimmering vitality of the brushwork, make this one of the most memorable examples of aristocratic baroque portraiture.

Music and Dance at the Court of Louis XIV

The court at Versailles was the setting for an extraordinary outpouring of music, theater, and dance. To provide musical entertainments for state dinners, balls, and operatic performances, Louis established a permanent orchestra, the first in European history. Its director, the Italian-born (but French-educated) Jean-Baptiste Lully (1632–1687), also headed the French Academy of Music. Often called the "father of French opera," Lully oversaw all phases of musical performance, from writing scores and conducting the orchestra to training the chorus and staging operatic productions. Many of Lully's operas were based on themes from classical mythology. Their semidivine heroes, prototypes of Louis himself, flattered his image as ruler.

Lully's operas shared the pomp and splendor of Le Brun's frescoes, the strict clarity of Poussin's paintings, and the formal correctness of classical drama. Though Lully's compositions were generally lacking in spontaneity and warmth of feeling, they were faithful to the neoclassical unity of words and music. Lully modified the music of the recitative to follow precisely and with great clarity the inflections of the spoken word. He also introduced to opera the "French overture," an instrumental form that featured contrasts between a slow first part in homophonic texture and a fast, contrapuntal second part. Under Lully's

leadership, French opera also developed its most characteristic feature: the inclusion of formal dance.

At the court of Louis XIV, dancing and fencing were the touchstones of aristocratic grace. All members of the upper class were expected to perform the basic court dances, including the very popular *minuet*, and the courtier who could not dance was judged rude and inept. Like his father, Louis XIII, who had commissioned and participated in extravagantly expensive ballets, Louis XIV was a superb dancer. Dressed as the sun, he danced the lead in the 1653 performance of the *Ballet de la Nuit* (Figure **21.16**). Of lasting significance was Louis' contribution to the birth of professional dance and the transformation of court dance into an independent artform. During the late seventeenth century, French ballet masters of the Royal Academy of Dance established rules for the five positions that have become the basis for classical dance. Clarity, balance, and proportion, along with studied technique—elements characteristic of classicism in general—became the ideals of the classical ballet.

By 1685 female dancers were permitted to join the previously all-male French dance ensembles in staged performances. And in 1700 Raoul Auget Feuillet published a

Figure 21.16 King Louis XIV as the sun in the 1653 *Ballet de la Nuit.* Bibliothèque Nationale, Paris.

system of abstract symbols for recording specific dance steps and movements, thus facilitating the art of **choreography**. Ballet, itself a metaphor for the strict etiquette and ceremony of court life, enriched all aspects of the French theater. However, since classical ballet demanded a rigorous attention to proper form, it soon became too specialized for any but professionals to perform, and so there developed the gap between performer and audience that exists to this day in the art of dance.

Seventeenth-Century French Literature

As with most forms of artistic expression in seventeenth-century France, in literature neoclassical precepts of form and content held sway. French writers addressed questions of human dignity and morality in a language that was clear, polished, and precise. Their prose is marked by refinement, good taste, and the concentrated presentation of ideas.

One literary genre that typified the neoclassical spirit was the **maxim**. A maxim is a short, concise, and often witty saying, usually drawn from experience and offering some practical advice. Witty sayings that distilled wisdom into a few words were popular in many cultures, including those of the Hebrews, the Greeks, and the Africans. But in seventeenth-century France, the cautionary or moralizing aphorism was exalted as the ideal means of teaching good sense and decorum. Terse and lean, the maxim exalted precision of language and thought. France's greatest maxim writer was François de La Rochefoucauld (1613–1680), a nobleman who had participated in a revolt against Louis XIV early in his reign. Withdrawing from court society, La Rochefoucauld wrote with a cynicism that reflected his conviction that self-interest, hypocrisy, and greed motivated the behavior of most human beings—including and especially the aristocrats of his day. As the following maxims illustrate, however, La Rochefoucauld's insights into human behavior apply equally well to individuals of all social classes and to any age.

READING 4.4 From La Rochefoucauld's *Maxims* (1664)

Truth does less good in the world than its appearances do harm.

Love of justice in most men is only a fear of encountering injustice.

We often do good that we may do harm with impunity.

As it is the mark of great minds to convey much in few words, so small minds are skilled at talking at length and saying little.

Virtue would not go nearly so far if vanity did not keep her company.

We confess to small faults to create the impression that we have no great ones.

To be rational is not to use reason by chance, but to recognize it, distinguish it, appreciate it.

We all have strength enough to endure the misfortunes of others.

We are never so happy or so unhappy as we imagine we are.

Our minds are lazier than our bodies.

Quarrels would not last long were the wrong all on one side.

Q What is the effect of brevity in these maxims?

Q Which of these maxims might apply to the characters in Reading 4.5 (Molière)?

Like La Rochefoucauld's maxims, but on a larger scale, French drama, too, reflected the neoclassical effort to restrain passionate feeling by means of cool objectivity and common sense. The leading French tragedian of the seventeenth century, Jean Racine (1639–1699), wrote plays that treated high-minded themes in an elevated language. Racine added to Aristotle's unities of action and time (see chapter 4) a strict unity of place, thus manifesting his abiding commitment to intellectual control. In the play *Phèdre* (1677), itself based on Greek models, Racine explored the conflict between human passions (Phaedra's "unnatural" infatuation with her stepson) and human reason (Phaedra's sense of duty as the wife of Theseus, king of Athens). As in all of Racine's tragedies of passion, *Phèdre* illustrates the disastrous consequences of emotional indulgence—a weakness especially peculiar to Racine's female characters. Indeed, while Racine created some of the most dramatic female roles in neoclassical theater, he usually pictured women as weak, irrational, and cruel.

Molière's Human Comedy

Jean-Baptiste Poquelin (1622–1673), whose stage name was Molière, was France's leading comic dramatist. The son of a wealthy upholsterer, he abandoned a career in law in favor of acting and play writing. He learned much from the *commedia dell'arte*, a form of improvised Italian street theater that depended on buffoonery, slapstick humor, and pantomime. Molière's plays involve simple story lines that bring to life the comic foibles of such stock characters as the miser, the hypochondriac, the hypocrite, the misanthrope, and the would-be gentleman. The last of these is the subject of one of Molière's last plays, *Le Bourgeois Gentilhomme* ("The Tradesman Turned Gentleman"). The plot involves a wealthy tradesman (Monsieur Jourdain) who, aspiring to nobility, hires a variety of tutors to school him in the trappings of upper-class respectability. The play's fabric of deception and self-deception is complicated by Jourdain's refusal to accept his daughter's choice of a partner, the handsome but poor Cléonte. Only after Cléonte appears disguised as the son of the Grand Turk does the unwitting merchant bless the betrothal. Essentially a farce or comedy of manners, Molière's play (like La Rochefoucauld's maxims) holds up to ridicule the fundamental flaws of human behavior, which might be corrected by applying the classical norms of reason and moderation. By contrasting incidents of hypocrisy, pomposity, and greed with the solid, good sense demonstrated, for instance, by Mr. Jourdain's wife, Molière probes the excesses of passion and vanity that enfeeble human dignity. *Le Bourgeois Gentilhomme* was designed as a **comédie-ballet**, a dramatic performance that incorporated interludes of song and dance (in a manner similar to modern musical comedy). Lully provided the music, choreographed the ballet, and directed the entire production, which, like many other of Molière's plays, was well received by the king and his court, a court that lavishly and regularly received the ambassadors of "exotic" countries, such as Turkey.

But even beyond Versailles, Molière's hilarious comedy had wide appeal. French aristocrats, convinced that they were above imitation, embraced the play. So did upper-middle-class patrons who, while claiming an increasingly prominent place in the social order, refused to see themselves as merchants longing to be aristocrats. Women found themselves endowed in Molière's play with confidence and guile, while servants discovered themselves invested with admirable common sense. The comedy, for all its farce, reflected the emerging class structure of early modern European society, with its firmly drawn lines between sexes and classes. In Act II, Scene XIV of *Le Bourgeois Gentilhomme*, Mr. Jourdain—himself descended from shopkeepers—refuses to allow his daughter to marry anyone other than a gentleman. To prevent her from marrying "below" her, he boasts, "I have riches enough for my daughter; all I need is honors, so I shall make her a marquise." To this, his wife exclaims, "'Tis a thing to which I shall never consent. Your marriages with people above you are always subject to wretched vexations. I don't want my daughter to have a husband that can reproach her with her parents, and children that will be ashamed to call me grandma. If she should come to call on me in her fine lady's equipage, and fall by chance to bow to any of the neighbors, they would be sure to say a hundred ill-natured things. . . . I don't want all this cackle, and, in a word, I want a man who shall be beholden to me for my daughter, and to whom I can say: "Sit down there, son-in-law, and have dinner with me."

Mr. Jourdain snaps back, "Those are the sentiments of a petty soul, willing to stay forever in a mean station. Don't talk back to me any more. My daughter shall be a marquise, in spite of all the world, and if you provoke me, I'll make her a duchess."

With unparalleled comic wit, *Le Bourgeois Gentilhomme* captured the spirit of the seventeenth century—its class tensions and social contradictions, along with its ambitions and high expectations. Yet, for all its value as a mirror of a particular time and place, *Le Bourgeois Gentilhomme* is universal and timeless. The limitations of space forbid the inclusion of the play in its entirety. However, portions of the first and second acts offer a representative sampling of Molière's rollicking exposition of human nature.

READING 4.5 From Molière's *Le Bourgeois Gentilhomme* (1670)

Characters

Mr. Jourdain	His Scholar
Mrs. Jourdain, *his wife*	A Dancing-Master
Lucile, *his daughter*	A Fencing-Master
Cléonte, *suitor of Lucile*	A Philosophy-Master
Dorimene, *a marquise*	A Master-Tailor
Dorante, *a count, in love with Dorimene*	A Journeyman-Tailor
	Two lackeys
Nicole, *servant to Mr. Jourdain*	Musicians, Dancers, Cooks, Journeymen-Tailors, and other characters to dance in the interludes
Coveille, valet to Cléonte	
A Music-Master	

The scene is at Paris

ACT I

The scene is at Paris

ACT I

Overture, played by a full orchestra; in the middle of the stage the Music-Master's Scholar, seated at a table, is composing the air for a serenade which Mr. Jourdain has ordered.

Scene I

Music-Master, Dancing-Master, Three Singers, Two Violinists, Four Dancers

Music-Master (*To the singers*): Here, step inside, and wait until he comes. 1

Dancing-Master (*To the dancers*): And you too, this way.

Music-Master (To his scholar): Is it finished?

Scholar: Yes.

Music-Master: Let's see . . . That's good.

Dancing-Master: Is it something new?

Music-Master: Yes, 'tis the air for a serenade which I have had him compose, while waiting for our gentleman to wake up.

Dancing-Master: May I see it? 10

Music-Master: You shall hear it, with the words, when he comes. He won't be long.

Dancing-Master: You and I have no lack of occupation now.

Music-Master: That's true. We have found a man here who is just what we both needed. He's a nice little source of income for us, this Mr. Jourdain, with his visions of nobility and gallantry that he has got into his noddle. And 'twould be a fine thing for your dancing and my music if everybody were like him.

Dancing-Master: No, no, not quite; I could wish, for his 20 sake, that he had some true understanding of the good things we bring him.

Music-Master: 'Tis true he understands them ill, but he pays for them well; and that is what the arts need most nowadays.

Dancing-Master: For my part, I'll own, I must be fed somewhat on fame. I am sensitive to applause, and I feel that in all the fine arts 'tis a grievous torture to show one's talents before fools, and to endure the barbarous judgments of a dunce upon our compositions. There's great pleasure, I tell you, 30 in working for people who are capable of feeling the refinements of art, who know how to give a flattering reception to the beauties of your work, and recompense your toil by titillating praise. Yes, the most agreeable reward possible for what we do, is to see it understood, to see it caressed by applause that honors us. Nothing else, methinks, can pay us so well for all our labors; and enlightened praise gives exquisite delight.

Music-Master: I grant you that, and I relish it as you do. There is surely nothing more gratifying than such praise as you speak of; but man cannot live on applause. Mere praise won't buy you an estate; it takes something more solid. And the best way to praise, is to praise with open hands. Our fellow, to be sure, is a man of little wit, who discourses at random about anything and everything, and never applauds but at the wrong time. But his money sets right the errors of his mind; there is judgment in his purse; his praises pass current; and this ignorant shopkeeper is worth more to us, as you very well see, than the enlightened lord who introduced us to his house. **50**

Dancing-Master: There is some truth in what you say; but methinks you set too much store by money; and self-interest is something so base that no gentleman should ever show a leaning towards it.

Music-Master: Yet I haven't seen you refuse the money our fellow offers you.

Dancing-Master: Certainly not; but neither do I find therein all my happiness; and I could still wish that with his wealth he had good taste to boot.

Music-Master: I could wish so too; and 'tis to that end that we are both working, as best we may. But in any case, he gives **60** us the means to make ourselves known in the world; he shall pay for others, and others shall praise for him.

Dancing-Master: Here he comes.

[Act I, Scene II: Mr. Jourdain converses with his music- and dancing-masters, who dispute as to which is the more important art: music or dance. A dialogue in music, written by the music-master, follows, then a ballet choreographed by the dancing-master.

Act II, Scene I: Mr. Jourdain dances the minuet for the dancing-master, and then learns how to make a "proper" bow.]

ACT II, Scene II
Mr. Jourdain, Music-Master, Dancing-Master, Lackey

Lackey: Sir, here is your fencing-master. **1**

Mr. Jourdain: Tell him to come in and give me my lesson here. (*To the music-master and dancing-master*) I want you to see me perform.

Scene III
Mr. Jourdain, Fencing-Master, Music-Master, Dancing-Master, a Lackey with two foils

Fencing-Master (*Taking the two foils from the lackey and giving one of them to Mr. Jourdain*): Now, sir, your salute. The body erect. The weight slightly on the left thigh. The legs not so far apart. The feet in line. The wrist in line with the thigh. The point of your sword in line with your shoulder. The arm not quite so far extended. The left hand on a level **10** with the eye. The left shoulder farther back. Head up. A

bold look. Advance. The body steady. Engage my sword in quart[1] and finish the thrust. One, two. Recover. Again, your feet firm. One, two. Retreat. When you thrust, sir, your sword must move first, and your body be held well back, and sideways. One, two. Now, engage my sword in tierce,[2] and finish the thrust. Advance. Your body steady. Advance. Now, from that position. One, two. Recover. Again. One, two. Retreat. On guard, sir, on guard (*the fencing-master gives him several thrusts*), on guard. **20**

Mr. Jourdain: Well?

Music-Master: You do wonders.

Fencing-Master: I've told you already: the whole secret of arms consists in two things only: hitting and not being hit. And as I proved to you the other day by demonstrative logic, it is impossible that you should be hit if you know how to turn aside your adversary's sword from the line of your body; and that depends merely on a slight movement of the wrist, inwards or outwards.

Mr. Jourdain: So, then, without any courage, one may be **30** sure of killing his man and not being killed?

Fencing-Master: Certainly. Didn't you see the demonstration of it?

Mr. Jourdain: Yes.

Fencing-Master: And by this you may see how highly our profession should be esteemed in the State; and how far the science of arms excels all other sciences that are of no use, like dancing, music . . .

Dancing-Master: Softly, Mr. Swordsman; don't speak disrespectfully of dancing. **40**

Music-Master: Learn, pray, to appreciate better the excellences of music.

Fencing-Master: You are absurd fellows, to think of comparing your sciences with mine.

Music-Master: Just see the man of consequence!

Dancing-Master: The ridiculous animal, with his padded stomacher![3]

Fencing-Master: My little dancing-master, I will make you dance to a tune of my own, and you, little songster, I will make you sing out lustily. **50**

Dancing-Master: Mr. Ironmonger,[4] I'll teach you your own trade.

Mr. Jourdain (*To the dancing-master*): Are you mad, to pick a quarrel with him, when he knows tierce and quart and can kill a man by demonstrative logic?

Dancing-Master: A fig for his demonstrative logic, and his tierce and his quart.

Mr. Jourdain (*To the dancing-master*): Softly, I tell you.

Fencing-Master (*To the dancing-master*): What, little Master Impudence! **60**

Mr. Jourdain: Hey! my dear fencing-master.

Dancing-Master (*To the fencing-master*): What, you great cart-horse!

Mr. Jourdain: Hey, my dear dancing-master.

Fencing-Master: If I once fall upon you . . .

---

[1] A defensive posture in the art of fencing.
[2] Another fencing posture.
[3] Protection used in fencing.
[4] A dealer in hardware.

Mr. Jourdain (*To the fencing-master*): Gently.

Dancing-Master: If I once lay hands on you . . .

Mr. Jourdain (*To the dancing-master*): So, so.

Fencing-Master: I will give you such a dressing . . .

Mr. Jourdain (*To the fencing-master*): I beg you.   70

Dancing-Master: I will give you such a drubbing[5] . . .

Mr. Jourdain (*To the dancing-master*): I beseech you . . .

Music-Master: Let us teach him manners a little.

Mr. Jourdain: Good Heavens! do stop.

Scene IV

Professor of Philosophy, Mr. Jourdain, Music-Master, Dancing-Master, Fencing-Master, Lackey

Mr. Jourdain: Oho! Mr. Philosopher, you've arrived in the nick of time with your philosophy. Do come and set these people here at peace.

The Philosopher: How now? What is the matter, gentlemen?

Mr. Jourdain: They have put themselves in a passion about the precedence of their professions, and even insulted   80 each other and almost come to blows.

The Philosopher: O fie, gentlemen! Should a man so lose his self-control? Have you not read the learned treatise which Seneca composed, *Of Anger*?[6] Is there anything more base or shameful than this passion, which of a man makes a savage beast? Should not reason be mistress of all our emotions?

Dancing-Master: How, how, sir! Here he comes and insults us both, by condemning dancing, which I practice, and music, which is his profession.

The Philosopher: A wise man is above all the insults that   90 can be offered him; and the chief answer which we should make to all offences, is calmness and patience.

Fencing-Master: They both have the insolence to think of comparing their professions with mine!

The Philosopher: Should that move you? 'Tis not for vainglory and precedence that men should contend; what really distinguishes us from each other is wisdom and virtue.

Dancing-Master: I maintain to his face that dancing is a science which cannot be too highly honored.

Music-Master: And I, that music is a science which all   100 ages have reverenced.

Fencing-Master: And I maintain, against both of them, that the science of fencing is the finest and most indispensable of all sciences.

The Philosopher: But what then becomes of philosophy? I think you are all three mighty impertinent to speak with such arrogance before me, and impudently to give the name of science to things which ought not even to be honored with the name of art, and which may best be classed together as pitiful trades, whether of prize-fighters, ballad-mongers, or   110 mountebanks.[7]

Fencing-Master: Go to, dog of a philosopher.

Music-Master: Go to, beggarly pedagogue.

Dancing-Master: Go to, past master pedant.

The Philosopher: What, you rascally knaves! . . .

(*He falls upon them, and they all three belabor him with blows.*)

Mr. Jourdain: Mr. Philosopher!

The Philosopher: Villains! varlets! insolent vermin!

Mr. Jourdain: Mr. Philosopher!

Fencing-Master: Plague take the beast!

Mr. Jourdain: Gentlemen!

The Philosopher: Brazen-faced ruffians!   120

Mr. Jourdain: Mr. Philosopher!

Dancing-Master: Deuce take the old pack-mule!

Mr. Jourdain: Gentlemen!

The Philosopher: Scoundrels!

Mr. Jourdain: Mr. Philosopher!

Music-Master: Devil take the impertinent puppy!

Mr. Jourdain: Gentlemen!

The Philosopher: Thieves! vagabonds! rogues! impostors!

Mr. Jourdain: Mr. Philosopher! Gentlemen! Mr. Philosopher!

Gentlemen! Mr. Philosopher!   130

(*Exit fighting.*)

Scene V

Mr. Jourdain, Lackey

Mr. Jourdain: Oh! fight as much as you please; I can't help it, and I won't go spoil my gown trying to part you. I should be mad to thrust myself among them and get some blow that might do me a mischief.

Scene VI

The Philosopher, Mr. Jourdain, Lackey

The Philosopher (*Straightening his collar*): Now for our lesson.

Mr. Jourdain: Oh! sir, I am sorry for the blows you got.

The Philosopher: That's nothing. A philosopher knows how to take things aright; and I shall compose a satire against them   140 in Juvenal's manner,[8] which will cut them up properly. But let that pass. What do you want to learn?

Mr. Jourdain: Everything I can; for I have the greatest desire conceivable to be learned; it throws me in a rage to think that my father and mother did not make me study all the sciences when I was young.

The Philosopher: That is a reasonable sentiment; *nam, sine doctrina, vita est quasi mortis imago.* You understand that, for of course you know Latin.

Mr. Jourdain: Yes; but play that I don't know it; and explain   150 what it means.

The Philosopher: It means that, *without learning, life is almost an image of death.*

Mr. Jourdain: That same Latin's in the right.

The Philosopher: Have you not some foundations, some rudiments of knowledge?

Mr. Jourdain: Oh! yes, I can read and write.

The Philosopher: Where will you please to have us begin? Shall I teach you logic?

Mr. Jourdain: What may that same logic be?   160

The Philosopher: 'Tis the science that teaches the three operations of the mind.

---

[5]A beating

[6]A treatise by the first-century Roman stoic, Lucius Annaeus Seneca (see chapter 6).

[7]Charlatans or quacks.

---

[8]A Roman satirist of the early second century (see chapter 6).

Mr. Jourdain: And who are they, these three operations of the mind?

The Philosopher: The first, the second, and the third. The first is to conceive aright, by means of the universals; the second, to judge aright, by means of the categories; and the third, to draw deductions aright, by means of the figures: *Barbara, Celarent, Darii, Ferio, Baralipton.*[9]

Mr. Jourdain: There's a pack of crabbed words. This logic 170
doesn't suit me at all. Let's learn something else that's prettier.

The Philosopher: Will you learn ethics?

Mr. Jourdain: Ethics?

The Philosopher: Yes.

Mr. Jourdain: What is your ethics about?

The Philosopher: It treats of happiness, teaches men to moderate their passions, and . . .

Mr. Jourdain: No; no more of that. I am choleric as the whole pack of devils, ethics or no ethics; no, sir, I'll be angry to my heart's content, whenever I have a mind to it. 180

The Philosopher: Is it physics you want to learn?

Mr. Jourdain: And what has this physics to say for itself?

The Philosopher: Physics is the science which explains the principles of natural phenomena, and the properties of bodies; which treats of the nature of the elements, metals, minerals, stones, plants, and animals, and teaches us the causes of all such things as meteors, the rainbow, St. Elmo's fire,[10] comets, lightning, thunder, thunderbolts, rain, snow, hail, winds, and whirlwinds.

Mr. Jourdain: There's too much jingle-jangle in that, too 190
much hurly-burly.

The Philosopher: Then what to do you want me to teach you?

Mr. Jourdain: Teach me spelling.

The Philosopher: With all my heart.

Mr. Jourdain: And afterward, you shall teach me the almanac, so as to know when there's a moon, and when there isn't.

The Philosopher: Very well. To follow up your line of thought logically, and treat this matter in true philosophic 200
fashion, we must begin, according to the proper order of things, by an exact knowledge of the nature of the letters, and the different method of pronouncing each one. And on that head I must tell you that the letters are divided into vowels, so called—*vowels*—because they express the sounds of the voice alone; and consonants, so called—*con-sonants*—because they sound with the vowels, and only mark the different articulations of the voice. There are five vowels, or voices: A, E, I, O, U.

Mr. Jourdain: I understand all that. 210

The Philosopher: The vowel A is formed by opening the mouth wide: A.

Mr. Jourdain: A, A. Yes.

The Philosopher: The vowel E is formed by lifting the lower jaw nearer to the upper: A, E.

Mr. Jourdain: A, E; A, E. On my word, 'tis so. Ah! how fine!

---

[9]Part of a series of Latin names used by medieval logicians to help remember the valid forms of syllogisms.

[10]Electrical discharges seen by sailors before and after storms at sea and named after the patron saint of sailors.

The Philosopher: And the vowel I, by bringing the jaws still nearer together, and stretching the corners of the mouth toward the ears: A, E, I.

Mr. Jourdain: A, E, I, I, I, I. That is true. Science forever! 220

The Philosopher: The vowel O is formed by opening the jaws, and drawing in the lips at the corners: O.

Mr. Jourdain: O, O. Nothing could be more correct: A, E, I, O, I, O. 'Tis admirable! I, O; I, O.

The Philosopher: The opening of the mouth looks exactly like a little circle, representing an O.

Mr. Jourdain: O, O, O. You are right. O. Ah! What a fine thing it is to know something!

The Philosopher: The vowel U is formed by bringing the teeth together without letting them quite touch, and thrusting 230
out the lips, at the same time bringing them together without quite shutting them: U.

Mr. Jourdain: U, U. Nothing could be truer: U.

The Philosopher: Your lips are extended as if you were pouting; therefore if you wish to make a face at anyone, and mock at him, you have only to say U.

Mr. Jourdain: U, U. 'Tis true. Ah! would I had studied sooner, to know all that!

The Philosopher: To-morrow, we will consider the other letters, namely the consonants. 240

Mr. Jourdain: Are there just as curious things about them as about these?

The Philosopher: Certainly. The consonant D, for instance, is pronounced by clapping the tip of the tongue just above the upper teeth: D.

Mr. Jourdain: D, D. Yes! Oh! what fine things! what fine things!

The Philosopher: The F, by resting the upper teeth on the lower lip: F.

Mr. Jourdain: F, F. 'Tis the very truth. Oh! father and mother 250
of me, what a grudge I owe you!

The Philosopher: And the R by lifting the tip of the tongue to the roof of the mouth; so that being grazed by the air, which comes out sharply, it yields to it, yet keeps returning to the same point, and so makes a sort of trilling: R, Ra.

Mr. Jourdain: R, R, Ra, R, R, R, R, R, Ra. That is fine. Oh! what a learned man you are, and how much time I've lost! R, R, R, Ra.

The Philosopher: I will explain all these curious things to you thoroughly. 260

Mr. Jourdain: Do, I beg you. But now, I must tell you a great secret. I am in love with a person of very high rank, and I wish you would help me to write her something in a little love note which I'll drop at her feet.

The Philosopher: Excellent!

Mr. Jourdain: 'Twill be very gallant, will it not?

The Philosopher: Surely. Do you want to write to her in verse?

Mr. Jourdain: No, no; none of your verse.

The Philosopher: You want mere prose? 270

Mr. Jourdain: No, I will have neither prose nor verse.

The Philosopher: It must needs be one or the other.

Mr. Jourdain: Why?

The Philosopher: For this reason, that there is nothing but prose or verse to express oneself by.

Mr. Jourdain: There is nothing but prose or verse?

The Philosopher: No, sir. All that is not prose is verse, and all that is not verse is prose.

Mr. Jourdain: But when we talk, what is that, say?

The Philosopher: Prose. 280

Mr. Jourdain: What! When I say: "Nicole, bring me my slippers and give me my nightcap," that's prose?

The Philosopher: Yes, sir.

Mr. Jourdain: Oh my word, I've been speaking prose these forty years, and never knew it; I am infinitely obliged to you for having informed me of this. Now I want to write to her in a note: *Fair Marquise,*[11] *your fair eyes make me die of love*; but I want it to be put in gallant fashion, and neatly turned.

The Philosopher: Say that the fires of her eyes reduce your heart to ashes; that night and day you suffer for her all the 290 tortures of a. . .

Mr. Jourdain: No, no, no, I want none of all that. I will have nothing but what I told you: *Fair Marquise, your fair eyes make me die of love.*

The Philosopher: You must enlarge upon the matter a little.

Mr. Jourdain: No, I tell you. I'll have none but those very words in the note, but put in a fashionable way, arranged as they should be. Pray tell me over the different ways they can be put, so that I may see.

The Philosopher: You can first of all put them as you said: 300 *Fair Marquise, your fair eyes make me die of love.*
Or else: *Of love to die me make, fair Marquise, your fair eyes.*
Or else: *Your fair eyes of love me make, fair Marquise, to die.*
Or else: *To die your fair eyes, fair Marquise, of love me make.*
Or else: *Me make your fair eyes die, fair Marquise, of love.*

Mr. Jourdain: But which of all these ways is the best?

The Philosopher: The way you said it: *Fair Marquise, your fair eyes make me die of love.*

Mr. Jourdain: And yet I never studied, and I did it at the first try. I thank you with all my heart, and beg you to come 310 again to-morrow early.

The Philosopher: I shall not fail to.

Scene VII
Mr. Jourdain, Lackey

Mr. Jourdain (*To the lackey*): What! Haven't my clothes come yet?

Lackey: No, sir.

Mr. Jourdain: That cursed tailor makes me wait a long while, on a day when I'm so busy. I am furious. May the quartan ague[12] wring this villain of a tailor unmercifully! To the devil with the tailor! Plague choke the tailor! If I had him here now, that wretch of a tailor, that dog of a tailor, that scoundrel 320 of a tailor, I'd. . .

Scene VIII
Mr. Jourdain, A Master-Tailor; A Journeyman-Tailor, *carrying Mr. Jourdain's suit*; Lackey

Mr. Jourdain: Ah! so there you are! I was just going to get angry with you.

Master-Tailor: I could not come sooner. I had twenty men at work on your clothes.

Mr. Jourdain: You sent me some silk stockings so tight that I had dreadful work getting them on, and there are two stitches broke in them already.

Master-Tailor: If anything, they will grow only too loose.

Mr. Jourdain: Yes, if I keep on breaking out stitches. And 330 you made me some shoes that pinch horribly.

Master-Tailor: Not at all, sir.

Mr. Jourdain: What! Not at all?

Master-Tailor: No, they do not pinch you.

Mr. Jourdain: I tell you they do pinch me.

Master-Tailor: You imagine it.

Mr. Jourdain: I imagine it because I feel it. A fine way of talking!

Master-Tailor: There, this is one of the very handsomest and best matched of court costumes. 'Tis a masterpiece to 340 have invented a suit that is dignified, yet not of black; and I'd give the most cultured tailors six trials and defy them to equal it.

Mr. Jourdain: What's this? You have put the flowers upside down.

Master-Tailor: You didn't tell me you wanted them right end up.

Mr. Jourdain: Was there any need to tell you that?

Master-Tailor: Why, of course. All persons of quality wear them this way. 350

Mr. Jourdain: Persons of quality wear the flowers upside down?

Master-Tailor: Yes, sir.

Mr. Jourdain: Oh! that's all right then.

Master-Tailor: If you wish, I will put them right end up.

Mr. Jourdain: No, no.

Master-Tailor: You have only to say the word.

Mr. Jourdain: No, I tell you; you did rightly. Do you think the clothes will fit me?

Master-Tailor: A pretty question! I defy any painter, with 360 his brush, to make you a closer fit. I have in my shop a fellow that is the greatest genius in the world for setting up a pair of German breeches; and another who is the hero of our age for the cut of a doublet.[13]

Mr. Jourdain: Are the wig and the feathers just as they should be?

Master-Tailor: Everything is just right.

Mr. Jourdain (*Looking at the tailor's suit*): Ah! ah! Mr. Tailor here is some of the cloth from my last suit you made me. I know it perfectly. 370

Master-Tailor: The cloth seemed to me so fine that I thought well to cut a suit for myself out of it.

Mr. Jourdain: Yes; but you ought not to have cabbaged[14] it out of mine.

Master-Tailor: Will you put on your suit?

Mr. Jourdain: Yes; let me have it.

Master-Tailor: Wait. That is not the way to do things. I have brought my men with me to dress you to music; clothes such as these must be put on with ceremony. Ho! enter, you fellows.

[11]The wife of a nobleman ranking below a duke and above an earl or count.
[12]An intermittent fever.

[13]A man's close-fitting jacket.
[14]Stolen or filched.

Scene IX

Mr. Jourdain, Master-Tailor, Journeyman-Tailor; Dancers, *in the costume of journeymen-tailors*; Lackey

Master-Tailor (*To his journeymen*): Put on the gentleman's **380** suit, in the style you use for persons of quality.

First Ballet

Enter four journeymen-tailors, two of whom pull off Mr. Jourdain's breeches that he has on for his exercise, and the other two his jacket; then they put on his new suit; and Mr. Jourdain walks about among them, showing off his suit, to see if it is all right. All this to the accompaniment of full orchestra.

Journeyman-Tailor: Noble Sir, please give the tailor's men something to drink.

Mr. Jourdain: What did you call me?

Journeyman-Tailor: Noble Sir. **390**

Mr. Jourdain: Noble Sir! That is what it is to dress as a person of quality! You may go clothed as a tradesman all your days, and nobody will call you Noble Sir. (*Giving him money*) There, that's for Noble Sir.

Journeyman-Tailor: My Lord, we are greatly obliged to you.

Mr. Jourdain: My Lord! Oh! oh! My Lord! Wait, friend; My Lord deserves something, 'tis no mean word, My Lord! There, there's what His Lordship gives you.

Journeyman-Tailor: My Lord, we will all go and drink Your Grace's health. **400**

Mr. Jourdain: Your Grace! Oh! oh! oh! wait; don't go. Your Grace, to me! (*Aside*) Faith, if he goes as far as Your Highness he'll empty my purse. (*Aloud*) There, there's for Your Grace.

Journeyman-Tailor: My Lord, we thank you most humbly for your generosity.

Mr. Jourdain: He did well to stop. I was just going to give it all to him.

Q How does Molière poke fun at aristocratic values?

Q How does he treat middle-class aspirations?

Absolute Power and the Aristocratic Style Beyond Europe

Fueled by curiosity and commercial ambition, cross-cultural contacts between Europe and Asia flourished during the early modern era. In the 1700s, ambassadors of the Shah (the word means "king") of Persia and of other Asian potentates were splendidly received at Versailles, while, at the same time, Christian missionaries and official representatives of the European monarchs found their way to Hindu, Buddhist, and Muslim lands. France had long maintained diplomatic ties with the Ottoman Turks, the Muslim successors of the Seljuk Turks in Southwest Asia, North Africa, and parts of southeastern Europe (see Map 21.1). So powerful were the Ottoman forces and so vast were their territories that one of Louis' ancestors, Francis I, had attempted to tip the balance of power in Western Europe by forming, in 1536, an "unholy" alliance with the great Muslim leader Suleiman (1494–1566).

Under Suleiman's rule the Ottoman Empire, which stretched across North Africa and the ancient Fertile Crescent (see Map 21.1), became a model of Muslim absolutism. Unlimited power in matters political and religious lay in Suleiman's hands. Known in Turkish history as the "Lawgiver," Suleiman oversaw the establishment of a legal code that fixed specific penalties for routine crimes and introduced the concept of balanced financial budgets. State revenues some eighty times those of France permitted Suleiman to undertake an extensive program of architectural and urban improvement in Mecca, Constantinople, and Jerusalem. A goldsmith and a poet of some esteem, Suleiman initiated a golden age of literature and art. Pomp and luxury characterized Suleiman's court, and the arts that flourished under his patronage shared with those of seventeenth-century France a taste for the ornate and a high degree of technical skill (Figure **21.17**). Suleiman, whom Europeans called "the Magnificent," personally oversaw the activities of official court poets, painters, architects, and musicians. He established a model for imperial patronage that ensured the triumph of the aristocratic style not only in Turkish lands but in all parts of his multiethnic empire.

Neither absolutism nor its manifestation in the arts were the invention of Suleiman, any more than they were the creation of Louis XIV. Suleiman's ancestors, as well as his successors and their rivals, were equally autocratic. During the seventeenth century, as the Ottoman Empire lost initiative, Muslims of the Safavid dynasty rose to power in Persia under the astute leadership of Shah Abbas

Figure 21.17 Ceremonial canteen, Ottoman Empire, second half of the sixteenth century. Gold decorated with jade plaques and gems. Topkapi Sarayi Museum, Istanbul.

(1557–1629). Shah Abbas united a multiethnic population to make theocratic Persia (present-day Iran) the political, economic, and cultural leader of Asia. By the year 1600, Persian silk rivaled that of China at European markets. Carpet weaving became a national industry that employed more than twenty-five thousand people in the capital city of Isfahan alone. Persian tapestries, intricately woven in silk and wool (Figure **21.18**), and finely ornamented ceramics were avidly sought across the world, and

Figure 21.18 Kirman shrub rug, Persia, seventeenth century. Silk and wool, 10 ft. 1 in. × 4 ft. 7 in. Philadelphia Museum of Art. The Joseph Lees Williams Memorial Collection.

Persian manuscripts embellished with brightly printed illustrations came to be imitated throughout Asia. The arts were as much an adjunct to the majesty of Shah Abbas as they had been to Suleiman and would be to Louis XIV.

In the field of architecture, the outstanding monument to Safavid wealth and power was the Imperial Mosque, commissioned by Shah Abbas for the city of Isfahan (Figure **21.19**). Completed in 1637, this magnificent structure, flanked by two minarets, encloses a square main hall covered by a splendid dome that rises to 177 feet. The surfaces of the mosque, both inside and out, are covered with colored glazed tiles (compare to the Ishtar Gate of ancient Babylon, see Figure 2.11) ornamented with calligraphic inscriptions and delicate blue and yellow floral motifs. French aristocrats in the service of Louis XIV brought back to France enthusiastic reports of the Imperial Mosque—a fact that has led scholars to detect the influence of Persian art on some of Louis' more lavish enterprises at Versailles.

Absolute Power and the Aristocratic Style in India

Muslims had ruled parts of India for almost a thousand years, but it was not until the sixteenth century that the Muslim dynasty known as the Moguls (the name derives from "Mongol") succeeded in uniting all of India (see Map 21.1). Distant cousins of the Safavid princes, the Moguls created an Indian empire and ruled India as absolute monarchs from 1526 to 1707. They imported Persian culture and language into India in much the same way that Louis XIV brought Italian culture into France. The creators of a cultural style that blended Muslim, Hindu, Turkish, Persian, Arabic, and African traditions, the Moguls encouraged the development of an aristocratic style, which—like that of the Sun King—served as an adjunct to majesty.

The founder of the Mogul empire, Akbar (1542–1605), came to the throne at the age of thirteen and laid the foundations for a luxurious court style that his son and grandson would perpetuate. India's most dynamic ruler since Emperor Asoka of the third century B.C.E., Akbar ruled over a court consisting of thousands of courtiers, servants, wives, and concubines. He exercised political

Science and Technology

1717 inoculation against smallpox is introduced in Europe (from Ottoman Turkey)

1736 expansion of the Indian shipbuilding industry in Bombay

1780 a European version of Chinese silk-reeling machines is introduced in Bengal

1781 Turkish methods for producing high-quality cloth are copied in England

1790 India uses military rockets based on Ottoman technology in warfare

Figure 21.19 Imperial Mosque, Isfahan, Iran, 1637. Surface decorated with colored glazed tiles, height of dome 177 ft. © E. Böhm, Mainz.

control over feudal noblemen and court officials who, unlike their French counterparts, received paid salaries. Amidst the primarily Hindu population, the Muslim emperor tirelessly pursued a policy of religious toleration, a position that complemented his own quest for a synthesis of faiths that would surpass the teaching of any one religion. To this end, he brought to his court learned representatives of Christianity, Judaism, Hinduism, and other religions to debate with Muslim theologians. He also made

every effort to rid India of such outmoded traditions as the immolation of wives on their husbands' funeral pyres. Despite Akbar's reforms, however, the lower classes and especially the peasants were taxed heavily (as were the French peasants under Louis) to finance the luxuries of the upper-class elite.

In the seventeenth century, the Moguls governed the wealthiest state in the world, a state whose revenues were ten times greater than those of France. Akbar commissioned magnificent works of music, poetry, painting, and architecture—the tangible expressions of princely affluence and taste. As was the case in Louis' court, most of these exquisite objects were designed for secular, not liturgical, use. A state studio of more than one hundred artists working under Persian masters created a library of more than 24,000 illuminated manuscripts, the contents of which ranged from love poetry to Hindu epics and religious tales. One Mogul innovation was the practice of recording and illustrating first-hand accounts of specific historical events. A miniature celebrating the birth of Akbar's son, Jahangir, shows courtiers rejoicing: dancers

Figure 21.20 *Rejoicing at the Birth of Prince Salim in 1569*. Manuscript illustration from the Akbar-Nama. The Chester Beatty Library, Dublin.

sway to the rhythms of a musical ensemble (consisting of male and female instrumentalists), while bread and alms are distributed outside the palace gate (Figure 21.20). Such miniatures reveal the brilliant union of delicate line, rich color, and strong surface patterns—features that also dominate Asian carpet designs. The absence of Western perspective gives the scene a flat, decorative quality.

The Patronage of Jahangir and Shah Jahan Under the rule of Akbar's son, Jahangir (ruled 1605–1627), aristocratic court portraiture came into fashion in India. The new genre reflects the influence of European painting, which had been eagerly embraced by the Moguls, and suggests the gradual relaxation of Muslim prohibition against the representation of the human figure. Relatively small in comparison with the aristocratic portraits executed by Rigaud or van Dyck (see Figures 21.1, 22.1), the painted likeness of Jahangir (the name means "world seizer") reflects the will to glorify royalty in a realistic and psychologically probing manner (Figure 21.21). The artist Bichitr (fl. 1625), whose self-portrait appears in the lower left corner, shows the Shah enthroned atop an elaborate hourglass throne, a reference to the brevity of life and to Jahangir's declining health. Jahangir welcomes a sufi (a Muslim mystic), who stands in the company of a Turkish dignitary and the European King James I of England. Four Western-style angels frame the scene: the upper two seem to lament the impermanence of worldly power (as suggested in the inscription above them), while the bottom two inscribe the base of the hourglass with the prayer, "O Shah, may the span of your life be a thousand years." Just as Louis XIV assumed the guise of the Sun King, so Jahangir—as notorious for his overconsumption of wine and opium as Louis was for fine food and sex—is apotheosized by a huge halo consisting of the sun and the moon.

Well before the seventeenth century, Mogul rulers had initiated the tradition of building huge ceremonial and administrative complexes, veritable cities in themselves. Such complexes symbolized Muslim wealth and authority in India, but, as in France, they were also political manifestations of the cult of royalty. Akbar had personally overseen the construction of a palace complex near Agra, which, comparable with Versailles, featured an elaborate residence surrounded by courtyards and mosques, as well as by formal gardens and fountains

Figure 21.21 (right) *Jahangir Preferring a Sufi Shaikh to Kings*, from the *Leningrad Album of Bichitr*, seventeenth century. Color and gold, 10 × 7⅞ in. Courtesy of the Freer Gallery of Art, Smithsonian Institution, Washington, D.C. (42.15V).

watered by means of artificial conduits. The garden, a this-worldly counterpart of the Garden of Paradise described in the Quran (see chapter 10) and a welcome refuge from India's intense heat, was a characteristic feature of the Mogul palace complex.

Inspired by the elaborate ceremonial centers built by his father and his grandfather, Shah Jahan (1627–1666) commissioned the most sumptuous of all Mogul palaces, the Shahjahanabad (present-day Old Delhi). The red sandstone walls of the Shahjahanabad (nicknamed the "Red Fort") enclosed a palatial residence of white marble, flanked by magnificent gardens, public and private audience halls, courtyards, pavilions, baths, and the largest mosque in India (Figure **21.22**). The Red Fort's 3:4 rectangular plan was bisected by an axis that led through successive courts to the public audience hall, a pattern that anticipated the rigid symmetry of Versailles (compare Figure 21.2).

The hot Indian climate inclined Mogul architects to open up interior space by means of foliated arcades (see chapter 10) and latticed screens through which breezes might blow uninterrupted. These graceful architectural features distinguish the Shah's palace at the Red Fort (Figure **21.23**). The most ornate of all Mogul interiors, Shah Jahan's audience hall consists of white marble arcades and ceilings decorated with geometric and floral patterns popular in Mogul embroidery, a craft traditionally dominated by women. The rich designs consist of inlaid precious and semiprecious stones (***pietra dura***), a type of mosaic work that the Moguls had borrowed from Italy. At the center of the hall, the Shah once sat on the prized (but no longer existing) Peacock Throne, fashioned in solid gold and studded with emeralds,

Figure 21.22 Anonymous Delhi artist, *The Red Fort*, ca. 1820. The building dates from the Shah Jahan period, after 1638. Courtesy of the British Library, London.

Figure 21.23 Foliated arcades and perforated monolithic screens in the Red Fort (Shahjahanabad), Delhi, Shah Jahan period, after 1638.

rubies, diamonds, and pearls. Above the throne (which served as the imperial throne of India until it was plundered by Persian warriors in 1732) was a canopy on which stood two gold peacocks, and above the canopy, around the ceiling of the hall, were inscribed the words, "If there is a paradise on the face of the earth, It is this, oh! it is this, oh! it is this."

Surpassing the splendor of the palace at Delhi (badly damaged by the British army during the nineteenth century) is Shah Jahan's most magnificent gift to world architecture: the Taj Mahal (Figure **21.24**). Shah Jahan built the Taj Mahal as a mausoleum to honor the memory of his favorite wife, Mumtaz Mahal (the name means "light of the world"). When Mumtaz died giving birth to their fourteenth child, her husband, legend has it, was inconsolable. He directed his architects to construct alongside the Jumna River a glorious tomb, a twin to one he planned for himself on the adjoining riverbank. Fabricated in cream-colored marble, the Taj rises majestically above a tree-lined pool that mirrors its elegant silhouette so that the mausoleum seems to be floating in air. Although the individual elements of the structure—minarets, bulbous domes, and octagonal base—recall Byzantine and Persian prototypes (see chapter 9 and Figure 21.19), its total effect

is unique: shadowy voids and bright solids play against one another on the surface of the exterior, while delicate patterns of light and dark animate the latticed marble screens and exquisitely carved walls of the interior. The garden complex, divided into quadrants by waterways and broad footpaths, is an earthly recreation of the Muslim garden of paradise. The Taj Mahal is the product of some twenty thousand West Asian builders and craftsmen working under the direction of a Persian architect. It is a brilliant fusion of the best aspects of Byzantine, Muslim, and Hindu traditions and, hence, an emblem of Islamic cohesion. But it is also an extravagant expression of conjugal devotion and, to generations of Western visitors, an eloquent tribute to romantic love.

The Decline of the Islamic Empires

As these pages suggest, during the sixteenth and seventeenth centuries the aristocratic courts of Islam ruled vast parts of Asia, including India and the Near East (see Map 21.1). By the mid-eighteenth century, however, the great empires of the Ottomans, the Safavids, and the Moguls were either destroyed or in fatal decline. India came under the rule of Great Britain and parts of the Ottoman Empire were lost to the control of other European powers. While the Islamic empires had depended on the West for modern weapons, they could not compete with the West's rapidly advancing commercialism and military technology. Conservative Muslim elements vigorously resisted all aspects of Western culture, including Western science and Christian learning. Threatened by the culture of the Christian West, some Muslim clerics even opposed the printing of books. Movements of Muslim revivalism would grow more militant in the following centuries, as Islam—once the imperial leader of the Asian world—struggled against European colonialism and the inevitable forces of modernism.

Absolute Power and the Aristocratic Style in China

From the earliest days of Chinese history, Chinese emperors—the "Sons of Heaven"—ruled on earth by divine authority, or, as the Chinese called it, "the Mandate of Heaven" (see chapter 3). In theory, all of China's emperors were absolute rulers. Nevertheless, over the centuries, their power was frequently contested by feudal lords, military generals, and government officials. In 1368, native Chinese rebels drove out the last of the Mongol rulers and established the Ming dynasty, which ruled China until 1644. The Ming dynasty governed the largest and most sophisticated empire on earth, an empire of some 120 million people. In the highly centralized Chinese state, Ming emperors oversaw a bureaucracy that included offices of finance, laws, military

affairs, and public works. They rebuilt the Great Wall (see chapter 7) and revived the ancient Chinese tradition of the examination system, which had been suspended by the Mongols. By the seventeenth century, however, the Ming had become autocrats who, like the foreigners they had displaced, took all power into their own hands. They transformed the civil service into a non-hereditary bureaucracy that did not dare to threaten the emperor's authority. The rigid court protocol that developed around the imperial rulers of the late Ming dynasty symbolized this shift toward autocracy. Officials, for instance, knelt in the presence of the emperor, who, as the Son of Heaven, sat on an elevated throne in the center of the imperial precinct.

Beset by court corruption and popular revolts, the Ming fell prey to the invading hordes of East Asians (descendants of Mongols, Turks, and other tribes) known as the Manchu. Under the rule of the Manchu, who established the Qing dynasty (1644–1911), the conditions of imperial autocracy intensified. As a symbol of submission, every Chinese male was required to adopt the Manchu hairstyle, by which one shaved the front of the head and wore a plaited pigtail at the back. Qing rulers retained the administrative traditions of their predecessors, but government posts were often sold rather than earned by merit. When the Qing dynasty reached its zenith—during the very last years that Louis XIV ruled France—it governed the largest, most populous, and one of the most unified states in the world (see Map 21.1). Despite internal peace, uprisings were common. They reflected the discontent of

Figure 21.24 Taj Mahal, Agra, India, 1623–1643. AKG Images, London/Jean-Louis Nou.

Figure 21.25 XU YANG, *Bird's-Eye View of the Capital*, 1770. Hanging scroll, ink and color on paper, 8 ft. 4¼ in. × 7 ft. 8 in. The Palace Museum, Beijing.

peasant masses beset by high taxes and rents and periodic famines. Like the lower classes of France and India, Chinese villagers and urban workers supported the luxuries of royal princes, government officials, and large landholders, who (as in France and India) were themselves exempt from taxation. The early Manchu rulers imitated their predecessors as royal sponsors of art and architecture. Like Louis XIV and Shah Jahan, the Chinese emperor and his huge retinue resided in an impressive ceremonial complex (Figure **21.25**). This metropolis, the symbol of entrenched

absolutism and the majesty of the ruler, was known as the Forbidden City—so-called because of its inaccessibility to ordinary Chinese citizens until 1925.

The Forbidden City Comparable in size and conception to Versailles in the West and to the Mogul palaces of India, the Forbidden City—a walled complex of palaces, tombs, and gardens located in Beijing—was the most elaborate imperial monument of the Ming and Qing eras. Construction on the imperial palace began under fifteenth-

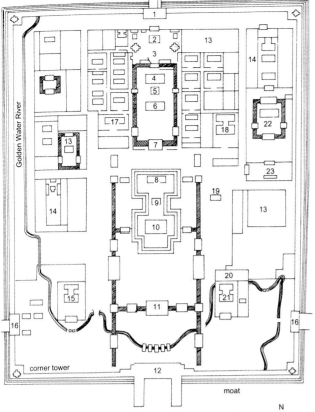

century Ming emperors and was continued by the Manchus. For almost 500 years, this vast ceremonial complex—which, like Versailles, is now a park and museum—was the administrative center of China and the home of no fewer than twenty-four Ming and Qing emperors, their families, and the members of their courts. By the eighteenth century, some 9,000 people, including guards, concubines, and domestic servants, resided within the complex.

Inside the ten-foot-high walls of the Forbidden City are royal meeting halls, grand avenues, broad courtyards, government offices, mansions of princes and dignitaries, artificial lakes, lush gardens, spacious temples, theaters, a library, and a printing house (Figure **21.26**). Entering from the south, one passes under the majestic, five-towered entranceway through a succession of courtyards and gates reminiscent of the intriguing boxes within boxes at which Chinese artisans excel. At the heart of the rectangular complex, one proceeds up the three-tiered stone terrace (Figure **21.27**), into the Hall of Supreme Harmony (approximately 200 by 100 feet), where the Sons of Heaven once sat, and beyond, to the imperial living quarters at the rear of the complex. Fragrant gardens, watered by fountains and artificial pools, once graced the private quarters of the royal officials. During the seventeenth century, courtyard gardening itself developed into a fine art. Often flanked by a covered walkway from which it could be viewed, the garden was an arrangement of seemingly random (but actually carefully placed) rocks, plants, and trees—a miniature version of the natural world. Like the Chinese landscape scroll, the Chinese garden was designed to be enjoyed progressively, as an object of gentle contemplation. Such gardens, with their winding, narrow

Figure 21.26 (above) Plan of the imperial palace, Forbidden City, Beijing, China.

1 Gate of Divine Pride
2 Pavilion of Imperial Peace
3 Imperial Garden
4 Palace of Earthly Tranquility
5 Hall of Union
6 Palace of Heavenly Purity
7 Gate of Heavenly Purity
8 Hall of the Preservation of Harmony
9 Hall of Perfect Harmony
10 Hall of Supreme Harmony
11 Gate of Supreme Harmony
12 Meridian Gate
13 Kitchens
14 Gardens
15 Former Imperial Printing House
16 Flower Gate
17 Palace of the Culture of the Mind
18 Hall of the Worship of the Ancestors
19 Pavilion of Arrows
20 Imperial Library
21 Palace of Culture
22 Palace of Peace and Longevity
23 Nine Dragon Screen

Figure 21.27 Three-tiered stone terrace and Hall of Supreme Harmony, Forbidden City, Beijing, China, Ming dynasty. Hall approx. 200 × 100 ft. Number 10 in Figure 21.26, the largest throne hall in the complex, is positioned centrally on the two-mile-long ceremonial axis. Gavin Hellier/Robert Harding World Images, London.

Figure 21.28 Flower vase, Qing dynasty. Chinese pottery, "peach-bloom" glaze, height 7¾ in. Courtesy of the Freer Gallery of Art, Smithsonian Institution, Washington, D.C. (42.20).

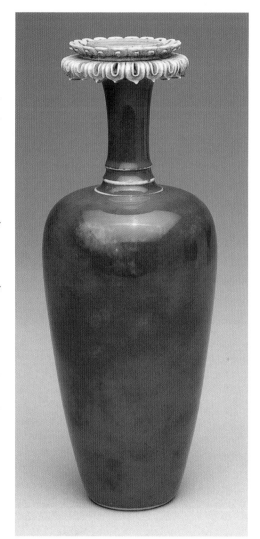

paths, delicate ferns, and sheltering bamboos, have become a hallmark of East Asian culture.

The Forbidden City was the nucleus of imperial power and the symbol of Chinese absolutism. Laid out with a gridiron regularity that rivaled Mogul and French palatial complexes, the arrangement of buildings, courtyards, gates, and terraces was uniquely Chinese. This ceremonial arrangement adheres to ancient Confucian principles of correctness and to the Chinese taste for self-enclosure. Buildings are lined up along the traditional north/south axis. Their relative sizes and functions are determined by the rigors of Chinese court procedure, a strict protocol based on rank, age, and gender. During the Ming Era, for instance, imperial legislation prescribed nine rooms for the emperor, seven for a prince, five for a court official, and three for an ordinary citizen. Most of the buildings of the Forbidden City are no more than a single story high, their walls serving only as screens that divide interior space. What the Chinese sacrificed in monumentality, however, they recovered in ornamental splendor and in the creation of an architecture that achieved harmony with (rather than dominance over) nature. Chinese architects preserved such traditional features as the rectangular hall with fully exposed wooden rafters and the pitched roof with projecting eaves and glazed yellow tiles—the latter symbolic of the mantle of heaven. Bronze lions and gilded dragons (symbols of royal power) guard the great halls and entrances. In the Forbidden City, as in all Chinese court culture prior to the twentieth century, a lavish aristocratic style enhanced the majesty of the ruler.

Imperial Patronage of the Arts The Ming and Manchu emperors were great patrons of the arts. They encouraged the traditional schools of landscape painting and oversaw the production of such luxury items as inlaid bronze vessels, carved ivories and jades, lacquer ware, embroidered silk, and painted ceramics. Chinese porcelains had been much sought-after since the seventh century; by the seventeenth century they were world famous, so much so that in the West the word "Ming" became synonymous with porcelain. (More generally, the word "china" has come to signify fine ceramics and tableware.)

Qing artists used bright colors more freely than in earlier times. Vessels with solid color glazes of ox-blood red and peach-blossom pink (Figure **21.28**) alternated with colorful landscapes filled with songbirds, flowering trees, human figures, and mythical animals. One Qing bowl ornamented with a rich five-color palette shows a group of elegantly attired men, women, and servants in a luxurious interior (Figure **21.29**). As this delightful scene suggests, neither in the porcelains nor in the paintings of this period did the Chinese develop any interest in the kinds of heroic and moralizing themes that dominated baroque art in the West. This difference notwithstanding, imperial tastes dictated the style of aristocratic art in China every bit as much as the royal academies of France influenced seventeenth-century French style. By 1680, there were over thirty official palace workshops serving the imperial court.

Figure 21.29 *Famille verte*, Qing dynasty, early eighteenth century. Foliated porcelain bowl, diameter 6½ in. Ashmolean Museum, Oxford, Department of Eastern Art.

Figure 21.30 (above) Incense burner in the shape of a *li* (tripod), Ming dynasty, fifteenth or possibly early sixteenth century. *Cloisonné* enamel, 7 ½ in. diameter. Courtesy of the Freer Gallery of Art, Smithsonian Institution, Washington, D.C. (F61.12).

Figure 21.31 Manchu style man's *jifu* (semi-formal court robe), Qing dynasty, second quarter eighteenth century. Silk and gold leaf over lacquered paper strips, 4 ft. 4 ¾ in x 6 ft. 2 ⅓ in. The Art Institute of Chicago.

Out of these workshops poured increasingly flamboyant works of art: gem-encrusted jewelry, carved wood and lacquerware, painted enamels, *cloisonné* vessels (Figure **21.30**), intricate jade carvings, and heavily embroidered silk and gold textiles (Figure **21.31**). Many of these objects found their way into Europe, where they inspired **chinoiserie**, a style reflecting the influence of Chinese art and a taste for Chinese items that, in the 1700s, developed into something of a mania. From China, by way of the Dutch, tea ("the Chinese drink") came into use in England, often smuggled into the country to avoid the high import tax. Fashionable tea service became the object of imitation in the West, most notably in the blue and white wares of Delft, Holland. Cultural exchange between East and West, however, was mutual: delegations of Jesuits, who arrived in China in 1601, introduced the rules of linear perspective to Chinese art, even as they transmitted to Europe (often by means of prints and engravings) a knowledge of Chinese techniques and goods. And French prints in turn prompted early Manchu rulers to build a Chinese version of Versailles, complete with fountains, at the imperial summer palace northwest of Beijing.

Chinese Literature and the Theater Arts Ming and Manchu rulers worked hard to preserve the rich literary heritage of China. Under Ming patronage, a group of two thousand scholars began the enormous task of collecting and copying

Figure 21.32 UNKNOWN ARTIST, portrait of Emperor Kangxi reading. Imperial Palace Museum, Beijing.

the most famous of China's literary and historical works. The Manchu contemporary of Louis XIV, Emperor Kangxi (1662–1722), hired 15,000 calligraphers and 360 editors to compile a vast assortment of dictionaries, encyclopedias, and a thirty-six-volume anthology of the Chinese classics. Kangxi, who ruled China for sixty years, is shown seated in his library against a background of stringbound books (Figure 21.32). Increasing numbers of literate middle-class men and women in China's growing cities demanded printed books for everyday use. These included almanacs, guides to letter writing, short stories, collections of proverbs and maxims, chronicles, ballads, and romances.

Novels, long works of fiction in the colloquial style, had emerged as early as the twelfth century in China and even earlier in Japan (see chapter 14); but in the Ming and Qing eras, this literary genre became ever more popular. The typical Chinese novel recounted historical events and often made fun of religious and secular authorities. In the early eighteenth century, Cao Xueqin produced China's greatest novel, *The Dream of the Red Chamber* (also known as *The Story of the Stone*). This 4,000-page work, which was to become the most popular example of Chinese fiction, is a love story involving two aristocratic Beijing families. Filled with realistic detail as well as fantastic dream sequences, the novel provides a fascinating picture of upper-class Qing society.

Plots drawn from popular novels such as *The Dream of the Red Chamber* provided the themes for staged performances, which always included mime, dance, and vocal and instrumental music. This type of theatrical performance—which Westerners might call "opera"—was the only form of drama that existed in China prior to the twentieth century (when, imitating Western drama, Chinese writers began to produce exclusively spoken plays). In the Chinese theater, performers were exclusively male, and male actors would play the parts of such stock characters as the coquette or the virtuous maid. Since troupes of players moved from city to city, elaborate costumes and stage scenery were minimal. Chinese theater made use of a system of conventions to indicate setting or circumstance: a chair might represent a mountain, a whip might signify that the actor was on horseback, and a black cloth might be used to indicate that a character was invisible. Colors symbolized conventional character types: red represented loyalty and dignity, white symbolized villainy or treachery, and so on. During the Ming Era, when sumptuous costumes and masklike makeup became popular, such earlier stage symbols and conventions were still preserved. Indeed, to this day, Chinese theater retains many traditional, highly stylized features.

Despite the differences in their origins, Chinese and European opera developed during the same era—the seventeenth century. And, by the late eighteenth century (when the first permanent Chinese opera company appeared in the capital city of Beijing), both attracted an increasingly wealthy social class. Both employed many artificial conventions and both employed male performers for female roles. Chinese music, however, sounded distinctly different from Western music. Rich in melodic and rhythmic nuances, Chinese opera shunned the dramatic contrasts in texture and timbre that have characterized Western opera (and Western music in general since the Renaissance). While European operas usually borrowed themes from Greco-Roman mythology and biblical history—themes often employed to glorify a royal patron or flatter upper-class tastes—Chinese operas mainly drew on a traditional repertory of love stories, social events, and the adventures of folk heroes. Such operas often featured stock characters resembling those of Molière's plays, and, like Molière's plays, they had wide and lasting popularity.

Absolute Power and the Aristocratic Style in Japan

By the seventeenth century, feudal Japan had taken the direction of a unified and centralized state led by members of the Tokugawa dynasty (1600–1868). In contrast to China, whose aristocracy consisted of a scholarly elite recruited through civil service examinations, Japan had an aristocracy that consisted of a warrior elite (the *samurai*)

See Music Listening Selection 14, CD One, an excerpt from a Chinese opera described in chapter 14.

recruited in battle (see chapter 14). In the style of Louis XIV, the Tokugawa *shogun* (general-in-chief) demanded that his feudal lords attend his court in Edo (modern-day Tokyo), from which center he enforced court etiquette as faithfully as he solidified political and economic control. Unique to Japan was its policy of isolation from the West (see chapter 20). In the 1630s, Tokugawa rulers initiated a policy of national seclusion. Determined to maintain internal stability and peace, they expelled foreigners and forbade citizens to travel abroad, thus sealing off Japan from the outside world.

While a large segment of Japan's peasantry led barely subsistent lives, the pleasure-loving court at Edo (a city of 1 million people by the year 1700) and the rising commercial classes of the towns enjoyed one of the most creative periods in Japanese history. In the Tokugawa court, the traditional Japanese decorative style reached new heights in multipaneled screens (used to divide interior space), hand-painted scrolls, ceramics (including the decorative porcelains known as "Imari ware"), and lacquer boxes used for the tea ceremony. Japan's aristocratic style is epitomized in the Edo Era's brightly painted multifold screens, adorned with stylized flowers, birds, or landscape motifs. In the large six-paneled screen by Ogata Korin (ca. 1658–1716), pictured in Figure **21.33**, the Japanese love of bold, decorative shapes organized by means of a subtle balance of figures and ground (positive and negative space) evokes an astonishing purity of design. Such screens reveal a unique blend of elegant simplicity and luxury (the ground of the screen is gold leaf) that distinguishes the Japanese court style at its best.

Parallel with the flowering of the aristocratic style in Tokugawa Japan was the rise of popular culture and popular art. Between the mid-seventeenth and mid-eighteenth centuries, three of Japan's best-known modes of artistic expression emerged: *kabuki* theater, the woodblock print, and the light verse form known as the **haiku**. Kabuki theater evolved out of the popular dances and skits presented by troupes of female performers. Women's kabuki was banned after 1629, but male actors continued to work this popular form of urban entertainment by assuming all female roles. Kabuki drama—whose domestic, historical, and contemporary themes called for elaborate scenery and magnificent costumes—featured tales of romance marked by violent passions and "love suicides." It provided an alternative to the classical drama of Japan, the Nō play (see chapter 14), whose stylized action, traditional literary subjects, choral interludes, and masked players resembled Greek drama.

Often mirroring the expressive moods of kabuki, seventeenth- and eighteenth-century woodblock prints, with their actors, high-class courtesans, and leisure-time entertainments, scrutinize the "floating world" (*ukiyo*). *Ukiyo* describes the pleasures and delights of a neighborhood in Edo in which a variety of bawdy entertainments were readily available. *The Tale of the Floating World* (1665) by Asai Ruyoi picture it thus:

> Living only for the moment, turning our full
> attention to the pleasures of the moon, the snow,
> the cherry blossoms and the maples, singing songs,
> drinking wine, and diverting ourselves in just
> floating, floating, caring not a whit for the poverty
> staring us in the face, refusing to be disheartened,
> like a gourd floating along with the current:
> this is what we call *ukiyo*.

Figure 21.33 OGATA KORIN, *Irises at Yatsuhashi*, from the Tale of Ise (*Ise Monogatari*), Edo period. One of a pair of six-paneled screens, ink and color and gilded paper, with black lacquered frames, each screen 4 ft. 11 in x 11 ft. 3in. Nezu Institute of Fine Art, Tokyo.

Figure 21.34 TOSHUSAI SHARAKU, *Bust Portrait of the Actor Segawa Tomisaburo as Yadorigi, the Wife of Ogishi Kurando*, 1794–1795. Woodblock print, 14½ × 9¼ in. Photograph © 1997, The Art Institution of Chicago, All Rights Reserved. Clarence Buckingham Collection, 1928.1056.

wealthy merchants as a paradigm of the cultivated life. The four-hour tea ceremony is choreographed according to a strict set of rules and formal etiquette. A unique synthesis of theater and ritual, along with the arts of ceramics, textiles, and flower-arranging, it remains a sacramental expression of Japanese culture.

A mainstay of Zen monastic life, tea and the etiquette of tea-drinking coincided with a revival of Zen painting among eighteenth-century artist–monks. Zen calligraphers did not consider their paintings as works of art, but as acts of meditation involving intense concentration and focus. Absence of detail invited the beholder to complete the painting, and thus partake of the meditative process. One of the greatest Zen masters was Hakuin Ekaku (1685–1768), whose magnificent ink scrolls are noted for their vigorous yet subtle brush drawing. In *Two Blind Men Crossing a Log Bridge* (Figure **21.35**), Hakuin illustrates his vision of the precarious nature of the human journey to spiritual enlightenment: two monks, one with his sandals hanging on his staff so as to grasp the log's surface more directly, make their way unsteadily across the narrow bridge, which, like each Japanese character, is executed with a single, confident calligraphic brushstroke. Hakuin adds the accompanying poem:

> Both inner life and the floating world outside us
> Are like the blind man's round log bridge—
> An enlightened mind is the best guide.

In their improvisational brushwork, the ink scrolls of the Zen master differ from the stylized and elegantly patterned Edo screens. Yet, both share the Japanese preference for a stripped style of the utmost simplicity. Controlled simplicity also characterizes Tokugawa lyric verse forms, the most notable of which is the *haiku*. The *haiku*—a seventeen-syllable poem arranged in three lines of 5/7/5/ syllables—depends for its effectiveness on the absence of detail and the pairing of contrasting images. The unexpected contrast does not describe a condition or event, but rather evokes a mood or emotion. Much like the art of the Zen calligrapher, the *haiku* creates a provocative void between what is stated and what is left unsaid. In this void there lies an implied "truth," one that aims to close the gap between the world of things and the world of feelings. Witness the following five compositions by Japan's most famous *haiku* poet and Zen monk, Matsuo Bashō (1644–1694):

> The beginning of all art
> a song when planting a rice field
> in the country's inmost part.

◆

> The first day of the year:
> thoughts come—and there is loneliness;
> the autumn dusk is here.

◆

> Oh, these spring days!
> A nameless little mountain,
> wrapped in morning haze!

◆

Woodcut prints immortalizing celebrity actors and courtesans were purchased by patrons as souvenirs (Figure **21.34** and see Figure 31.11)—much as we might collect posters of famous personalities today.

Executed in black and white, or colored by hand or with inked blocks, such prints are evidence of Japanese virtuosity in calligraphic design. As with Korin's screens, these prints display a rare unity of simplicity, elegance, and control.

The Way of Tea and Zen A classic expression of the Japanese aesthetic of elegance and simplicity is the ritual tea ceremony—a unique synthesis of art, theater, and everyday ritual. Introduced into Japan from China during the ninth century, tea served as an aid to Buddhist meditation. By the sixteenth century the Way of Tea (as the philosophy of tea-drinking is called) was closely associated with Zen Buddhism, a strand of Buddhism that stresses the attainment of spiritual enlightenment through intuitive illumination (see chapter 8). With the cultivation of better types of tea plants, tea-drinking became widely practiced in Japanese society, gradually establishing itself among warriors and

Figure 21.35 HAKUIN EKAKU, *Two Blind Men Crossing a Log Bridge*, Edo Period (1615–1868). Hanging scroll, ink on paper, 11¹⁄₁₆ × 33 in. Kurt and Millie Gitter Collection.

I'd like enough drinks
    to put me to sleep—on stones
        covered with pinks.

◆

Leaning upon staves
    and white-haired—a whole family
        visiting the graves.*

SUMMARY

The aristocratic style in the arts of the seventeenth century reflects the influence of absolutism in the political history of the West, as well as in Central and East Asia. In Europe, the most notable figure of the Age of Absolutism was Louis XIV. Under Louis' leadership, the arts worked to serve the majesty of the crown. At Versailles, the classical baroque style—an amalgam of Greco-Roman subject matter, classical principles of design (often derived from Renaissance models), and baroque theatricality—became the vehicle of French royal authority. Luxury, grandeur, and technical refinement became the hallmarks of elitism.

Louis XIV was instrumental in founding most of the royal academies of France, whose members established neoclassical guidelines for painting, sculpture, music, literature, and dance. Poussin's canvases, Girardon's sculptures, La Rochefoucauld's maxims, Lully's operas, Racine's tragedies, and Molière's comedies all assert the neoclassical view that the mind must prevail over the passions. Under Louis' leadership, the ballet emerged as an independent artform and one that epitomized neoclassical order and grace. Outside of France, Velázquez and van Dyck painted elegant portraits that flattered aristocratic patrons, while Rubens produced dramatic allegories of royal authority.

In Southwest Asia, the Ottoman Emperor Suleiman established a pattern of princely patronage that was imitated by Muslim rulers for at least two centuries. The Persian Shah Abbas and the Mogul rulers of India—Akbar, Jahangir, and Shah Jahan—were great patrons of the arts and commissioned some of the most magnificent monuments in architectural history. Like Versailles in France, the Imperial Mosque at Isfahan, the Red Fort at Old Delhi, and the Taj Mahal—though serving different functions—epitomize the wealth, absolute authority, and artistic vision of a privileged minority. So too, the imperial complex at the Forbidden City in Beijing stands as a symbol of the absolutism of China's rulers. Finally, in the sheltered society of Tokugawa Japan, the decorative tradition in the arts reached new heights of sophistication and refinement.

Though the aristocratic style has a rich history whose origins may be traced back to the pharaohs of Egypt, that style held a particularly important place in the seventeenth century, when it served to legitimize and glorify the power of the ruling elite throughout Europe and Asia. Flamboyant and lavish, the aristocratic style touched all forms of intellectual and artistic expression.

---

*Henderson, Harold G. *An Introduction to Haiku*. Garden City, NY: Doubleday, 1958. Pages 25, 33, 23, 44, 49.

GLOSSARY

chinoiserie European imitation of Chinese art, architecture, and decorative motifs; also any objects that reflect such imitation

choreography the art of composing, arranging, and/or notating dance movements

comédie-ballet (French) a dramatic performance that features interludes of song and dance

haiku a light verse form consisting of seventeen syllables (three lines of five, seven, and five)

marquetry a decorative technique in which patterns are created on a wooden surface by means of inlaid wood, shell, or ivory

maxim a short, concise, and often witty saying

objet d'art (French) art object

pietra dura (Italian, "hard stone") an ornamental technique involving inlaid precious and semiprecious stones

salon (French, "drawing room") an elegant apartment or drawing room

CHAPTER 22

The Baroque in the Protestant North

"No man is an island entire of itself, every man is a piece of the continent, a part of the main."
John Donne

Throughout France, Italy, Spain, and other parts of the West, the baroque style mirrored the spirit of the Catholic Reformation; in Northern Europe, where Protestant loyalties remained strong, another manifestation of the style emerged. The differences between the two are easily observed in the arts: in Italy, church interiors were ornate and theatrical; but in England, the Netherlands, and northern Germany, where Protestants as a matter of faith were committed to private devotion rather than public ritual, churches were stripped of ornamentation, and the mood was more somber and intimate. Protestant devotionalism shared with Catholic mysticism an anti-intellectual bias, but Protestantism shunned all forms of theatrical display. In Northern Europe, where a largely Protestant population valued personal piety, the Bible exercised an especially significant influence on the arts. Pietism, a seventeenth-century religious movement that originated in Germany, encouraged Bible study as the principal means of cultivating the "inner light" of religious truth.

If religion was a shaping influence on the arts of the Protestant North, so too was the patronage of a rising middle class. Having benefited financially from worldwide commerce, merchants demanded an art that reflected their keen interest in secular life. And since princely patronage in the North did not slacken during the seventeenth century, the landmark examples of Northern European art pay tribute to the vitality of this wealthy commercial class.

The Rise of the English Commonwealth

In England, Queen Elizabeth I (1533–1603) was succeeded by the first Stuart monarch James I (1566–1625). A Scot, and a committed proponent of absolute monarchy, James claimed, "There are no privileges and immunities which can stand against a divinely appointed King." His son, Charles I (1600–1649; Figure **22.1**), shared his father's view that kings held a God-given right to rule. Charles alienated

Parliament by governing for more than a decade without its approval and antagonized the growing number of Puritans (English Calvinists who demanded church reform and greater strictness in religious observance). Allying with antiroyalist factions, mostly of the emergent middle class, the Puritans constituted a powerful political group. With the support of the Puritans, leaders in Parliament raised an army to oppose King Charles, ultimately defeating the royalist forces in a civil war that lasted from 1642 to 1648 and executing the king on charges of treason. The government that followed this civil war, led by the Puritan general Oliver Cromwell (1599–1658), was known as the "Commonwealth." Bearing the hallmarks of a republic, the new government issued a written constitution that proposed the formation of a national legislature elected by universal manhood suffrage. The Commonwealth, however, was unable to survive without military support. When Cromwell died, Stuart monarchs were invited to return to the throne; however, when the Stuart king James II (1633–1701) attempted to fill a new Parliament with his Catholic supporters, the opposition rebelled again. They expelled the king and offered the crown of England to William of Orange, ruler of the Netherlands, and his wife Mary, the Protestant daughter of James II. Following the "Glorious Revolution" of 1688, Parliament enacted a Bill of Rights prohibiting the king from suspending parliamentary laws or interfering with the ordinary course of justice. The Bill of Rights was followed by the Toleration Act of 1689, which guaranteed freedom of worship to non-Anglican sects. By 1689, Parliament's authority to limit the power of the English monarch was firmly established. The "bloodless revolution" reestablished constitutional monarchy and won a victory for popular sovereignty.

The King James Bible

These dramatic political developments, so closely tied to religious issues, occurred in the years following one of the most influential cultural events of the seventeenth century:

Figure 22.1 ANTHONY VAN DYCK, *Charles I on Horseback*, ca. 1638. Oil on canvas, 12 ft. × 9 ft. 7in. National Gallery, London

the new English translation of the Bible. If, indeed, tradition is formed by the perpetuation of systems of ideas, then, surely, English tradition and Western European culture in general owe a major debt to the 1611 publication of the King James version of the Bible. Drawing on a number of earlier English translations of Scripture made during the sixteenth century, a committee of fifty-four scholars recruited by James I of England produced an "authorized" English-language edition of the Old and New Testaments. This edition of Scripture emerged during the very decades in which Shakespeare was writing his last major dramas (see chapter 19)—a time when the English language

reached its peak in eloquence. Along with the writings of Shakespeare, the King James Bible had a shaping influence on the English language and on all subsequent English literature.

The new translation of Scripture preserved the spiritual fervor of the Old Testament Hebrew and the narrative vigor of the New Testament Greek. Like Shakespeare's poetry, the language of the King James Bible is majestic and compelling. Some appreciation of these qualities may be gleaned from comparing the two following translations. The first, a sixteenth-century translation based on Saint Jerome's Latin Vulgate edition and published in the city of Douay in France in 1609, lacks the concise language, the poetic imagery, and the lyrical rhythms of the King James version (the second example), which, though deeply indebted to a number of sixteenth-century English translations, drew directly on manuscripts written in the original Hebrew.

READING 4.6   The Twenty-Third Psalm

From the Douay Bible (1609)

Our Lord ruleth me, and nothing shall be wanting to me; in place of pasture there he hath placed me.

Upon the water of refection he hath brought me up; he hath converted my soul.

He hath conducted me upon the paths of justice, for his name.

For although I shall walk in the midst of the shadow of death, I will not fear evils; because thou art with me.

Thy rod and thy staff, they have comforted me.

Thou hast prepared in my sight a table against them that trouble me.

Thou hast fatted my head with oil, and my chalice inebriating, how goodly is it!

And thy mercy shall follow me all the days of my life.

And that I may dwell in the house of our Lord in longitude of days.

From the King James Bible (1611)

The Lord is my shepherd; I shall not want.

He maketh me to lie down in green pastures: he leadeth me beside the still waters.

He restoreth my soul: he leadeth me in the paths of righteousness for his name's sake.

Yea, though I walk through the valley of the shadow of death, I will fear no evil: for thou art with me; thy rod and thy staff they comfort me.

Thou preparest a table before me in the presence of mine enemies: thou anointest my head with oil; my cup runneth over.

Surely goodness and mercy shall follow me all the days of my life: and I will dwell in the house of the Lord for ever.

Q What aspects of the King James version of the Twenty-Third Psalm make this translation memorable?

English Literature of the Seventeenth Century

John Donne

One of the most eloquent voices of religious devotionalism in the Protestant North was that of the poet John Donne (1571–1631). Born and raised as a Roman Catholic, Donne studied at Oxford and Cambridge, but he renounced Catholicism when he was in his twenties. He traveled widely, entered Parliament in 1601, and converted to

Anglicanism fourteen years later, soon becoming a priest of the Church of England.

A formidable preacher as well as a man of great intellectual prowess, Donne wrote eloquent sermons that challenged the parishioners at Saint Paul's Cathedral in London (Figure **22.2**), where he acted as dean. At Saint Paul's, Donne developed the sermon as a vehicle for philosophic meditation. In *Meditation 17* (an excerpt from which follows), Donne pictures humankind—in typically baroque terms—as part of a vast, cosmic plan. His image of human beings as "chapters" in the larger "book" of God's design is an example of Donne's affection for unusual, extended metaphors.

READING 4.7   From Donne's *Meditation 17* (1623)

All mankind is of one author, and is one volume; when one man   1
dies, one chapter is not torn out of the book, but translated into
a better language; and every chapter must be so translated. God
employs several translators; some pieces are translated by age,
some by sickness, some by war, some by justice; but God's hand   5
is in every translation, and his hand shall bind up all our
scattered leaves again for that library where every book shall lie
open to one another. As therefore the bell that rings to a
sermon calls not upon the preacher only but upon the
congregation to come, so this bell calls us all. . . . No man is an   10
island entire of itself; every man is a piece of the continent, a
part of the main. If a clod be washed away by the sea, Europe is
the less, as well as if a promontory were, as well as if a manor
of thy friend's or of thine own were. Any man's death diminishes
me, because I am involved in mankind, and therefore never send   15
to know for whom the bell tolls; it tolls for thee.

Q What three metaphors are invoked in *Meditation 17*?

The tolling bell that figures so powerfully in the last lines of Donne's *Meditation* makes reference to an age-old tradition (perpetuated at Saint Paul's) of ringing the church bells to announce the death of a parishioner. Donne's poetry was as unconventional as his prose: both abound in "conceits," that is, elaborate metaphors that compare two apparently dissimilar objects or emotions, often with the intention of shocking or surprising. In that the conceits of Donne (and other seventeenth-century writers) borrowed words and images from the new science (see chapter 23), critics called these devices and the poetry they embellished "metaphysical." Metaphysical poetry reflects the baroque affection for dramatic contrast, for frequent and unexpected shifts of viewpoint, and for the dramatic synthesis of discordant images. These features are apparent in some of Donne's finest works, including the group of religious poems known as the *Holy Sonnets*. In the first of the following two sonnets, Donne challenges Death for conceiving itself as powerful and influential. Instead of regarding Death, according to convention, as a "mighty

Figure 22.2 CHRISTOPHER WREN, West façade of Saint Paul's Cathedral, London, 1675–1710. Width approx. 90 ft. © Angelo Hornak, London.

and dreadful" ruler, Donne demeans it as a slave who keeps bad company ("poison, war, and sickness"); he concludes with the artful device of Death itself "dying." Donne's defiance of Death stands in contrast to the submissive tone of medieval preachers (see chapter 12), but his view of physical death as "a short sleep" from which "we wake eternally" is confidently Christian.

In the second sonnet, Donne compares himself to a fortress that has been seized by the enemies of the Lord. Donne describes Reason as the ruler ("Your viceroy in me") who has failed to defend the fortress. He now pleads with God to "ravish" and "imprison" him. The poem abounds in intriguing paradoxes that link sinfulness with deliverance, conquest with liberation, and imprisonment with freedom. Donne's unexpected juxtapositions and paradoxical images are typical of English metaphysical poetry, but his rejection of conventional poetic language in favor of a conversational tone (much celebrated by modern poets) represents a revolutionary development in European literature.

READING 4.8 From Donne's *Holy Sonnets* (1610)

Death be not proud, though some have called thee   1
Mighty and dreadful, for thou art not so;
For those whom thou think'st thou dost overthrow
Die not, poor Death, nor yet canst thou kill me.
From rest and sleep, which but thy pictures be,   5
Much pleasure, then from thee much more must flow,
And soonest our best men with thee do go,
Rest of their bones and souls' delivery.
Thou art slave to fate, chance, kings, and desperate men,
And dost with poison, war, and sickness dwell,   10
And poppy[1], or charms[2] can make us sleep as well,
And better than thy stroke; why swell'st[3] thou then?
One short sleep past, we wake eternally,
And Death shall be no more; Death, thou shalt die.

—— ◆ ——

Batter my heart, three-personed God; for You   15
As yet but knock, breath, shine, and seek to mend;
That I may rise, and stand, o'erthrow me, and bend
Your force, to break, blow, burn, and make me new.
I, like an usurped town to another due,
Labour to admit You, but oh! to no end;   20
Reason, Your viceroy in me, me should defend,
But is captived and proves weak or untrue.
Yet dearly I love You, and would be loved fain,[4]
But am betrothed unto Your enemy.
Divorce me, untie, or break that knot again,   25
Take me to You, imprison me, for I
Except You enthrall me, never shall be free;
Nor ever chaste, except You ravish me.

Q Why might these sonnets be called "metaphysical?"

Q Is faith, in the second sonnet, a matter of knowledge or belief?

The Genius of John Milton

John Milton (1608–1674) was a devout Puritan and a defender of the Cromwellian Commonwealth that collapsed in 1658. His career as a humanist and poet began at Cambridge University and continued throughout his eleven-year tenure as secretary to the English Council of State. Though shy and retiring, Milton became a political activist and a persistent defender of religious, political, and intellectual freedom. He challenged English society with expository prose essays on a number of controversial subjects. In one pamphlet, he defended divorce between couples who were spiritually and temperamentally incompatible—a subject possibly inspired by his first wife's unexpected decision to abandon him briefly just after their marriage. In other prose works, Milton opposed Parliament's effort to control free speech and freedom of the press. "Who kills a man kills a reasonable creature," wrote Milton, "but he who destroys a good book, kills reason itself."

Milton's verse compositions include lyric poems and elegies, but the greatest of his contributions are his two epic poems: *Paradise Lost* and *Paradise Regained*. Milton wrote both of these monumental poems during the last decades of his life, when he was totally blind—a condition he erroneously attributed to long nights of reading. Legend has it that he dictated the poems to his two young daughters. In *Paradise Lost* Milton created a cosmic (and earth-centered) vision of Heaven, Hell, and Paradise comparable to that drawn by Dante (see chapter 12) but more philosophic in its concern with the issues of knowledge, sin, and free will. Considered the greatest of modern epics, *Paradise Lost* is impressive in its vast intellectual sweep, its wide-ranging allusions to history and literature, and its effort to address matters of time, space, and causality.

Milton was already fifty years old when he resolved to compose a modern epic that rivaled the majesty of the classic works of Homer and Virgil. At the outset, he considered various themes, one of which was the story of King Arthur. But he settled instead on a Christian subject that allowed him to examine an issue particularly dear to his Protestant sensibilities: the meaning of evil in a universe created by a benevolent God. The twelve books of *Paradise Lost* retell the story of the fall of Adam and Eve, beginning with the activities of the rebellious archangel Satan and culminating in the expulsion of the First Parents from Paradise. The poem concludes with the angel Michael's explanation to Adam of how fallen Man, through Christ, will recover immortality. This august theme, rooted in biblical history, permitted Milton to explore questions of human knowledge, freedom, and morality and, ultimately, to "justify the ways of God to Men."

Central in this cosmic drama is the figure of Satan, who is painted larger than life. Milton vividly recounts the demon's passage from Hell to Earth and the fall of the rebel angels—a lengthy account that was probably inspired by the English Civil War. The titanic Satan is a metaphor for the Puritan conception of evil in the world. Less vividly drawn, Adam is an expression of Protestant pessimism—a figure who, for all his majesty, is incapable of holding on to Paradise. *Paradise Lost* may be considered a Christian parable of the human condition. In its cosmic scope and verbal exuberance, it is also a mirror of the baroque imagination.

Paradise Lost rivals the achievements of Shakespeare. Like Shakespeare, Milton used blank verse: unrhymed lines of ten syllables each with accents on every second syllable. This form allowed Milton to carry the thread of a single thought past the end of the line and thereby group ideas in rich verse paragraphs. The language of *Paradise Lost* is intentionally lofty; it is designed to convey epic breadth and to narrate (as Milton promised) "things unattempted yet in prose or rhyme." The following excerpts

---

[1]Opium.
[2]Sleeping potion.
[3]Puff with pride.
[4]Willingly.

convey some sense of the power and majesty of Milton's verse. In the first twenty-six lines of Book I, Milton announces the subject of the poem: the loss of humankind's spiritual innocence. The second excerpt, also from Book I, relates the manner in which Satan tears himself from Hell's burning lake and proudly assumes his place as ruler of the fallen legions. In the third excerpt (from Book IX), Adam resolves to perish with his beloved partner, Eve, by imitating her in eating the Forbidden Fruit. Milton's description of "the wanton Eve" and her "fatal trespass" (l. 71) perpetuated the misogynistic trope of flawed womankind well into the late nineteenth century. Finally, in the passage from Book XII, Adam hears the angel Michael's prophetic description of humankind's destiny and prepares to leave Paradise.

READING 4.9 From Milton's *Paradise Lost* (1667)

Book I

Of man's first disobedience, and the fruit	1
Of that forbidden tree, whose mortal taste	
Brought death into the world, and all our woe,	
With loss of Eden, till one greater Man[1]	
Restore us, and regain the blissful seat,	
Sing Heav'nly Muse, that on the secret top	
Of Oreb, or of Sinai,[2] didst inspire	
That shepherd, who first taught the chosen seed,	
In the beginning how the heav'ns and earth	
Rose out of chaos: or if Sion hill	10
Delight thee more, and Siloa's brook[3] that flowed	
Fast by the oracle of God; I thence	
Invoke thy aid to my advent'rous song,	
That with no middle flight intends to soar	
Above th' Aonian mount,[4] while it pursues	
Things unattempted yet in prose or rhyme.	
And chiefly thou O Spirit, that dost prefer	
Before all temples th' upright heart and pure,	
Instruct me, for thou know'st; thou from the first	
Wast present, and with mighty wings outspread	20
Dove-like sat'st brooding on the vast abyss	
And mad'st it pregnant: what in me is dark	
Illumine, what is low raise and support;	
That to the highth of this great argument	
I may assert Eternal Providence,	
And justify the ways of God to men.	

. . . .

---

[1]Christ.

[2]As was the case with epic poets of old, Milton here invokes a divine source of inspiration. Milton's muse, however, is an abstraction of Judeo-Christian wisdom, identified with the muse that inspired Moses at Mount Horeb (Deut. 4.10) or on Mount Sinai (Exod. 19.20).

[3]A spring near Mount Zion in Jerusalem where, in the Hebrew Bible, God spoke to his people.

[4]In Greece, the Muses were thought to live on Mount Helicon, also known as the "Aonian mountain."

Forthwith upright he rears from off the pool	
His mighty stature; on each hand the flames	
Driv'n backward slope their pointing spires, and rolled	
In billows, leave i' th' midst a horrid vale.	30
Then with expanded wings he steers his flight	
Aloft, incumbent on the dusty air	
That felt unusual weight, till on dry land	
He lights, if it were land that ever burned	
With solid, as the lake with liquid fire,	
And such appeared in hue; as when the force	
Of subterranean wind transports a hill	
Torn from Pelorus,[5] or the shattered side	
Of thund'ring Etna, whose combustible	
And fuelled entrails thence conceiving fire,	40
Sublimed with mineral fury, aid the winds,	
And leave a singèd bottom all involved	
With stench and smoke: such resting found the sole	
Of unblest feet. Him followed his next mate,	
Both glorying to have escaped the Stygian[6] flood	
As gods, and by their own recovered strength,	
Not by the sufferance of supernal power.	
"Is this the region, this the soil, the clime,"	
Said then the lost Archangel, "this the seat	
That we must change for heav'n, this mournful gloom	50
For that celestial light? Be it so, since he	
Who now is sovran[7] can dispose and bid	
What shall be right: farthest from him is best	
Whom reason hath equaled, force hath made supreme	
Above his equals. Farewell, happy fields,	
Where joy for ever dwells: hail horrors, hail,	
Infernal world, and thou, profoundest hell	
Receive thy new possessor: one who brings	
A mind not to be changed by place or time.	
The mind is its own place, and in itself	60
Can make a heav'n of hell, a hell of heav'n.	
What matter where, if I be still the same,	
And what I should be, all but less than he	
Whom thunder hath made greater? Here at least	
We shall be free; th' Almighty hath not built	
Here for his envy, will not drive us hence:	
Here may we reign secure, and in my choice	
To reign is worth ambition though in hell:	
Better to reign in hell, than serve in heav'n."	

. . . .

Book IX

On th' other side, Adam, soon as he heard	70
The fatal trespass done by Eve, amazed,[8]	
Astonied[9] stood and blank, while horror chill	
Ran through his veins, and all his joints relaxed;	
From his slack hand the garland wreathed for Eve	
Down dropped, and all the faded roses shed:	

---

[5]A promontory near the volcanic Mount Etna in Sicily.

[6]Referring to the River Styx, in Greek mythology the principal river of the Underworld.

[7]Sovereign.

[8]Confused, terror-stricken.

[9]Stunned.

Speechless he stood and pale, till thus at length
First to himself he inward silence broke.
    "O fairest of creation, last and best
Of all God's works, creature in whom excelled
Whatever can to sight or thought be formed,   80
Holy, divine, good, amiable, or sweet!
How art thou lost, how on a sudden lost,
Defaced, deflow'red, and now to death devote?[10]
Rather how hast thou yielded to transgress
The strict forbiddance, how to violate
The sacred fruit forbidd'n! some cursèd fraud
Of enemy hath beguiled thee, yet unknown,
And me with thee hath ruined, for with thee
Certain my resolution is to die;
How can I live without thee, how forgo   90
Thy sweet converse and love so dearly joined,
To live again in these wild woods forlorn?
Should God create another Eve, and I
Another rib afford, yet loss of thee
Would never from my heart; no no, I feel
The link of nature draw me: flesh of flesh,
Bone of my bone thou art, and from thy state
Mine never shall be parted, bliss or woe."
    So having said, as one from sad dismay
Recomforted,[11] and after thoughts disturbed   100
Submitting to what seemed remédiless,
Thus in calm mood his words to Eve he turned.
    "Bold deed thou hast presumed, advent'rous Eve,
And peril great provoked, who thus hast dared
Had it been only coveting to eye
That sacred fruit, sacred to abstinence,
Much more to taste it under ban to touch.
But past who can recall, or done undo?
Not God omnipotent, nor fate; yet so
Perhaps thou shalt not die, perhaps the fact[12]   110
Is not so heinous now, foretasted fruit,
Profaned first by the serpent, by him first
Made common and unhallowed ere our taste;
Nor yet on him found deadly, he yet lives,
Lives, as thou saidst, and gains to live as man
Higher degree of life, inducement strong
To us, as likely tasting to attain
Proportional ascent, which cannot be
But to be gods, or angels demi-gods.
Nor can I think that God, Creator wise,   120
Though threat'ning, will in earnest so destroy
Us his prime creatures, dignified so high,
Set over all his works, which in our fall,
For us created, needs with us must fail,
Dependent made; so God shall uncreate,
Be frustrate, do, undo, and labor lose,
Not well conceived of God, who though his power
Creation could repeat, yet would be loath
Us to abolish, lest the Adversary
Triumph and say; 'Fickle their state whom God   130

Most favors, who can please him long? Me first
He ruined, now mankind; whom will he next?'
Matter of scorn, not to be given the Foe.
However I with thee have fixed my lot,
Certain to undergo like doom; if death
Consort with thee, death is to me as life;
So forcible within my heart I feel
The bond of nature draw me to my own.
My own in thee, for what thou art is mine;
Our state cannot be severed, we are one,   140
One flesh: to lose thee were to lose myself."

.   .   .   .

Book XII

[. . . to the Angel] Adam last replied.
    "How soon hath thy prediction, seer blest,
Measured this transient world, the race of time,
Till time stand fixed: beyond is all abyss,
Eternity, whose end no eye can reach.
Greatly instructed I shall hence depart,
Greatly in peace of thought, and have my fill
Of knowledge, what this vessel can contain;
Beyond which was my folly to aspire.   150
Henceforth I learn, that to obey is best,
And love with fear the only God, to walk
As in his presence, ever to observe
His providence, and on him sole depend,
Merciful over all his works, with good
Still overcoming evil, and by small
Accomplishing great things, by things deemed weak
Subverting worldly strong, and worldly wise
By simply meek; that suffering for truth's sake
Is fortitude to highest victory,   160
And to the faithful death the gate of life;
Taught this by his example whom I now
Acknowledge my Redeemer ever blest."
    To whom thus also th' angel last replied:
"This having learnt, thou hast attained the sum
Of wisdom; hope no higher, though all the stars
Thou knew'st by name, and all th' ethereal powers,
All secrets of the deep, all nature's works,
Or works of God in heav'n, air, earth, or sea,
And all the riches of this world enjoy'dst,   170
And all the rule, one empire; only add
Deeds to thy knowledge answerable, add faith,
Add virtue, patience, temperance, add love,
By name to come called charity, the soul
Of all the rest: then wilt thou not be loath
To leave this Paradise, but shalt possess
A paradise within thee, happier far.
Let us descend now therefore from this top
Of speculation; for the hour precise
Exacts our parting hence; and see the guards,   180
By me encamped on yonder hill, expect
Their motion,[13] at whose front a flaming sword,

---

[10]Devoted, doomed.
[11]Comforted, refreshed.
[12]Crime, deed.

---

[13]Await their marching orders.
[14]Departure.

In signal of remove,[14] waves fiercely round;
We may no longer stay: go, waken Eve;
Her also I with gentle dreams have calmed
Portending good, and all her spirits composed
To meek submission: thou at season fit
Let her with thee partake what thou hast heard,
Chiefly what may concern her faith to know,
The great deliverance by her seed to come   **190**
(For by the Woman's Seed) on all mankind.
That ye may live, which will be many days,
Both in one faith unanimous though sad,
With cause for evils past, yet much more cheered
With meditation on the happy end."

> **Q** Describe the appearance and the personality of Satan (Book I).
>
> **Q** Why does Adam decide to stay with the fallen Eve (Book IX)?
>
> **Q** What message does the angel give to Adam (Book XII)?

The London of Christopher Wren

London at the time of Donne and Milton was a city of vast extremes. England's commercial activities in India and the Americas made its capital a center for stock exchanges, insurance firms, and joint-stock companies. Yet living amongst the wealthy Londoners, a great number of people remained poor. One-fourth of London's 250,000 inhabitants could neither read nor write; meanwhile, English intellectuals advanced scientific learning. For some time Londoners enjoyed some of the finest libraries and theaters in Western Europe, but, under the Puritan-dominated Parliament of the 1640s, stage plays were suppressed, and many old theaters, including Shakespeare's Globe, were torn down. The restoration of the monarchy in 1660 brought with it a revived interest in drama and in the construction of indoor theaters (as opposed to the open-air theaters of Shakespeare's time).

In 1666, a devastating fire tore through London and destroyed three-quarters of the city, including 13,000 homes, eighty-seven parish churches, and the cathedral church of Saint Paul's, where John Donne had served as dean some decades earlier. Following the fire, there was an upsurge of large-scale building activity and a general effort to modernize London. The architect Christopher Wren (1632–1723) played a leading role in this effort. A child prodigy in mathematics, then an experimental scientist and professor of astronomy at London and Oxford, Wren was one of the founding fathers of the Royal Society of London for Improving Natural Knowledge. Following the Great Fire, Wren prepared designs for the reconstruction of London. Although his plans for new city streets (based on Rome) were rejected, he was commissioned to rebuild more than fifty churches, including Saint Paul's—the first church in Christendom to be completed in the lifetime of its architect.

Wren's early designs for Saint Paul's featured the Greek-cross plan that Michelangelo had proposed for Saint Peter's in Rome (see chapter 17). However, the clergy of Saint Paul's preferred a Latin-cross structure. The final design was a compromise that combined classical, Gothic, Renaissance, and baroque architectural features. Saint Paul's dramatic two-story façade, with its ornate twin clock towers and its strong surface contrasts of light and dark (see Figure 22.2), looks back to Borromini (see Figure 20.19), but its massive scale and overall design—a large dome set upon a Latin-cross basilica—are reminiscent of Saint Peter's (see Figure 20.14). As at Saint Peter's, Wren's dome, which physically resembles Bramante's Tempietto (see Figure 17.33), is equal in its diameter (102 feet) to the combined width of the nave and side-aisles. The dimensions of the cathedral are colossal: 366 feet from ground level to the top of the lantern cross (Saint Peter's reaches 452 feet).

Wren envisioned a dome that was both impressive from the outside and easily visible from the inside. He came up with an inventive and complex device: two domes, one exterior (made of timber covered with lead) and the other interior (made of light brick), are supported by a third, cone-shaped, middle dome, which is hidden between the other two (Figure **22.3**). The monumental silhouette of Wren's dome, which became the model for the United States capitol, remains an impressive presence on the London skyline. From within the church, there is the equally impressive illusionism of the *trompe l'oeil* heavens

Figure 22.3 Cross-section of Saint Paul's showing Wren's three domes.

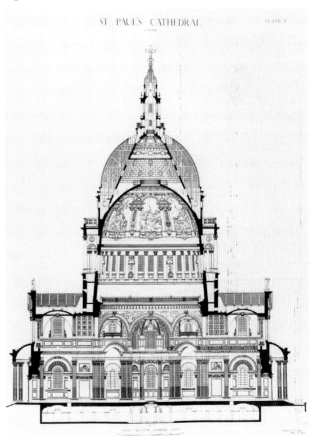

Figure 22.4 REMBRANDT VAN RIJN, *The Return of the Prodigal Son*, ca. 1662–1668. Oil on canvas, 8 ft. 8 in. × 6 ft. 8 in.
Hermitage Museum, Saint Petersburg, Russia / Bridgeman Art Library, London.

painted on the inner surface of the central cupola. Like Milton's *Paradise Lost*, Wren's Saint Paul's is a majestic synthesis of classical and Christian traditions, while its huge size, dramatic exterior, and light-filled interior are baroque in conception and effect.

Rembrandt and Protestant Devotionalism

In the Netherlands, developments in painting rivaled those in English architecture. Among the great artists of the Protestant North, Rembrandt van Rijn (1606–1669) stands out as a figure of towering stature and talent. His contribution to the humanistic tradition is better understood in the context of his time and place.

Since 1560, when Spain had invaded the Dutch Lowlands, the seventeen provinces of the Netherlands had been engaged in a bitter struggle against the Catholic forces of the Spanish king Philip II. In 1579, after years of bloodshed, the Dutch forced Philip's armies to withdraw. In 1581, the seven provinces of the North Netherlands declared their independence. By the end of the century the predominantly Calvinist Dutch Republic (later called "Holland") was a self-governing state and one of the most commercially active territories in Western Europe. Dutch shipbuilders produced some of the finest trading vessels on the high seas, while skilled Dutch seamen brought those vessels to all parts of the world. In Amsterdam, as in hundreds of other Dutch towns, merchants and craftspeople shared the responsibilities of local government, profiting handsomely from the smooth-running, primarily maritime, economy.

The autonomous towns of the North Netherlands, many of which supported fine universities, fostered freedom of thought and a high rate of literacy. Hardworking, thrifty, and independent-minded, the seventeenth-century Dutch enjoyed a degree of independence and material prosperity unmatched elsewhere in the world. Their proletarian tastes, along with a profound appreciation for the physical comforts of home and hearth, inspired their preference for such secular subjects as portraits, still lifes, landscapes, and scenes of domestic life (see chapter 23). While the arts in Italy reflected the Mediterranean love for outdoor display, in the North, where a harsher climate prevailed, artistic expression centered on the domestic interior. And, in the North, where the remains of ancient Greece and Rome were fewer, the classical heritage figured less visibly in the arts.

Since Calvinism strongly discouraged the use of religious icons, sculpture was uncommon in the Protestant North. But paintings, especially those with scriptural subjects, were favored sources of seventeenth-century moral knowledge and instruction. The Old Testament was particularly popular among the Dutch, who viewed themselves as God's "chosen" people, elected to triumph over Spain. In this milieu emerged Amsterdam's leading painter, Rembrandt van Rijn. The Leyden-born Rembrandt rose to fame as a painter of biblical subjects that were uncommon in Catholic art. His moving representation of *The Return*

of the Prodigal Son (Figure **22.4**), for instance, shows the moment when the wayward son in Jesus' parable returns home in rags and, humbly kneeling before his father, receives forgiveness (Luke 15:11–32). The figures of father and son, bathed in golden light, form an off-center triangle balanced by the sharply lit vertical figure to the right. The composition is thus "open" and asymmetrical, rather than "closed" and symmetrical in the manner of High Renaissance art (see chapter 17). As if to symbolize spiritual revelation itself, Rembrandt "pulls" figures out of the shadowy depths of the background. His rich contrasts between bright **impasto** areas (produced by building up thick layers of paint) and dark, brooding passages work to increase the dramatic impact of the composition. Rembrandt learned much about theatrical staging from Caravaggio, but, in his simpler, more restrained compositions, Rembrandt reaches further below surface appearances to explore the psychological depths of his subjects.

Rembrandt's unidealized treatment of sacred subject matter belonged to a long tradition of religious devotionalism (see chapter 15), but his sympathetic depiction of the poor and the persecuted was uniquely Protestant. His Anabaptist upbringing, with its fundamentalist approach to Scripture and its solemn attention to the role of individual conscience in daily life, surely contributed to Rembrandt's preference for portraying biblical subjects in literal, human terms. The people of the streets provided him with a cast of characters, and his Bible narratives abound with the faces of Spanish and Jewish refugees, whom he regularly sketched in the ghettos of Amsterdam.

Rembrandt's technical virtuosity as a draftsman made him more famous in his own time as a printmaker than as a painter. His medium of choice was **etching** (Figure **22.5**). Like the woodcuts and engravings of his Northern European predecessors Dürer and Holbein (see chapter 19),

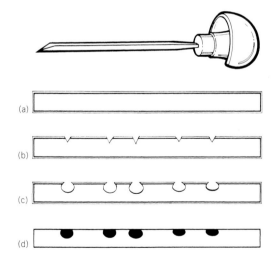

Figure 22.5 Etching is an intaglio printing process. A metal plate is coated with resin (a) then images are scratched through the coating with a burin, or graver (b). Acid is applied, which "eats" or etches the metal exposed by the scratches (c). The resin is then removed and ink is rubbed into the etched lines on the metal plate (d). After the plate is wiped clean, it is pressed onto the paper and the ink-filled lines are deposited on the paper surface. Other intaglio processes include engraving and aquatint. From Richard Phipps and Richard Wink, *Invitation to the Gallery*. Copyright © 1987 Wm. C. Brown Publishers, Dubuque, Iowa. All rights reserved. Reprinted by permission.

Figure 22.6 (above) **REMBRANDT VAN RIJN**, *Christ Preaching* ("The Hundred-Guilder Print"), ca. 1648–1650. Etching, 11 × 15½ in. Rijksmuseum, Amsterdam.

Figure 22.7 (right) **REMBRANDT VAN RIJN**, detail of *Christ Preaching* ("The Hundred-Guilder Print"), ca. 1648–1650.

Rembrandt's etchings met the demands of middle-class patrons who sought private devotional images that—by comparison with paintings—were inexpensive. A consummate and prolific printmaker, Rembrandt used the **burin** (a steel cutting tool) to develop dramatic contrasts of rich darks and emphatic lights. *Christ Preaching* (Figure **22.6**)—also known as "The Hundred-Guilder Print," because it sold for one hundred Dutch guilders in a seventeenth-century auction—illustrates parts of the Gospel of Matthew. In the etching, Rembrandt depicts Jesus addressing the members of the Jewish community: the sick and the lame (foreground), "the little children" (middle left), the ill and infirm (right), and an assembly of Pharisees (far left). With an extraordinary economy of line—no more than a few deft strokes of the pen—the artist brings to life the lot of the poor, the downtrodden, and the aged (Figure **22.7**). So colloquial is Rembrandt's handling of the biblical story that it seems an event that might have taken place in Rembrandt's time and place, or in ours.

The Music of the Protestant North

Handel and the English Oratorio

If the Protestant North produced memorable literature and art, it also generated great music. The careers of two extraordinary German composers, George Frideric Handel (1685–1756) and Johann Sebastian Bach (1685–1750), represent the flowering of the baroque style in Northern European music.

Born in the Lutheran trading city of Halle, Germany, George Frideric Handel was determined to pursue his childhood musical talents. When his father, who intended for him a career in law, refused to provide him with a musical instrument, he smuggled a small clavichord into the attic. After proving himself at the keyboard and as a successful violinist and composer in the courts of Hamburg, Rome, Paris, Naples, and Venice, he emigrated to London in 1710 and became a British citizen in 1726. Like many of his contemporaries, Handel began his career as a student of Italian opera. He composed forty-six operas in Italian and four in his native German. He also produced a prodigious number of instrumental works. But it was for his development of the **oratorio** that he earned fame among the English, who called him "England's greatest composer."

An oratorio is the musical setting of a long sacred or epic text that is performed in concert by a narrator, soloists, chorus, and orchestra (Figure **22.8**). Like operas, oratorios are large in scale and dramatic in intent but, unlike opera, they are produced without scenery, costumes, or dramatic action. Soloists and chorus assume the roles of the main characters in the narrative. The word "oratorio" refers to a church chapel, and most oratorios are religious in content; however, they were never intended for church services. Rather, they were performed in public concert halls. With the oratorio came the shift from music written and performed for church or court to music composed for concert halls (or opera houses) and enjoyed by the general public. Appropriately, in the late seventeenth century, public

Figure 22.8 Performance of an oratorio; Handel (far right) is conducting. Woodcut.

concerts (and entrance fees) made their first appearance in the social history of music.

In his lifetime, Handel composed more than thirty oratorios. Like Rembrandt and Milton (whose verses he borrowed for the oratorio *Samson*), Handel brought Scripture to life. The most famous of Handel's oratorios is *Messiah*, which was written in the English of the King James Bible. Composed, remarkably enough, in twenty-four days, it was performed for the first time in Dublin in 1742. It received instant acclaim. One of the most moving pieces of choral music ever written, *Messiah* celebrates the birth, death, and resurrection of Jesus. Unlike most of Handel's oratorios, it is not a biblical dramatization but rather a collection of verses from the Old and New Testaments. The first part of the piece recounts Old Testament prophecies of a Savior, the second relates the suffering and death of Jesus, and the third rejoices in the redemption of humankind through Christ's resurrection.

Messiah is typical of the baroque sensibility: indeed, the epic proportions of its score and libretto call to mind Milton's *Paradise Lost*. It is also baroque in its style, which features vigorous contrasts of tempo and dynamics and dramatic interaction between participating ensembles—solo voices, chorus, and instruments. A master of theatrical effects, Handel employed word painting and other affective devices throughout the piece. For example, the music for the last words of the sentence, "All we, like sheep, have gone astray," consists of deliberately divergent melodic lines. The best-loved choral work in the English language, *Messiah* has outlasted its age. In many Christian communities, it has become traditional to perform the piece during both the Christmas and Easter seasons. The jubilant "Hallelujah Chorus" (which ends the second of the three parts of the oratorio) still brings audiences to their feet, as it did King George II of England, who introduced this tradition by rising from his seat when he first heard it performed in London in 1743.

Handel's *Messiah* features polyphonic textures at the start of many of the choruses, such as the "For unto us, a Child is born." Nevertheless, like Handel's other oratorios, much of *Messiah* is essentially **homophonic**; that is, its musical organization depends on the use of a dominant melody supported by chordal accompaniment. The homophonic organization of melody and chords differed dramatically from the uninterrupted polyphonic interweaving of voices that characterized most music prior to the seventeenth century. The chords in a homophonic composition serve to support—or, in the visual sense, to "spotlight"—a primary melody. In the seventeenth century, there evolved a form of musical shorthand that allowed musicians to fill in the harmony for the principal melody of a homophonic piece. The **figured bass**, as this shorthand was called, consisted of a line of music with numbers written below it to indicate the harmony accompanying the primary melody. The use of the figured bass (also called the "continuo," since it played throughout the piece) was one of the main features of baroque music.

Bach and Religious Music

Johann Sebastian Bach (Figure **22.9**) was born in the small town of Eisenach, very near the castle in which Martin Luther—hiding from the wrath of the Roman papacy—had first translated the Bible into German. Unlike the cosmopolitan Handel, Bach never strayed more than a couple of hundred miles from his birthplace; the last twenty-seven years of his career were spent in nearby Leipzig. Nor did he depart from his Protestant roots: Luther's teachings and Lutheran hymn tunes were Bach's major sources of religious inspiration, and the organ—the principal instrument of Protestant church music—was one of his favorite instruments. The Germans were the masters of the organ, and Bach was acknowledged to be the finest of organ virtuosi. He even served as a consultant for the construction of baroque organs, whose ornately embellished casings made them the glory of many Protestant churches (Figure **22.10**). As organ master and choir director of the Lutheran Church of Saint Thomas in Leipzig, Bach assumed the responsibility of composing music for each of the Sunday services and for holy days. A pious Lutheran, who, in the course of two marriages, fathered twenty children (five of whom became notable musicians), Bach humbly dedicated his compositions "to the glory of God."

Bach's religious vocal music included such forms as the oratorio, the Mass, and the **cantata**. The cantata is a multimovement work with a text in verse sung by chorus and soloists and accompanied by a musical instrument or instruments. Like the oratorio, the cantata may be sacred or secular in subject matter and lyric or dramatic in style.

Figure 22.9 ELIAS GOTTLOB HAUSSMAN, *Johann Sebastian Bach*, 1746. Oil on canvas. William H. Scheide Library, Princeton University.

Bach composed cantatas as musical commentaries on the daily scriptural lessons of the Lutheran church service. Unparalleled in their florid counterpoint, Bach's 195 surviving cantatas were usually inspired by the simple melodies of Lutheran chorales, with their regular rhythms and rugged melodies. Cantata No. 80 is based on Luther's "A Mighty Fortress is Our God," the most important hymn of the Lutheran church (see chapter 19). Bach drew on Protestant chorales not only for his cantatas but as the basis for many of his instrumental compositions (see chapter 23), including the 170 organ **preludes** that he composed to precede and set the mood for congregational singing.

At the apex of Bach's achievement in vocal music is the *Passion According to Saint Matthew*, an oratorio written

for the Good Friday service at the Church of Saint Thomas in Leipzig. This majestic piece of religious music consists of the sung texts of chapters 26 and 27 of Matthew's Gospel, which describe Christ's Passion: the events between the Last Supper and the Resurrection. The biblical verses alternate with narrative commentary from a text written by a local German poet. Bach's combination of Bible and moral commentary dramatizes Scripture with eloquence and expressive power.

The *Passion According to Saint Matthew* is written for a double chorus whose members take the parts of the disciples, the Pharisees, and other characters in the biblical account. The chorus alternates with a solo tenor who narrates, and other soloists (representing Matthew, Jesus, Judas, and others) who sing the arias and recitatives. Two orchestras accompany the voices. The three-and-a-half-

See Music Listening Selections at end of chapter.

hour-long piece consists of two parts, the first originally to be sung before the Vespers sermon and the second after it. In Bach's time, the church congregation participated in the performance of the choral portions, thus adding to the sheer volume of sound produced by choirs and orchestras. Performed today in the church or in the concert hall, Bach's oratorio still conveys the devotional spirit of the Protestant North. In its imaginative use of Scripture, as well as in its vivid tonal color and dramatic force, the *Passion According to Saint Matthew* compares with the best of Rembrandt's Bible narratives, Handel's *Messiah*, and Milton's *Paradise Lost*.

SUMMARY

In seventeenth-century Northern Europe, a unique set of circumstances shaped the progress of the baroque style. These circumstances featured the dominance of Protestantism, with its strong scriptural and devotional emphasis, rising commercialism, and—especially in England and Holland—passionate antiauthoritarian efforts to sustain personal rights and political liberties. The study of sacred Scripture was central to the ideals of Pietism and Protestant belief. Consequently, Northern baroque artistic expression turned inward to the personal and subjective, rather than outward to public spectacles of religious display.

In the literary domain, the King James translation of the Bible brought the English language to new heights of eloquence. The Anglican John Donne and the Puritan John Milton produced poetry that reflected Protestant perspectives of morality, evil, and death. Donne's metaphysical poetry featured ingenious conceits and paradoxes. Milton's *Paradise Lost*, the last great epic poem in Western literature, recast the heritage of the Hebrew Bible according to Puritan views of sin and salvation. The poem's cosmic scope, colossal proportions, and majestic language exemplify the baroque spirit in the Protestant North.

The religious works of the Dutch master Rembrandt van Rijn present a visual parallel to these literary landmarks. Rembrandt illustrated the contents of Holy Scripture in paintings, drawings, and etchings that were at once realistic, theatrical, and psychologically profound. With bold compositions and an inventive use of light, he described sacred events as though they were occurring in his own time and place.

The genius of Rembrandt was matched in music by the German masters Johann Sebastian Bach and George Frideric Handel. Handel dramatized scriptural narrative by means of the oratorio, a new musical form that typified the baroque taste for rich color and dramatic effect. Handel's *Messiah*, an early landmark in homophonic composition, remains one of the most stirring examples of choral music. Handel's Lutheran contemporary, Johann Sebastian Bach, dedicated much of his life to composing music that honored God. His cantatas and his preludes employ melodies borrowed largely from Lutheran hymns. In the *Passion According to Saint Matthew*, Bach brought polyphonic choral music to new heights of dramatic grandeur. Like Milton's *Paradise Lost* and the paintings of Rembrandt, Bach's music invested Protestant Christianity with a sublime and deeply personal sense of human tragedy. In all, the contributions of Milton, Rembrandt, Handel, and Bach constitute the crowning achievements of the baroque style in the Protestant North.

MUSIC LISTENING SELECTIONS

CD Two Selection 3 Handel, *Messiah*, "Hallelujah Chorus," 1742.
CD Two Selection 4 Bach, Cantata No. 80, "Ein feste Burg ist unser Gott" ("A Mighty Fortress is Our God"), Chorale, 1724.

GLOSSARY

burin a steel tool used for engraving and incising

cantata (Italian, *cantare* = "to sing") a multimovement composition for voices and instrumental accompaniment; smaller in scale than the *oratorio*

etching a kind of engraving in which a metal plate is covered with resin, then incised with a *burin*; acid is applied to "eat" away the exposed lines, which are inked before the plate is wiped clean and printed; see Figure 22.5

figured bass in baroque music, the line of music with numbers written below (or above) it to indicate the required harmonies, usually improvised in the form of keyboard chords accompanying the melody; also called "continuo"

homophony a musical texture consisting of a dominant melody supported by chordal accompaniment that is far less important than the melody; compare polyphony (see Glossary, chapter 13)

impasto a style in painting in which the paint is applied thickly or heavily

oratorio (Latin, *oratorium* = "church chapel") a musical setting of a long text, either religious or secular, for soloists, chorus, narrator, and orchestra; usually performed without scenery, costumes, or dramatic action

prelude a piece of instrumental music that introduces either a church service or another piece of music

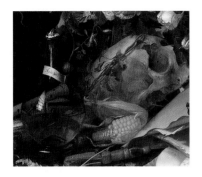

CHAPTER 23

The Scientific Revolution and the New Learning

"Human knowledge and human power meet in one; for where the cause is not known, the effect cannot be produced."
Francis Bacon

While the seventeenth century was a period of religious turbulence and heightened spirituality, it was also an age of scientific discovery and development. The Scientific Revolution that occurred in Europe between approximately 1600 and 1750 was not entirely sudden, nor were its foundations exclusively European. It owed much to a long history of science and technology that reached back to ancient Egypt, China, and Islam, to the construction of pyramids and cathedrals, the formulation of Euclidean geometry, and the invention of the windmill, the magnetic compass, and the printing press. As Renaissance artist–scientists diligently investigated the visible world, the will to control nature by means of practical knowledge gained impetus in the West. Following the pioneering efforts of Leonardo da Vinci, the Flemish physician Andreas Vesalius (1514–1574) dissected cadavers to make an accurate record of the human anatomy. The Swiss alchemist Philippus Ambrosius Paracelsus (1493–1541) compounded medical remedies from minerals rather than from the older, botanical substances. And, on the evidence of mathematical calculations, the Polish humanist, physician, and astronomer Nicolas Copernicus (1473–1543) opposed the traditional **geocentric** (earth-centered) model of the cosmos. He advanced the **heliocentric** (sun-centered) theory, according to which the earth and all the other planets circle around the sun (Figure **23.1**).

The Scientific Revolution

Those who launched the Scientific Revolution differed from their Asian and European predecessors in effectively combining the tools of mathematics and experimentation.

Figure 23.1 The cosmos on the right, dating from the sixteenth century, shows a geocentric universe. The version on the left, from Copernicus' *De revolutionibus orbium coelestium* (1543), shows a heliocentric universe.

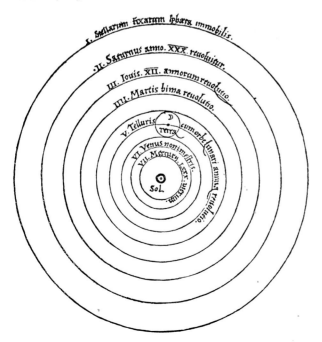

They invented new instruments with which to measure more precisely natural phenomena, to test scientific hypotheses, and to predict the operations of nature. They also differed from their predecessors in asserting that *scientia* (the Latin word for "knowledge") existed separate and apart from divine power and authority. If medieval intellectuals viewed the universe as the extension of an absolute and eternal God, modern scientists regarded it as a mechanism that operated according to its own laws, laws that were discoverable by human beings. Modern scientists took nature out of the hands of poets and priests and put it inside the laboratory.

Kepler and Galileo

Even before the second century C.E., when the Greek geographer Ptolemy published his theory of a geometric universe, learned individuals regarded the earth as fixed in space and spherical in shape. They envisioned the earth at the center of a series of endlessly turning crystalline spheres, one for each of the celestial bodies: the Moon, Mercury, Venus, the Sun, Mars, Jupiter, and Saturn—a cosmology enshrined in Dante's *Divine Comedy* (see chapter 12). According to Aristotle, movement in nature was the work of a *prime mover* or, in the later, Christian view, of some supernatural force. During the one hundred years following the publication of Copernicus' treatise *On the Revolution of the Heavenly Spheres* in 1543, these earlier theories came under scrutiny. Early in the seventeenth century, the German mathematician Johannes Kepler (1571–1630) made detailed records of planetary movements which substantiated the heliocentric theory. Challenging the conventional assumption that the planetary orbits had to be perfectly circular, Kepler also showed that the five known planets moved around the sun in elliptical paths. He argued that the magnetic force emitted by the sun determined the movements of the planets and their distances from the sun. Kepler's new physics, which advanced the idea of a universe in motion, contradicted the Aristotelian notion of a fixed and unchanging cosmos. It also stood in opposition to the Bible—where, for example, the Hebrew hero Joshua is described as making the sun stand still (Joshua 10: 12–13), a miraculous event that could have occurred only if the sun normally moved around the earth. Although Catholics and Protestants were at odds on many theological matters, in defending the inviolable truth of Scripture against the claims of the new science, they were united.

In Italy, Kepler's contemporary Galileo Galilei (1564–1642) was experimenting with matters of terrestrial motion. His assertions concerning motion and gravity stood contrary to long-held opinions based on Aristotle. Whether or not Galileo actually dropped different-sized weights from the top of the leaning Tower of Pisa—as legend has it—in an effort to determine rates of speed relative to mass, the Florentine astronomer formulated the *law of falling bodies*, which proclaimed that the earth's gravity attracts all objects—regardless of shape, size, or density—at the same rate of acceleration. In 1608, shortly after the publication of this theorem, a Dutch lensmaker invented an instrument that magnified objects seen at a great distance. Perfected by Galileo, the telescope literally revealed new worlds. Through its lens, one could see the craters of the moon, the rings of Saturn, and the moons of Jupiter, which, Galileo observed, operated exactly like earth's moon. The telescope turned the heliocentric theory into fact.

Galileo's discoveries immediately aroused opposition from Catholics and Protestants committed to maintaining orthodox Christian beliefs, especially as set forth in Scripture. Not only did the theory of a heliocentric universe contradict God's word and challenge the Christian concept of a stable and finite universe, it also deprived human beings of their central place in that universe. The heliocentric theory made humanity seem incidental to God's plan and the heavens seem material and "corruptible." Such an idea did not go unchallenged. The first institutional attack on "the new science" occurred in 1600, when the Catholic Inquisition tried, condemned, and publicly executed the Italian astronomer Giordano Bruno, who had asserted that the universe was infinite and without center. Bruno had also suggested that other solar systems might exist in space. Sixteen years after Bruno was burned at the stake, Rome issued an edict that condemned Copernican astronomy as "false and contrary to Holy Scripture" and the writings of Copernicus were put on the Catholic Index of Forbidden Books. Galileo added to the controversy by making his own findings public; and more so because he wrote in the everyday Italian rather than in Latin, the traditional language of Western authority.

More inflammatory still in the eyes of the Church was the publication of Galileo's *Dialogue Concerning the Two Principal Systems of the World* (1632), a fictional conversation between a Copernican and the defenders of the old order, one of whom resembled the pope. Earlier in his career, when it had become evident that his gravitational theories contradicted Aristotle, Galileo had been forced to give up his position as mathematics professor at the University of Pisa. Now, ill with kidney stones and arthritis, he was dragged to Rome and brought before the Inquisition. After a long and unpleasant trial, Church officials, threatening torture, forced the aging astronomer to "admit his errors." Legend has it that after publicly denying that the earth moved around the sun, he muttered under his breath, "Eppur si muove" ("But it *does* move!"). Though condemned to indefinite imprisonment, Galileo was permitted to reside—under "house arrest"—in a villa outside of Florence. Imprisonment, however, did not daunt his ingenuity or his sense of awe. On developing the

Science and Technology

1608 Galileo improves the design of Dutch telescopes to obtain three-power magnification

1609 Hans Lippershey and Zacharias Janssen invent the compound microscope

1619 William Harvey accurately traces the circulation of the blood

Figure 23.2 JOSEPH WRIGHT, *An Experiment on a Bird in the Air Pump*, 1768. Oil on canvas, 5 ft. 11⅝ in. × 7 ft. 11¾ in. National Gallery, London. The experiment shown here involves a glass bowl from which the air is removed, thus depriving the bird of oxygen.

compound microscope, he marveled, "I have observed many tiny animals. . . among which the flea is quite horrible, the gnat and the moth very beautiful; and with great satisfaction I have seen how flies and other little animals can walk attached to mirrors, upside down." His books banned by the Church, Galileo continued to receive personal visits from eminent figures, including the English poet, John Milton.

Despite unrelenting Church opposition, scientists pressed on to devise new instruments for measurement and new procedures for experimentation and analysis. The slide rule, the magnet, the microscope, the mercury barometer, and the air pump (Figure **23.2**) were among the many products of the European quest to calculate, investigate, predict, and ultimately master nature. Seventeenth-century Western scientists investigated the workings of the human eye and explored the genesis and propagation of light, thus advancing the science of optics beyond the frontiers of Islamic and Renaissance scholarship. They accurately described the action of gases and the circulation of the blood. And they devised the branches of higher mathematics known as coordinate geometry, trigonometry, and infinitesimal calculus, by means of which modern scientists might analyze the phenomena of space and motion.

The New Learning

Bacon and the Empirical Method

One of the most characteristic features of the Scientific Revolution was its glorification of the empirical method, a manner of inquiry that depended on direct observation and experimentation. Natural phenomena, argued seventeenth-century scientists, provided evidence from which one might draw general conclusions or axioms, according to a process known as **inductive reasoning**. The leading advocate for the new learning was the English scientist and politician Francis Bacon (1561–1626). In 1620, Bacon published his *Novum Organum* ("New Method"), an impassioned plea for objectivity and clear thinking and the strongest defense of the empirical method ever written. "Man, being the servant and interpreter of Nature," wrote Bacon, "can do and understand so much and so much only as he has observed in fact or in thought of the course of Nature: beyond this he neither knows anything nor can do anything."

Bacon argued that human beings might become "the masters and possessors of Nature" only by means of scientific study guided by precise methods. He promoted an objective system of experimentation, tabulation, and record keeping that became the touchstone of modern

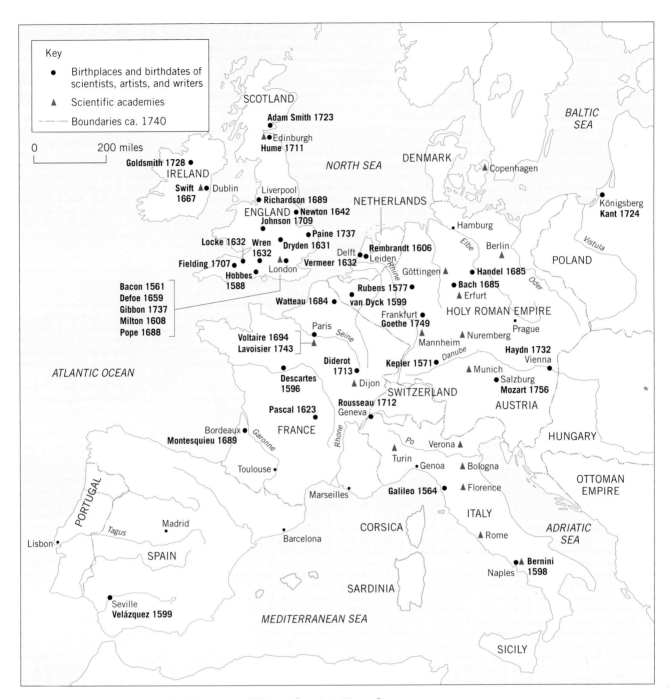

Map 23.1 The Intellectual Revolution of the Seventeenth and Eighteenth Centuries in Western Europe.

scientific inquiry. Unlike earlier humanists, Bacon turned his back on Aristotle and classical science. A prophet of the new learning, he sought to eliminate errors in reasoning derived from blind adherence to traditional sources of authority and religious belief. In an era dominated by fervent spirituality, he demanded a separation of religion and science. "In every age," observed Bacon, "Natural Philosophy has had a troublesome adversary . . . namely, superstition, and the blind and immoderate zeal of religion." Opposing all obstacles to the progress of science, he championed knowledge as the most powerful tool for material achievement. In advancing his strategy for the acquisition of knowledge, Bacon warned against four "false notions" (or Idols, as he called them), which, as the following excerpts from his *Novum Organum*

illustrate, he condemned as hindrances to clear and objective thinking.

READING 4.10 From Bacon's *Novum Organum* (1620)

36

One method of delivery alone remains to us; which is simply this: we must lead men to the particulars themselves, and their series and order; while men on their side must force themselves for a while to lay their notions by and begin to familiarize themselves with facts.

The idols and false notions which are now in possession of the human understanding, and have taken deep root therein, not only so beset men's minds that truth can hardly find entrance, but even after entrance obtained, they will again in the very instauration[1] of the sciences meet and trouble us, unless men being forewarned of danger fortify themselves as far as may be against their assaults.

39

There are four classes of Idols which beset men's minds. To these for distinction's sake I have assigned names,—calling the first class *Idols of the Tribe*; the second, *Idols of the Cave*; the third, *Idols of the Marketplace*; the fourth, *Idols of the Theatre*.

41

The Idols of the Tribe have their foundation in human nature itself, and in the tribe or race of men. For it is a false assertion that the sense of man is the measure of things. On the contrary, all perceptions as well of the sense as of the mind are according to the measure of the individual and not according to the measure of the universe. And the human understanding is like a false mirror, which, receiving rays irregularly, distorts and discolors the nature of things by mingling its own nature with it.

42

The Idols of the Cave are the idols of the individual man. For every one (besides the errors common to human nature in general) has a cave or den of his own, which refracts and discolors the light of nature; owing either to his own proper and peculiar nature; or to his education and conversation with others; or to the reading of books, and the authority of those whom he esteems and admires; or to the differences of impressions, accordingly as they take place in a mind preoccupied and predisposed or in a mind indifferent and settled; or the like. So that the spirit of man (according as it is meted out to different individuals) is in fact a thing variable and full of perturbation, and governed as it were by chance. Whence it was well observed by Heraclitus[2] that men look for sciences in their own lesser worlds, and not in the greater or common world.

43

There are also Idols formed by the intercourse and association of men with each other, which I call Idols of the Marketplace, on account of the commerce and consort of men there. For it is by discourse that men associate; and words are imposed according to the apprehension of the vulgar. And therefore the ill and unfit choice of words wonderfully obstructs the understanding. Nor do the definitions or explanations wherewith in some things learned men are wont to guard and defend themselves, by any means set the matter right. But words plainly force and overrule the understanding, and throw all into confusion, and lead men away into numberless empty controversies and idle fancies.

44

Lastly, there are Idols which have immigrated into men's minds from the various dogmas of philosophies, and also from wrong laws of demonstration. These I call Idols of the Theatre; because in my judgment all the received systems are but so many stage-plays, representing worlds of their own creation after an unreal and scenic fashion. Nor is it only of the systems now in vogue, or only of the ancient sects and philosophies, that I speak; for many more plays of the same kind may yet be composed and in like artificial manner set forth; seeing that errors the most widely different have nevertheless causes for the most part alike. Neither again do I mean this only of entire systems, but also of many principles and axioms in science, which by tradition, credulity, and negligence have come to be received.

 Q How does the notion of an "idol" serve Bacon's purpose in writing this treatise?

Bacon observes that every culture and every age has "worshiped" the Idols. *Idols of the Tribe* are deceptive ideas that have their foundations in human nature (such as our natural inclination to accept and believe what we prefer to be true). He points to the fact that human understanding is self-reflective; it functions like a "false mirror," distorting universal truth. Privately held fallacies (*Idols of the Cave*), on the other hand, derive from individual educations and backgrounds. One may assert, for instance, that one or another religion is "the true faith," that certain racial or ethnic groups are superior to others, or that women should be judged by a different set of standards than those applied to men. The errors resulting from human association and communication, the *Idols of the Marketplace*, arise, according to Bacon, from an "ill or unfit choice of words." For example: the use of the noun "mankind" to designate all human beings. Finally, *Idols of the Theatre* are false dogmas perpetuated by social and political philosophies and institutions. Bacon probably would have regarded "divine right monarchy" (see chapter 21) and "separate but equal education" as examples of these. To purge the mind of prejudice and false thinking, one must, argued Bacon, destroy the Idols.

Bacon's clarion call for objectivity and experimentation inspired the founding in 1645 of the Royal Society of London for Improving Natural Knowledge. The first of many such European and American societies for scientific advancement, the Royal Society has, over the centuries, attracted thousands of members. Their achievements have confirmed one nineteenth-century historian's assessment of Bacon as "the man that moved the minds that moved the world."

Science and Technology

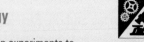

1626 Francis Bacon uses snow in experiments to refrigerate chickens

1637 René Descartes introduces analytic geometry

1645 Otto von Guericke perfects the air pump

1656 Christian Huygens develops the first accurate pendulum clock

1660 Anton van Leeuwenhoek discovers microscopic protozoa

---

[1]Reorganization or renewal.

[2]A Greek philosopher of ca. 500 B.C.E., who taught that all of nature was in a state of flux.

While Bacon wrote his scientific treatises in Latin, he used English for essays on law, rhetoric, and intellectual life. In *The Advancement of Learning* (1605), a sketch of his key ideas concerning methods for acquiring and classifying knowledge, and in the essay *Of Studies*, Bacon demonstrated the masterful use of prose as a tool for theorizing. Written in the poetic prose of the early seventeenth century, *Of Studies* describes the ways in which books serve the individual and society at large. In the excerpt that follows, Bacon eloquently defends reading as a source of pleasure, but, equally important, as a source of practical knowledge and power.

READING 4.11 From Bacon's *Of Studies* from *Essays* (1625)

Studies serve for delight, for ornament, and for ability. Their chief use for delight is in privateness and retiring; for ornament, is in discourse; and for ability, is in the judgment and disposition of business. For expert men can execute, and perhaps judge of particulars, one by one; but the general counsels and the plots and marshalling of affairs come best from those that are learned. To spend too much time in studies is sloth; to use them too much for ornament is affectation; to make judgment wholly by their rules is the humor of a scholar. They perfect nature, and are perfected by experience: for 10 natural abilities are like natural plants, that need pruning by study; . . . Read not to contradict and confute; nor to believe and take for granted; nor to find talk and discourse, but to weigh and consider. Some books are to be tasted, others to be swallowed, and some few to be chewed and digested; that is, some books are to be read only in parts; others to be read, but not curiously; and some few to be read wholly, and with diligence and attention. . . . Reading maketh a full man; conference a ready man; and writing an exact man. And therefore, if a man write little, he had need have a great 20 memory; if he confer little, he had need have a present wit; and if he read little, he had need have much cunning, to seem to know that he does not. Histories make men wise; poets witty; mathematics subtile; natural philosophy deep; moral [philosophy] grave; logic and rhetoric able to contend. . . .

Q In what ways do "studies," according to Bacon, "perfect nature?"
Q What, in his view, are the benefits of reading, verbal discourse, and writing?

Descartes and the Birth of Modern Philosophy

Born in France, René Descartes (1596–1650; Figure **23.3**) is regarded as the founder of modern Western philosophy and the father of analytic geometry. His writings revived the ancient Greek quest to discover how one knows what one knows, and his methods made the discipline of philosophy wholly independent of theology.

Whereas Bacon gave priority to knowledge gained through the senses, Descartes, the supreme rationalist, valued abstract reasoning and mathematical speculation.

Figure 23.3 FRANS HALS, *Portrait of René Descartes*, 1649. Oil on wood, 7½ × 5½ in. Royal Museum of Fine Arts, Copenhagen.

Descartes did not deny the importance of the senses in the search for truth, but he observed that our senses might deceive us. As an alternative to inductive reasoning, he championed the procedure for investigation called **deductive reasoning**. The reverse of the inductive method, the deductive process began with clearly established general premises and moved toward the establishment of particular truths. In the *Discourse on the Method of Rightly Conducting the Reason and Seeking for Truth in the Sciences*, perhaps the most important of all his philosophic works, Descartes set forth his rules for reasoning: never accept anything as true that you do not clearly know to be true; dissect a problem into as many parts as possible; reason from simple to complex knowledge; and finally, draw complete and exhaustive conclusions. Descartes began the *Discourse* by systematically calling everything into doubt. He then proceeded to identify the first thing that he could not doubt—his existence as a thinking individual. This one clear and distinct idea of himself as a "thinking thing," expressed in the proposition "Cogito, ergo sum" ("I think, therefore I am"), became Descartes' "first principle" and the premise for all of his major arguments.

For Descartes, the clear and unbiased mind was the source of all natural understanding. "Except [for] our own thoughts," he insisted, "there is nothing absolutely in our power." Having established rational consciousness as the only sure point of departure for knowledge, Descartes proceeded to examine the world. He made a clear distinction between physical and psychical phenomena, that is, between matter and mind, and between body and soul. According to this dualistic model, the human body operates much like a computer, with the immaterial mind (the software) "informing" the physical components of the body (the hardware). The **Cartesian** view of the human mind as a thinking substance distinct from the human body dominated European philosophic thought until the end of the nineteenth century and still has some strong adherents today.

READING 4.12 From Descartes' *Discourse on Method* (Part IV) (1637)

... I do not know that I ought to tell you of the first meditations   1
there made by me, for they are so metaphysical and so unusual
that they may perhaps not be acceptable to everyone. And yet
at the same time, in order that one may judge whether the
foundations which I have laid are sufficiently secure, I find
myself constrained in some measure to refer to them. For a long
time I had remarked that it is sometimes requisite in common
life to follow opinions which one knows to be most uncertain,
exactly as though they were indisputable, as has been said
above. But because in this case I wished to give myself entirely   10
to the search after Truth, I thought that it was necessary for me
to take an apparently opposite course, and to reject as
absolutely false everything as to which I could imagine the least
ground of doubt, in order to see if afterwards there remained
anything in my belief that was entirely certain. Thus, because
our senses sometimes deceive us, I wished to suppose that
nothing is just as they cause us to imagine it to be; and because
there are men who deceive themselves in their reasoning and
fall into paralogisms,[1] even concerning the simplest matters of
geometry, and judging that I was as subject to error as was any   20
other, I rejected as false all the reasons formerly accepted by
me as demonstrations. And since all the same thoughts and
conceptions which we have while awake may also come to us
in sleep, without any of them being at that time true, I resolved
to assume that everything that ever entered into my mind was
no more true than the illusions of my dreams. But immediately
afterwards I noticed that whilst I thus wished to think all things
false, it was absolutely essential that the "I" who thought this
should be somewhat, and remarking that this truth "*I think,
therefore I am*" was so certain and so assured that all the most   30
extravagant suppositions brought forward by the sceptics
were incapable of shaking it, I came to the conclusion that I
could receive it without scruple as the first principle of the
Philosophy for which I was seeking.

And then, examining attentively that which I was, I saw that I
could conceive that I had no body, and that there was no world nor
place where I might be; but yet that I could not for all that
conceive that I was not. On the contrary, I saw from the very
fact that I thought of doubting the truth of other things, it very
evidently and certainly followed that I was; on the other hand if   40
I had only ceased from thinking, even if all the rest of what I
had ever imagined had really existed, I should have no reason
for thinking that I had existed. From that I knew that I was a

---

[1]Fallacious arguments.

substance the whole essence or nature of which is to think, and
that for its existence there is no need of any place, nor does it
depend on any material thing; so that this "me," that is to say,
the soul by which I am what I am, is entirely distinct from body, and
is even more easy to know than is the latter; and even if body
were not, the soul would not cease to be what it is.

After this I considered generally what in a proposition is   50
requisite in order to be true and certain; for since I had just
discovered one which I knew to be such, I thought that I ought
also to know in what this certainly consisted. And having
remarked that there was nothing at all in the statement "*I think,
therefore I am*" which assures me of having thereby made a
true assertion, excepting that I see very clearly that to think it is
necessary to be, I came to the conclusion that I might assume,
as a general rule, that the things which we conceive very clearly
and distinctly are all true—remembering, however, that there is
some difficulty in ascertaining which are those that we   60
distinctly conceive.

Following upon this, and reflecting on the fact that I
doubted, and that consequently my existence was not quite
perfect (for I saw clearly that it was a greater perfection to
know than to doubt), I resolved to inquire whence I had learnt
to think of anything more perfect than I myself was; and I
recognised very clearly that this conception must proceed from
some nature which was really more perfect. As to the thoughts
which I had of many other things outside of me, like the
heavens, the earth, light, heat, and a thousand others, I had   70
not so much difficulty in knowing whence they came, because,
remarking nothing in them which seemed to render them
superior to me, I could believe that, if they were true, they
were dependencies upon my nature, in so far as it possessed
some perfection; and if they were not true, that I held them
from nought, that is to say, that they were in me because I had
something lacking in my nature. But this could not apply to the
idea of a Being more perfect than my own, for to hold it from
nought would be manifestly impossible; and because it is no
less contradictory to say of the more perfect that it is what   80
results from and depends on the less perfect, than to say that
there is something which proceeds from nothing, it was
equally impossible that I should hold it from myself. In this way
it could but follow that it had been placed in me by a Nature
which was really more perfect than mine could be, and which
even had within itself all the perfections of which I could form
any idea—that is to say, to put it in a word, which was God. . . .

 Q How does Descartes arrive at his distinction between mind and matter?
Q Why does he conclude that he is "a substance the whole essence or nature of which is to think?"

Religion and the New Learning

The new learning, a composite of scientific method and rational inquiry, presented its own challenge to traditional religion. From "self-evident" propositions, Descartes arrived at conclusions to which empirical confirmation was irrelevant. His rationalism—like Plato's—involved a process of the mind independent of the senses. Reasoning that the concept of perfection ("something more perfect than myself") had to proceed from "some Nature which in reality was more perfect," Descartes "proved" the existence of God as Absolute Substance. Since something cannot proceed from nothing, argued Descartes, the idea of God held by human beings must come from God. Moreover, the idea of Perfection (God) embraces the idea of existence, for, if something is perfect, it must exist. Raised by Jesuits, Descartes believed in the existence of a Supreme Creator, but he shared with many seventeenth-century intellectuals the view that God was neither Caretaker nor personal Redeemer. Instead, Descartes identified God with "the mathematical order of nature." The idea that God did not interfere with the laws of humanity and nature was central to **deism**, a system of thought advocating a "natural" religion based on human reason rather than revelation. Deists purged religion of superstition, myth, and ritual. They viewed God as a master mechanic who had created the universe, then stepped aside and allowed his World-Machine to run unattended.

Unlike Bacon, Descartes did not envision any conflict between science and religion. He optimistically concluded that "all our ideas or notions contain in them some truth; for otherwise it could not be that God, who is wholly perfect and veracious, should have placed them in us." Like other deists of his time, Descartes held that to follow reason was to follow God.

Spinoza and Pascal

In Amsterdam, a city whose reputation for freedom of thought had attracted Descartes—he lived there between 1628 and 1649—the Jewish philosopher Baruch Spinoza (1632–1677) addressed the question of the new science versus the old faith. Stripping God of his traditional role as Creator (and consequently finding himself ousted from the local synagogue), Spinoza claimed "God exists only philosophically." God is neither behind, nor beyond, nor separate from nature but, rather, identical with nature. Every physical thing, including human beings, is an expression of God in some variation of mind combined with matter. In a pantheistic spirit reminiscent of Hinduism and Daoism, Spinoza held that the greatest good was the union of the human mind with the whole of nature.

For the French physicist–mathematician Blaise Pascal (1623–1662), on the other hand, science and religion were irreconcilable. Having undergone a mystical experience that converted him to devout Roman Catholicism, he believed that the path to God was through the heart rather than through the head. Although reason might yield a true understanding of nature, it could in no way prove God's existence. We are capable, wrote Pascal, of "certain knowledge and of absolute ignorance." In his collected meditations on human nature, called simply *Pensées* ("Thoughts"), Pascal proposed a wager that challenged the indifference of skeptics: if God does *not* exist, skeptics lose nothing by believing in him, but if God *does* exist, they reap eternal life. The spiritual quest for purpose and

value in a vast, impersonal universe moved the precision-minded Pascal—inventor of a machine that anticipated the digital calculator—to confess: "The eternal silence of these infinite spaces frightens me."

Locke and the Culmination of the Empirical Tradition

The writings of the English philosopher and physician John Locke (1632–1704) firmly defended the empirical tradition in seventeenth-century thought. Written seventy years after Bacon's *Novum Organum*, Locke's *Essay Concerning Human Understanding* (1690) confirmed his predecessor's thesis that everything one knows derives from sensory experience. According to Locke, the human mind at birth is a *tabula rasa* ("blank slate") upon which experience—consisting of sensation, followed by reflection—writes the script. No innate moral principles or ideas exist; rather, human knowledge consists of the progressive accumulation of the evidence of the senses.

The implications of Locke's principles of knowledge moved European and (later) American thought to assume an optimistic view of human destiny. For, if experience influences human knowledge and behavior, argues the empiricist, then, surely, improving the social environment will work to perfect the human condition. Locke's ideas became basic to eighteenth-century liberalism, as well as to all political ideologies that held that human knowledge, if properly applied, would produce happiness for humankind (see chapter 24).

READING 4.13 From Locke's *Essay Concerning Human Understanding* (1690)

Idea is the Object of Thinking.—Every man being conscious **1** to himself that he thinks, and that which his mind is applied about whilst thinking, being the ideas that are there, it is past doubt that men have in their minds several ideas, such as are those expressed by the words whiteness, hardness, sweetness, thinking, motion, man, elephant, army, drunkenness, and others. It is in the first place then to be inquired how he comes by them. I know it is a received doctrine that men have native ideas and original characters stamped upon their minds in their very first being. This opinion I have at large examined already, **10** and I suppose what I have [already] said . . . will be much more easily admitted when I have shown whence the understanding may get all the ideas it has, and by what ways and degrees they may come into the mind; for which I shall appeal to every one's own observation and experience.

All Ideas come from Sensation or Reflection.—Let us then suppose the mind to be, as we say, white paper, void of all characters, without any ideas; how comes it to be furnished? Whence comes it by that vast store which the busy and boundless fancy of man has painted on it with an almost endless **20** variety? Whence has it all the materials of reason and knowledge? To this I answer in one word, from experience; in that all our knowledge is founded, and from that it ultimately derives itself. Our observation employed either about external sensible objects, or about the internal operations of our minds, perceived and reflected on by ourselves, is that which supplies our understandings with all the materials of thinking. These two are the fountains of knowledge from whence all the ideas we have or can naturally have do spring.

The Objects of Sensation, one Source of Ideas.—First, our **30** senses, conversant about particular sensible objects, do convey into the mind several distinct perceptions of things, according to those various ways wherein those objects do affect them: and thus we come by those ideas we have, of yellow, white, heat, cold, soft, hard, bitter, sweet, and all those which we call sensible qualities; which when I say the senses convey into the mind, I mean, they from external objects convey into the mind what produces there those perceptions. This great source of most of the ideas we have, depending wholly upon our senses, and derived by them to the **40** understanding, I call Sensation.

The Operations of our Minds, the other Source of them.— Secondly, the other fountain, from which experience furnishes the understanding with ideas, is the perception of the operations of our own mind within us, as it is employed about the ideas it has got; which operations, when the soul comes to reflect on and consider, do furnish the understanding with another set of ideas, which could not be had from things without; and such are perception, thinking, doubting, believing, reasoning, knowing, willing, and all the different actings of our **50** own minds; which we being conscious of, and observing in ourselves, do from these receive into our understandings as distinct ideas, as we do from bodies affecting our senses. This source of ideas every man has wholly in himself; and though it be not sense, as having nothing to do with external objects, yet it is very like it, and might properly enough be called internal sense. But as I call the other Sensation, so I call this Reflection, the ideas it affords being such only as the mind gets by reflecting on its own operations within itself. By reflection then, in the following part of this discourse, I would **60** be understood to mean that notice which the mind takes of its own operations, and the manner of them; by reason whereof there come to be ideas of these operations in the understanding. These two, I say, viz., external material things, as the objects of sensation; and the operations of our own minds within, as the objects of reflection; are to me the only originals from whence all our ideas take their beginnings. . . .

All our Ideas are of the one or the other of these.— The understanding seems to me not to have the least glimmering of **70** any ideas which it doth not receive from one of these two. External objects furnish the mind with the ideas of sensible qualities, which are all those different perceptions they produce in us; and the mind furnishes the understanding with ideas of its own operations.

These, when we have taken a full survey of them, and their several modes, combinations, and relations, we shall find to contain all our whole stock of ideas; and that we have nothing in our minds, which did not come in one of these two ways. Let any one examine his own thoughts, and thoroughly search into **80** his understanding; and then let him tell me, whether all the original ideas he has there, are any other than of the objects of his senses, or of the operations of his mind, considered as objects of his reflection: and how great a mass of knowledge soever he imagines to be lodged there, he will, upon taking a

strict view, see that he has not any idea in his mind, but what one of these two have imprinted. . . .

 Q. How does Locke's regard for the senses differ from Descartes'? On what aspects of the mind's operations might they agree?

Newton's Scientific Synthesis

The work of the great English astronomer and mathematician Isaac Newton (1642–1727) represents the culminating synthesis of seventeenth-century physics and mathematics. A tireless student of the sciences (so intent on his studies that he often forgot to eat), Newton moved the new learning from its speculative and empirical phases (represented by Copernicus and Galileo, respectively) to the stage of codification. He brought Kepler's laws of celestial mechanics and Galileo's terrestrial law of falling bodies into an all-embracing theory of universal gravitation that described every physical movement in the universe—from the operation of the tides to the effects of a planet upon its moons. In 1687 Newton published his monumental treatise on gravitation and the three laws of motion: the *Philosophiae Naturalis Principia Mathematica* ("Mathematical Principles of Natural Philosophy").[1] Newton's *Principia*, the fundamentals of which went unchallenged until the late nineteenth century, promoted the idea of a uniform and intelligible universe that operated as systematically as a well-oiled machine. With this five hundred and fifty page work, written in a mere eighteen months, he not only desanctified nature; he proved that nature's laws applied equally to terrestrial and celestial matter. The *Principia* replaced Aristotle's description of the physical world with simple mathematical equations that would become the basis of modern physics. It confirmed that by means of mathematical analysis and scientific observation, enlightened individuals might comprehend and control their world more completely than had ever before been possible. Newton's shaping influence on the spirit of the age is best described by his admiring British contemporary, Alexander Pope (see chapter 24): "Nature and Nature's Laws lay hid in Night./ God said, *Let Newton be!* And All was Light."

---

[1]The term "natural philosophy" meant primarily physics, astronomy, and the science of matter.

Science and Technology

1666 Isaac Newton uses a prism to analyze light

1671 Gottfried Wilhelm Leibniz invents a calculating machine that multiplies and divides

1684 Leibniz publishes his first paper on differential calculus

1687 Newton publishes his *Principia Mathematica*

Figure 23.4 JAN DAVIDSZ DE HEEM, *Still Life with View of the Sea*, 1646. Oil on canvas, 23⅜ × 36½ in. Courtesy of the Toledo Museum of Art, Ohio. Purchased with funds from the Libbey Endowment. Gift of Edward Drummond Libbey.

Figure 23.5 JAN VAN STEEN, *The Drawing Lesson*, 1665. Oil on canvas, 19⅜ × 16¼ in. The J. Paul Getty Museum, Los Angeles. Credit: © The J. Paul Getty Museum.

The Impact of the Scientific Revolution on Art

Northern Baroque Painting

If the new science engendered a spirit of objective inquiry in literature, it also inspired new directions in the visual arts. In the cities of seventeenth-century Holland, where Dutch lensmakers had produced the first telescopes and microscopes, artists paid obsessive attention to the appearance of the natural world. In still lifes, portraits, landscape, and scenes of everyday life—all secular subjects—Dutch masters practiced the "art of describing."[2] The almost photographic realism of such paintings as Jan Davidsz de Heem's *Still Life with View of the Sea* (Figure **23.4**) is typical of the new "Baconian" attention to the natural world: plump oysters and crabs, a succulent ham, ripe melons and peaches, and a gleaming tankard are all rendered with keen precision and detail. A distant view of the sea and a storm-tossed vessel in the background of the painting are less than subtle reminders that Dutch maritime activity financed the bounties of the dinner table.

Of the many master-painters working in seventeenth-century Holland, a good number were women. Often excluded from membership in the local guilds, they learned their trade by drawing from plaster-cast reproductions, as illustrated in a genre painting by Jan van Steen (Figure **23.5**) Forbidden to work from nude male models employed

---

[2]See Svetlana Alpers, *The Art of Describing: Dutch Art in the Seventeenth Century*. Chicago: University of Chicago Press, 1983.

in traditional studio training, they inclined to the painting of portraits and still-life subjects. Rachel Ruysch (1664–1750), the mother of ten children, produced precisely executed flower pieces for an international circle of patrons. Her works, which reflect the influence of newly available botanical prints, suggest the close relationship between late seventeenth-century science and art.

One of the most talented of Holland's female artists was Maria van Oosterwyck (1630–1693). Drawing on the tradition of exacting realism initiated by Jan van Eyck, van Oosterwyck brought a naturalist's passion for detail to her paintings. Her *Still Life* of 1668 includes a radiant Dutch tulip, a worn book, a meticulously painted globe, a rotting skull, various insects (including a moth and a microscopically precise fly), a mouse nibbling at some grain, and a wine carafe (left front) that reflects a minute image of the artist (Figure **23.6**). This illusionistic *tour de force*, while brilliantly decorative, makes symbolic reference to the transience of temporal existence. Ostensibly a celebration of earthly pleasures, the painting—a type known as **vanitas**—suggests the corruptibility of worldly goods, the futility of riches, and the inevitability of death.

In addition to still-life subjects, genre paintings (scenes of everyday life and especially family life) were in high demand in the Netherlands in the seventeenth century, generating a virtual Golden Age of Dutch art. The domestic scenes of Pieter de Hooch (1629–1684) show Dutch art to be societal—they are concerned with conviviality and companionship. In one painting, de Hooch uses a spacious courtyard filled with cool, bright light as the setting for such ordinary pleasures as pipe

Figure 23.6 MARIA VAN OOSTERWYCK, *Vanitas Still Life*, 1668. Oil on canvas, 29 × 35 in. Kunsthistorisches Museum, Vienna.

smoking and beer drinking (Figure **23.7**). He captures a mood of domestic intimacy in his loving attention to humble fact: the crumbling brick wall, the gleaming tankard, the homely matron, and the pudgy child. The strict verticals and horizontals of the composition—established with Cartesian clarity and precision—create a sense of tranquility and order.

Amateur musical performances, one of the major domestic entertainments of the seventeenth century, are the subject of many Northern baroque paintings, including de Hooch's *Portrait of a Family Making Music* (Figure **23.8**). The growing popularity of musical subjects reflects the emphasis on musical education and the rising number of private musical societies in the towns of the Dutch Republic. In the belief that music-listening and music-making were morally edifying (and thus more desirable than the all too popular pastime of drinking), many churches required musical recitals before and after services and encouraged instrumental and choral expression among members of the congregation. Holland was a center for the manufacture of musical instruments; the Dutch household pictured by de Hooch would have owned the bass viol, recorder, cittern (a type of lute), and violin on which the family performed, their rhythms closely measured by the portly, no-nonsense matron of the house.

Figure 23.7 (above) **PIETER DE HOOCH**, *A Dutch Courtyard*, 1658–1660. Oil on canvas, 26¾ × 23 in. © 1998 Board of Trustees, National Gallery of Art, Washington, D.C. Andrew W. Mellon Collection.

Figure 23.8 (right) **PIETER DE HOOCH**, *Portrait of a Family Making Music*, 1663. Oil on canvas, 38⅛ × 45¹⁵⁄₁₆ in. © The Cleveland Museum of Art 1998. Gift of the Hanna Fund (1951.355)

Figure 23.9 GERARD TER BORCH, *The Suitor's Visit*, ca. 1658. Oil on canvas, 31½ × 29⅝ in. © 1998 Board of Trustees, National Gallery of Art, Washington, D.C. Andrew W. Mellon Collection.

Music-making also figures in the delightful painting called *The Suitor's Visit* by Gerard ter Borch (1617–1681). The narrative is staged like a scene from a play: a well-dressed gentleman, who has just entered the parlor of a well-to-do middle-class family, bows before a young woman whose coy apprehension suggests that she is the object of courtship (Figure **23.9**). The father and the family dog take note of the tense moment, while a younger woman, absorbed in playing the lute, ignores the interruption. Ter Borch was famous for his virtuosity in painting silk and satin fabrics that subtly gleam from within the shadowy depths of domestic interiors. Equally impressive, however, was his ability to dignify an inconsequential social event with profound human meaning.

Vermeer and Dutch Painting

Seventeenth-century Dutch artists developed the naturalistic landscape (the very word derives from the Dutch *landschap*) as a major artistic subject. In landscape painting as in genre subjects, they described nature with a close attention to detail and a sensitivity to atmosphere that rivaled the landscapes of their Northern European predecessors, Dürer and Brueghel (see chapter 19). Unlike their seventeenth-century French contemporaries, Poussin and Claude Lorrain (see chapter 21), Dutch landscape painters depicted nature free of moralizing narratives; they brought to life a sense of place and the vastness of nature itself. Such is the case with the *View of Delft* (Figure **23.10**),

Figure 23.10 JAN VERMEER, *View of Delft*, 1658. Oil on canvas, 3 ft. 2¾ in. × 3 ft. 10 in. Mauritshuis, The Hague.

Figure 23.11 A *camera obscura*; the image formed by the lens and reflected by the mirror on the ground glass is traced by the artist.

paintings with the aid of a *camera obscura* (Figure **23.11**), an apparatus that anticipated the modern pinhole camera (while lacking the means of capturing the image on film). The blurred contours and small beads of light that twinkle on the surface of his canvases suggest the use of an optical lens.

Vermeer's favorite subjects—women, playing musical instruments, reading letters, or enjoying the company of suitors—are all depicted on small-sized canvases in a similar intimate interior (possibly that of his studio). Usually self-contained and self-possessed, and bathed in atmospheric light, they come to life in a strikingly personal manner. Light transforms Vermeer's *Woman Holding a Balance* (Figure **23.12**) from a mundane subject—the weighing of gold—into a lofty allegory; the need to balance material prosperity (symbolized by the jewels on the table) with the inevitability of one's destiny (marked by the painting of the Last Judgment that hangs on the back wall). In a manner that recalls the Arnolfini double portrait by his Netherlandish predecessor, Jan van Eyck (see Figure 17.12), light from a nearby window enters the room and subtly illuminates the subject. Vermeer's compositional strategy (used repeatedly in his interiors) here reinforces the allegorical theme of balance: light is set against dark, realistic details against broadly generalized shapes. Whether or not the painting was intended as

the only landscape painted by the Delft master, Jan Vermeer (1632–1675). An innkeeper and an art dealer, who produced fewer than forty canvases in his lifetime, Vermeer transformed everyday subjects by way of atmospheric space and evanescent light. His *View of Delft*, a topographical study of his native city, reveals a typically Dutch affection for the visible world, but it reflects the artist's delight in the physical effects of light on matter: the manner in which the silvery surface of the water is interrupted to reflect the density of boats and buildings, the way in which sunlight filters down to illuminate some segments of the city, while others are clouded into shade. Vermeer lowers the horizon line to give increased attention to the sky—a reflection perhaps of his interest in the new astronomy. Despite the filtered play of light, he fixes a single point of view at a precise moment in time and place. The broad horizon, however, seems to reach beyond the limits of the frame to suggest infinite space. Two groups of tiny figures (in the left foreground) invite us to share the view—as beholders and as minor players on the larger stage of nature.

It is likely that Vermeer and other Dutch masters shared an interest in the optical experiments of Galileo and Newton and in the optical devices (such as the *camera lucida*; see chapter 17) that facilitated an accurate and detailed depiction of the physical world. Scholars argue that Vermeer, the exemplar in an age of observation, executed his

Figure 23.12 JAN VERMEER, *Woman Holding a Balance*, ca. 1664. Oil on canvas, 16¾ × 15 in. © 1998 Board of Trustees, National Gallery of Art, Washington, D.C. The Widener Collection, 1962.

in chapter 22), dominated the genre of portraiture in seventeenth-century Dutch painting. Hals was the leading painter of Haarlem and one of the great realists of the Western portrait tradition. His talent lay in capturing the fleeting expressions that characterized the personality and physical presence of his sitters. Hals rendered the jaunty self-confidence of a courtly Dutch soldier (Figure **23.13**) with the same fidelity to nature that he used to convey the dour solemnity of the scholar-philosopher Descartes (see Figure 23.3). A master of the brush, Hals brought his forms to life by means of quick, loose, staccato brushstrokes and impasto highlights. Immediacy, spontaneity, and impulsive movement—features typical of baroque art—are captured in Hals' vigorous portraits.

These qualities also appear in the work of Judith Leyster (1609–1660), a Netherlandish artist from the province of Utrecht, whose canvases until the twentieth century were usually attributed to her colleague, Frans Hals. Leyster established a workshop in Haarlem and was one of only two females elected to the painters' guild of that city. Almost all her known paintings date from before her marriage at the age of twenty-six. Leyster's *Self-Portrait* achieves a sense of informality through the casual manner in which the artist turns away from her canvas as if to greet the viewer (Figure **23.14**). The laughing violinist that is the subject of the painting-within-the-painting provides an exuberant counterpoint to Leyster's robust visage, which

Figure 23.13 FRANS HALS, *The Laughing Cavalier*, 1624. Oil on canvas, 33¾ × 27 in. Reproduced by permission of the Trustees, the Wallace Collection, London.

an allegory, its exquisite intimacy and meditative mood are unique in Dutch art.

Dutch Portraiture

The vogue of portraiture in Northern baroque art reflected the self-conscious materialism of a rising middle class. Like the portraits of wealthy Renaissance aristocrats (see chapter 17), the painted likenesses of seventeenth-century Dutch burghers fulfilled the desire to immortalize one's worldly self. But in contrast to Italian portraits, the painted images of middle-class Dutch men and women are usually unidealized and often even unflattering. They capture a truth to nature reminiscent of late Roman portraiture (see chapter 6) but surpass even these in their self-scrutiny and probing, self-reflective character.

Two contemporaries, Frans Hals (1581–1666) and Rembrandt van Rijn (the latter introduced

Figure 23.14 JUDITH LEYSTER, *Self-Portrait*, ca. 1630. Oil on canvas, 29⅜ × 25⅛ in. © 1998 Board of Trustees, National Gallery of Art, Washington, D.C. Gift of Mr. and Mrs. Robert Woods Bliss.

conveys the self-confidence of a middle-class woman who competed with the best of Holland's masters and turned her art to profit. Leyster's portrait is a personal comment on the role of the artist as muse and artisan.

Hals' and Leyster's portraits are astute records of surface appearance and the social milieu. By comparison, Rembrandt's portraits are studies of the inner life of his sitters, uncompromising explorations of flesh and blood, rather than flattering accounts of rich costumes and grandiose architectural settings. A keen observer of human character and a master technician, Rembrandt became the leading portrait painter in the city of Amsterdam. The commissions he received at the beginning of his career exceeded his ability to fill them. But after a meteoric rise to fame, he saw his fortunes decline. Accumulated debts led to poverty, bankruptcy, and psychological depression—the last compounded by the loss of his beloved wife in 1642. The history of Rembrandt's career is mirrored in his self-portraits, over sixty of which survive; these are a kind of visual diary, a lifetime record of the artist's passionate enterprise in self-scrutiny. His *Self-Portrait* of 1661, with its slackened facial muscles and furrowed brow, directly engages the viewer with the image of a noble and yet utterly vulnerable personality (Figure **23.15**). Portraiture of this kind, which has no equivalent in any non-Western culture, may be considered among the outstanding examples of probing individualism.

Among the most lucrative of Rembrandt's commissions was the group portrait, a uniquely Dutch genre that commemorated the achievements of wealthy families, guild members, and militia officers. Some of these paintings, which measure more than 12 by 14 feet, reflect the baroque taste for colossal proportion and theatrical setting. But Rembrandt skillfully fused dramatic effect with sober, unidealized characterization. These features are especially obvious in *The Anatomy Lesson of Dr. Nicolaes Tulp* (1632), the painting that established Rembrandt's reputation as a master portraitist (Figure **23.16**). Rembrandt eliminated the posed look of the conventional group portrait by staging the scene as a dissection in progress. Here, as in his religious compositions (compare Figure 22.4), he manipulates light for dramatic purposes: he spotlights the dissected corpse in the foreground and balances the darker area on the right, dominated by the figure of the doctor, with a triangle formed by the illuminated heads of the students (whose names appear on the piece of paper held by the central figure). The faces of Tulp's students carry the force of individual personalities and capture the spirit of inquisitiveness peculiar to the Age of Science.

Baroque Instrumental Music

Until the sixteenth century, almost all music was written for the voice rather than for musical instruments. Even during the Renaissance, instrumental music was, for the most part, the result of substituting an instrument for a voice in music written for singing or dancing. The seventeenth century marked the rise of music that lacked an extramusical text. Like a mathematical equation or a geometric formula, the instrumental music of the early modern era carried no explicit narrative content—it was neither a vehicle of religious expression nor a means of supporting a secular vocalized text. Such music was written without consideration for the associational content traditionally provided by a set of sung lyrics. The idea of music as an aesthetic exercise, composed for its own sake

Figure 23.15 REMBRANDT VAN RIJN, *Self-Portrait as Saint Paul*, 1661. Oil on canvas, 35⅛ × 30⅜ in. Rijksmuseum, Amsterdam.

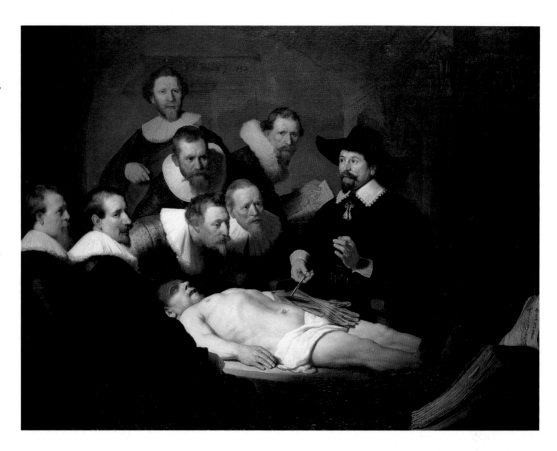

**Figure 23.16
REMBRANDT VAN
RIJN**, *The Anatomy
Lesson of Dr. Nicolaes
Tulp*, 1632. Oil on canvas,
5 ft. 3⅜ in. × 7 ft. 1¼ in.
Mauritshuis,
The Hague.

rather than to serve a religious or communal purpose, was a notable feature of the seventeenth century and one that distinguishes modern Western European music from the musical traditions of Asia and Africa.

Not surprisingly, the rise of instrumental music was accompanied by improvements in instruments and refinements in tuning. Indeed, instrumental music came to dominate musical composition at the very moment that Western musicians were perfecting such stringed instruments as the violin, viola, and cello (see Figure 23.8) and such keyboard instruments as the organ and harpsichord (Figure **23.17**). By the early eighteenth century, musicians were adopting the system of tuning known as **equal temperament**, whereby the octave was divided into twelve half-steps of equal size. The collection of preludes and fugues known as the *Well-Tempered* [tuned] *Clavier* (1722–1742) shows how Bach could take a technical development such as this uniform system of tuning and turn it into sublime music—he wrote two pieces in every possible key. The new attention paid to improving instruments and systematizing keys mirrored the efforts of scientists and philosophers to bring precision and uniformity to the tools and methods for scientific inquiry.

In the seventeenth century, northern Italy was the world center for the manufacture of violins. The Amati, Guarneri, and Stradivari families of Cremona, Italy, established the techniques of making quality violins that were sought in all of the great courts of Europe. Transmitted from father to son, the construction techniques used to produce these instruments were guarded so secretly that modern violinmakers have never successfully imitated them. Elsewhere, around 1650, earlier instruments were

Figure 23.17 JOHANNES COUCHET (maker), Flemish Harpsichord-double-banked; compass, four octaves, and a fifth F to C (each keyboard), ca. 1650. Case decorated with carving and gilt gesso work. The Metropolitan Museum of Art, New York. The Crosby Brown Collection of Musical Instruments, 1889 (89.4.2363).

standardized and refined. The ancient double-reed wind instrument known as the shawm, for instance, developed into the modern oboe. While amateur music-making was widespread, professional performance also took a great leap forward, as a new breed of virtuosi inspired the writing of treatises on performance techniques.

Three main types of composition—the sonata, the suite, and the concerto—dominated seventeenth-century instrumental music. All three reflect the baroque taste for dramatic contrasts in tempo and texture. The **sonata** (from the Italian word for "sounded," that is, music played and not sung) is a piece written for a few instruments—often no more than one or two. It usually consisted of three **movements** of contrasting tempo—fast/slow/fast—each based on a song or dance form of the time. The **suite**, written for any combination of instruments, is a sequence or series of movements derived from various European court or folk dances—for example, the sarabande, the pavane, the minuet, and the gigue, or jig. Henry Purcell (1659–1695) in England, François Couperin (1668–1733) in France (see chapter 26), and Johann Sebastian Bach (1685–1750) in Germany all contributed to the development of the suite as a musical genre. Finally, the **concerto** (from the same root as *concertato*, which describes opposing or contrasting bodies of sound; see chapter 20) is a composition consisting of two groups of instruments, one small and the other large, playing in "dialogue." The typical baroque concerto, the **concerto grosso** ("large concerto") featured several movements, whose number and kind varied considerably.

The leading Italian instrumental composer of the baroque era was Antonio Vivaldi (1678–1741), a Roman Catholic priest and the son of a prominent violinist at Saint Mark's Cathedral in Venice. Vivaldi wrote some 450 concertos. He systematized the concerto grosso into a three-movement form (fast/slow/fast) and increased the distinctions between solo and ensemble groups in each movement. Of the many exciting compositions Vivaldi wrote for solo violin and ensemble, the most glorious is *The Four Seasons*, a group of four violin concertos, each of which musically describes a single season. Vivaldi intended that this piece be "programmatic," that is, that it carry meaning outside of the music itself. As if to ensure that the music duplicate the descriptive power of the traditional vocal lines, he added poems at appropriate passages in the score for the instruction of the performers. At the section called "Spring," for instance, Vivaldi's verses describe "flowing streams" and "singing birds." While the music offers listeners the challenge of detecting such extramusical references to nature, the brilliance of this instrumental masterpiece lies not in its programmatic innovations but, rather, in its vibrant rhythms, its lyrical solos, and its exuberant "dialogues" between violin and small orchestra. Typical of the baroque concerto, a recurring melody known as the *ritornello* ("return") unifies the piece.

Rivaling Vivaldi's *Four Seasons* in their spiraling melodies and expansive rhythms are Bach's Brandenburg

Concertos, which the composer completed in 1721 on commission from Christian Ludwig, the Margrave of Brandenburg. Though there is no record that the six concertos were ever performed during Bach's lifetime, they were probably intended for performance by the Brandenburg court orchestra. The Brandenburg Concertos employ as soloists most of the principal instruments of the baroque orchestra: violin, oboe, recorder, trumpet, and harpsichord. Bach applied himself to developing rich contrasts of tone and texture between the two "contending" groups of instruments—note especially the massive sound of the entire ensemble versus the lighter sounds of the small sections in the first movement of the fourth concerto. Here, tightly drawn webs of counterpoint are spun between upper and lower instrumental parts, while musical lines, driven by an unflagging rhythm and energy, unfold majestically.

Only one year before he died, in 1749, Bach undertook one of the most monumental works of his career, a compelling example of baroque musical composition that came to be called *The Art of Fugue*. A **fugue** (literally "flight") is a polyphonic composition in which a single musical theme (or subject) is restated in sequential phrases. As in the more familiar canon known as a "round"—for instance, "Three Blind Mice"—a melody in one voice part is imitated in other voice parts, so that melody and repetitions overlap. The musical subject can be arranged to appear backward or inverted (or both), augmented (the time value of the notes doubled, so that the melody moves twice as slowly), or diminished (note values halved, so that the melody moves twice as fast). In the hands of a great composer, this form of imitative counterpoint wove a majestic tapestry of sound. Such is the case with Bach's *Art of Fugue*, in the last portion of which he went so far as to sign his name with a musical motif made up of the letters of his name—B flat, A, C, and B natural (pronounced as an H in German). Bach produced this *summa* of seventeenth-century musical science as a tool for instruction in the writing of fugues. However, even the listener who cannot read music or analyze the complexities of Bach's inventions is struck by the concentrated brilliance of each of his fugues. No less than Newton's codification of the laws of nature, *The Art of Fugue* was a triumphant expression of the Age of Science.

SUMMARY

During the seventeenth century, European scientists advanced a new picture of the cosmos. They showed that the earth, like the other planets, follows an elliptical and therefore irregular path around the sun, which stands at the center of the solar system. Clearly, the planet earth and its human inhabitants could no longer be regarded as the hub of a motionless universe. The progress of the Scientific Revolution moved from the stage of methodical speculation (represented by Copernicus and Kepler) to that of empirical confirmation (provided by Galileo's telescope) and, ultimately, to codification with Newton's

♩ See Music Listening Selections at end of chapter.

♩ See Music Listening Selections at end of chapter.

Principia. Between 1600 and 1750, many new scientific instruments were invented. The sciences of physics and astronomy, along with the language of higher mathematics, were firmly established.

While scientists demystified nature, the new learning provided a methodology for more accurately describing and predicting its operations. Francis Bacon championed induction and the empirical method, which gave priority to knowledge gained through the senses. John Locke defended the empirical tradition by claiming that all ideas came from sensation and reflection. Questioning the authority of the inductive method, René Descartes gave priority to deductive reasoning and mathematical analysis. Despite their differences, seventeenth-century intellectuals shared the deist notions of God as a master mechanic and the universe as a great machine that operated independently of divine intervention.

The Scientific Revolution and the new learning ushered in a phase of the baroque style marked by an empirical attention to detail, a fascination with light and space, and an increased demand for such subjects as still life, landscape, portraiture, and genre painting. The many examples of each testify to the secular preoccupations of middle-class patrons. In seventeenth-century art, cosmic landscapes such as Vermeer's *View of Delft* are balanced by the genre paintings of de Hooch and ter Borch, which explore the intimate pleasures of house and home, and by the psychologically penetrating portraits of Hals, Leyster, and Rembrandt.

Modern science also touched the art of music. During the seventeenth century, the violin and the organ were perfected, and keyboard instruments (and musical performance in general) benefited from the development of a uniform system of tuning. Treatises on the art of instrumental performance became increasingly popular. The seventeenth century saw the rise of wholly instrumental music and of such instrumental forms as the sonata, the suite, and the concerto. Vivaldi and Bach perfected the concerto grosso, while Bach exploited the art of the fugue in musical compositions whose complexity and brilliance remain unrivaled. These instrumental forms captured the exuberance of the baroque spirit, just as they summed up the dynamic intellectualism of the age.

MUSIC LISTENING SELECTIONS

CD Two Selection 5 Vivaldi, *The Four Seasons*, "Spring," Concerto in E Major, Op. 8, No. 1, first movement, 1725.

CD Two Selection 6 Bach, Brandenburg Concerto No. 4 in G Major, first movement, excerpt, 1721.

CD Two Selection 7 Bach, *The Art of Fugue*, Canon in the 12th, harpsichord, 1749–1750.

GLOSSARY

Cartesian of or relating to René Descartes or his philosophy

concerto (Italian, "opposing" or "competing") an instrumental composition consisting of one or more solo instruments and a larger group of instruments playing in "dialogue"

concerto grosso a "large concerto," the typical kind of baroque concerto, consisting of several movements

deductive reasoning a method of inquiry that begins with clearly established general premises and moves toward the establishment of particular truths

deism a movement or system of thought advocating natural religion based on human reason rather than revelation; deists describe God as Creator, but deny that God interferes with the laws of the universe

equal temperament a system of tuning that originated in the seventeenth century, whereby the octave is divided into twelve half-steps of equal size; since intervals have the same value in all keys, music may be played in any key, and a musician may change from one key to another with complete freedom.

fugue ("flight") a polyphonic composition in which a theme (or subject) is imitated, restated, and developed by successively entering voice parts

geocentric earth-centered

heliocentric sun-centered

inductive reasoning a method of inquiry that begins with direct observation and experimentation and moves toward the establishment of general conclusions or axioms

movement a major section in a long instrumental composition

ritornello (Italian, "a little return") in baroque music, an instrumental section that recurs throughout the movement

sonata an instrumental composition consisting of three movements of contrasting tempo, usually fast/slow/fast; see also Glossary, chapter 26

suite an instrumental composition consisting of a sequence or series of movements derived from court or folk dances

vanitas (Latin, "vanity") a type of still life consisting of objects that symbolize the brevity of life and the transience of earthly pleasures and achievements

PART 2

The Age of Enlightenment

The Age of Enlightenment, as the eighteenth century is often called, was a time of buoyant optimism. Educated Europeans envisioned themselves as the most civilized people in history: having survived a millennium of darkness, they now ushered in a new era of light—the light of reason. Reason, they optimistically predicted, would dispel the mists of human ignorance, superstition, and prejudice.

Eighteenth-century intellectuals were the heirs to Newtonian science. They viewed the universe as a great machine that operated according to unchanging "natural" laws. Just as Newton had systematized the laws of the physical universe, so these rationalists tried to regulate the laws of human behavior. Such practical powers, they argued, were not only attainable, but also essential to the progress and betterment of humankind. Enlightenment theorists—John Locke and Adam Smith in Great Britain, Jean-Jacques Rousseau in France, and Thomas Jefferson in America—articulated the fundamental concepts of natural law, political freedom, free enterprise, and the social contract between ruler and ruled; while other thinkers, such as Antoine Nicolas de Condorcet and Mary Wollstonecraft championed social equality and human progress. And although the major intellectual and cultural ideals of the Enlightenment did not directly touch the lives of millions of eighteenth-century peasants and villagers, they profoundly influenced the course of modern history, not only in the West, but, more recently, throughout the world.

During the eighteenth century, learning freed itself from the Church, and literacy became widespread. Among middle-class Europeans, ninety to one hundred percent of the males and almost seventy-five percent of the females could read and write. This new, more literate, middle class competed with a waning aristocracy for social and political prestige. The public interest in literature and the arts spurred the rise of the newspaper, the novel, and the symphony. Satire became a popular vehicle for dramatizing the contradictions between the polite society of the upper classes and the poverty and illiteracy of the lower classes. In educated circles, debate raged over the powers of rulers versus those of the ruled. And in France and North America, visionary treatises defended the unalienable rights of citizens and fanned the flames of revolt, culminating in violent revolutions. None of the age-old certitudes were left unexamined: the church hierarchy, the autocratic rule of kings and despots, the very social order—all fell under close scrutiny. By the pen and by the musket, the new order would be launched.

At the same time, the Age of Enlightenment was rich in the production of works of art and architecture, now increasingly commissioned by secular patrons. While the visual arts of the Enlightenment reflect some of the intellectual ideals of the era, they more closely mirror the shifting tastes and values of eighteenth-century society. The rococo style was an expression of aristocratic luxury and the delight in physical pleasure, while the neoclassical revival, inspired by a wealth of archeological discoveries, responded to the tempered rationalism and political idealism of reformers in France and the young American republic. The portrait, the visual counterpart of literary biography, continued to hold a prized place in Western art. Finally, in the birth of the symphony orchestra and in the development of classical forms of Western instrumental music, the eighteenth century made a lasting contribution to the humanistic tradition, one that continues to influence modern musical history.

(opposite) **JACQUES-LOUIS DAVID**, detail of *The Oath of the Horatii*, 1784. Oil on canvas, 10 ft. 10 in. × 14 ft. Louvre, Paris. © Photo Josse, Paris.

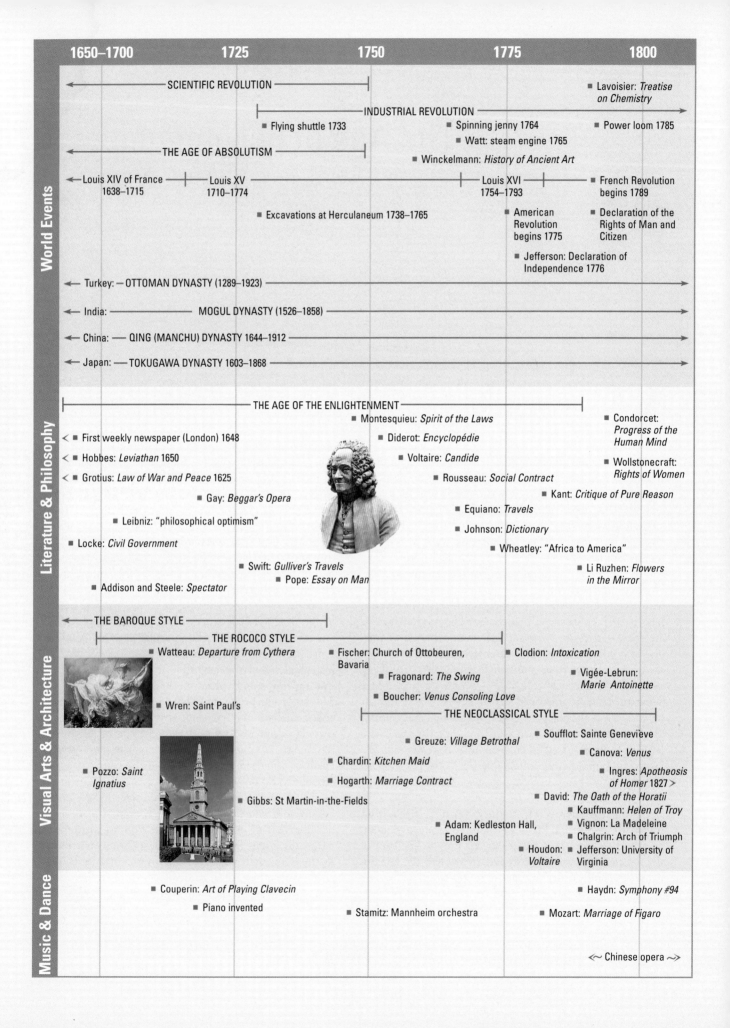

| 1650–1700 | 1725 | 1750 | 1775 | 1800 |

World Events

SCIENTIFIC REVOLUTION

■ Lavoisier: *Treatise on Chemistry*

INDUSTRIAL REVOLUTION

■ Flying shuttle 1733 ■ Spinning jenny 1764 ■ Power loom 1785

■ Watt: steam engine 1765

THE AGE OF ABSOLUTISM

■ Winckelmann: *History of Ancient Art*

← Louis XIV of France 1638–1715 — Louis XV 1710–1774 — Louis XVI 1754–1793 — ■ French Revolution begins 1789

■ Excavations at Herculaneum 1738–1765

■ American Revolution begins 1775

■ Declaration of the Rights of Man and Citizen

■ Jefferson: Declaration of Independence 1776

← Turkey: — OTTOMAN DYNASTY (1289–1923) →

← India: — MOGUL DYNASTY (1526–1858) →

← China: — QING (MANCHU) DYNASTY 1644–1912 →

← Japan: — TOKUGAWA DYNASTY 1603–1868 →

Literature & Philosophy

THE AGE OF THE ENLIGHTENMENT

■ Montesquieu: *Spirit of the Laws*

< ■ First weekly newspaper (London) 1648 ■ Diderot: *Encyclopédie*

< ■ Hobbes: *Leviathan* 1650 ■ Voltaire: *Candide*

< ■ Grotius: *Law of War and Peace* 1625 ■ Rousseau: *Social Contract*

■ Gay: *Beggar's Opera*

■ Leibniz: "philosophical optimism"

■ Locke: *Civil Government*

■ Condorcet: *Progress of the Human Mind*

■ Wollstonecraft: *Rights of Women*

■ Kant: *Critique of Pure Reason*

■ Equiano: *Travels*

■ Johnson: *Dictionary*

■ Wheatley: "Africa to America"

■ Swift: *Gulliver's Travels*

■ Pope: *Essay on Man*

■ Li Ruzhen: *Flowers in the Mirror*

■ Addison and Steele: *Spectator*

Visual Arts & Architecture

THE BAROQUE STYLE

THE ROCOCO STYLE

■ Watteau: *Departure from Cythera* ■ Fischer: Church of Ottobeuren, Bavaria ■ Clodion: *Intoxication*

■ Fragonard: *The Swing* ■ Vigée-Lebrun: *Marie Antoinette*

■ Wren: Saint Paul's ■ Boucher: *Venus Consoling Love*

THE NEOCLASSICAL STYLE

■ Greuze: *Village Betrothal* ■ Soufflot: Sainte Geneviève

■ Pozzo: *Saint Ignatius* ■ Chardin: *Kitchen Maid* ■ Canova: *Venus*

■ Hogarth: *Marriage Contract* ■ Ingres: *Apotheosis of Homer* 1827 >

■ Gibbs: St Martin-in-the-Fields ■ David: *The Oath of the Horatii*

■ Kauffmann: *Helen of Troy*

■ Adam: Kedleston Hall, England ■ Vignon: La Madeleine

■ Chalgrin: Arch of Triumph

■ Houdon: *Voltaire* ■ Jefferson: University of Virginia

Music & Dance

■ Couperin: *Art of Playing Clavecin* ■ Haydn: *Symphony #94*

■ Piano invented

■ Stamitz: Mannheim orchestra ■ Mozart: *Marriage of Figaro*

<~ Chinese opera ~>

CHAPTER 24

The Promise of Reason

"The time will ... come when the sun will shine only on free men who know no other master but their reason."
Antoine Nicolas de Condorcet

In the year 1680, a comet blazed across the skies over Western Europe. The English astronomer Edmund Halley (1656–1742) observed the celestial body, calculated its orbit, and predicted its future appearances. Stripped of its former role as a portent of catastrophe or a harbinger of natural calamity, Halley's comet now became merely another natural phenomenon, the behavior of which invited scientific investigation. This new, objective attitude toward nature and the accompanying confidence in the liberating role of reason were hallmarks of the Enlightenment—the period between 1687 (the date of Newton's *Principia*) and 1789 (the beginning of the French Revolution). The eighteenth century marks the divide between the essentially medieval view of the world as controlled by an omnipotent God and governed by the principles of faith, and the modern, secular view of the world as dominated by humankind and governed by the principles of reason. It also marks the beginning of an optimistic faith in the human ability to create a kind of happiness on earth that in former ages had been thought to exist only in heaven.

One of the principal preoccupations of Enlightenment thinkers was the study of human nature in scientific terms—without reference to divine authority. "Theology," wrote one Enlightenment skeptic, "is only ignorance of natural causes." Just as Halley explained the operations of the celestial bodies as a logical part of nature's mechanics, so eighteenth-century intellectuals explained human nature in terms of *natural law*. This unwritten and divinely sanctioned law of nature held that there are certain principles of right and wrong that all human beings, by way of reason, can discover and apply in the course of creating a just society. "Natural rights" included the right to life, liberty, property, and just treatment by the ruling order. Enlightenment thinkers argued that a true understanding of the human condition was the first step toward progress, that is, toward the gradual betterment of human life. It is

no wonder, then, that the eighteenth century saw the formation of the social sciences: anthropology, sociology, economics, and political science. These new disciplines, devoted to the study of humankind, optimistically confirmed that the promise of reason was the realization of an enlightened social order.

The Political Theories of Hobbes and Locke

An enlightened social order required a redefinition of the role of government and the rights of citizens. Not since the Golden Age of Athens had the relationship between the ruler and the ruled received so much intellectual attention as in the early modern era, the age of the rising European nation-state. During the sixteenth century, the political theorist Machiavelli had argued that the survival of the state was more important than the well-being of its citizens. Later in that century, the French lawyer Jean Bodin (1530–1596) employed biblical precepts and longstanding tradition to defend theories of divine right monarchy. In the seventeenth century, the Dutch statesman Hugo Grotius (1583–1645) proposed an all-embracing system of international law based on reason, which he identified with nature. Grotius' idea of a political contract based in natural law profoundly influenced the thinking of two of England's finest philosophers, Thomas Hobbes (1588–1679) and John Locke, the latter of whom we met in chapter 23 as a champion of the empirical method.

Hobbes and Locke took up the urgent question of human rights versus the sovereignty of the ruler. Shaken by the conflict between royalist and antiroyalist factions that had fueled the English Civil War (see chapter 22), both thinkers rejected the principle of divine right monarchy. Instead, they advanced the idea that government must be based in a **social contract**. For Hobbes, the social contract was a covenant among individuals who willingly surrendered a portion of their freedom to a governing authority or ruler, in whose hands should rest ultimate authority. Following Hobbes, Locke agreed that government must be formed by a contract that laid the basis for social order and individual happiness. But he believed that power must remain with the ruled.

The divergent positions of Hobbes and Locke proceeded from their contrasting perceptions of human nature. Whereas Locke described human beings as naturally equal, free, and capable (through reason) of defining the common good, Hobbes viewed human beings as selfish, greedy, and warlike. Without the state, he argued, human life was "solitary, poor, nasty, brutish, and short." Bound by an irrevocable and irreversible social contract, government under one individual or a ruling assembly was, according to Hobbes, society's only hope for peace and security. The collective safety of society lay in its willingness to submit to a higher authority, which Hobbes dubbed the "Leviathan," after the mythological marine monster described in the Bible. Hobbes aired these views in a treatise called the *Leviathan*, which he published in 1651—only two years after England's antiroyalist forces had beheaded the English monarch, Charles I.

READING 4.14 From Hobbes' *Leviathan* (1651)

Part I   Chapter 13: Of the Natural Condition of Mankind as Concerning their Felicity and Misery

Nature has made men so equal in the faculties of the body and mind as that, though there be found one man sometimes manifestly stronger in body or of quicker mind than another, yet, when all is reckoned together, the difference between man and man is not so considerable as that one man can thereupon claim to himself any benefit to which another may not pretend as well as he. For as to the strength of body, the weakest has strength to kill the strongest, either by secret machination or by confederacy with others that are in the same danger with himself. . . . 10

From this equality of ability arises equality of hope in the attaining of our ends. And therefore if any two men desire the same thing, which nevertheless they cannot both enjoy, they become enemies; and in the way to their end, which is principally their own conservation, and sometimes their delectation[1] only, endeavor to destroy or subdue one another. And from hence it comes to pass that where an invader has no more to fear than another man's single power, if one plant, sow, build, or possess a convenient seat, others may probably be expected to come prepared with forces united to dispossess 20 and deprive him, not only of the fruit of his labor, but also of his life or liberty. And the invader again is in the like danger of another. . . .

So that in the nature of man we find three principal causes of quarrel: first, competition; secondly, diffidence;[2] thirdly, glory.

The first makes men invade for gain, the second for safety, and the third for reputation. The first use violence to make

[1] Enjoyment; delight
[2] Lack of confidence

themselves masters of other men's persons, wives, children, and cattle; the second, to defend them; the third, for trifles, as a 30 word, a smile, a different opinion, and any other sign of undervalue, either direct in their persons or by reflection in their kindred, their friends, their nation, their profession, or their name.

Hereby it is manifest that, during the time men live without a common power to keep them all in awe, they are in that condition which is called war, and such a war as is of every man against every man. For WAR consists not in battle only, or the act of fighting, but in a tract of time wherein the will to contend by battle is sufficiently known; and therefore the notion of time is 40 to be considered in the nature of war as it is in the nature of weather. For as the nature of foul weather lies not in a shower or two of rain but in an inclination thereto of many days together, so the nature of war consists not in actual fighting but in the known disposition thereto, during all the time there is no assurance to the contrary. All other time is PEACE.

Whatsoever, therefore, is consequent to a time of war where every man is enemy to every man, the same is consequent to the time wherein men live without other security than what their own strength and their own invention shall furnish them 50 withal. In such condition there is no place for industry, because the fruit thereof is uncertain; and consequently no culture of the earth; no navigation nor use of the commodities that may be imported by sea; no commodious building; no instruments of moving and removing such things as require much force; no knowledge of the face of the earth; no account of time; no arts; no letters; no society; and, which is worst of all, continual fear and danger of violent death; and the life of man solitary, poor, nasty, brutish, and short. . . .

Part II   Chapter 17: Of the Causes, Generation, and Definition of a Commonwealth

The final cause, end, or design of men, who naturally love 60 liberty and dominion over others, in the introduction of that restraint upon themselves in which we see them live in commonwealths, is the foresight of their own preservation, and of a more contented life thereby—that is to say, of getting themselves out from that miserable condition of war which is necessarily consequent . . . to the natural passions of man when there is no visible power to keep them in awe and tie them by fear of punishment to the performance of their covenants and observations of [the] laws of nature. . . .

For the laws of nature—as *justice, equity, modesty, mercy,* 70 and, in sum, *doing to others as we would be done to*—of themselves, without the terror of some power to cause them to be observed, are contrary to our natural passions, that carry us to partiality, pride, revenge, and the like. And covenants without the sword are but words, and of no strength to secure a man at all. Therefore, notwithstanding the laws of nature . . ., if there be no power erected, or not great enough for our security, every man will—and may lawfully—rely on his own strength and art for caution against all other men. . . .

The only way to erect such a common power as may be able 80 to defend them from the invasion of foreigners and the injuries of one another, and thereby to secure them in such sort as that by their own industry and by the fruits of the earth they may nourish themselves and live contentedly, is to confer all their power and strength upon one man, or upon one assembly of men that may reduce all their wills, by plurality of voices, unto one will; which is as much as to say, to appoint one man or assembly of men to bear their person, and everyone to own and acknowledge to himself to be author of whatsoever he that so bears their person shall act or cause to be acted in those things **90** which concern the common peace and safety, and therein to submit their wills every one to his will, and their judgments to his judgment. This is more than consent or concord; it is a real unity of them all in one and the same person, made by covenant of every man with every man, in which manner as if every man should say to every man, *I authorize and give up my right of governing myself to this man, or to this assembly of men, on this condition, that you give up your right to him and authorize all his actions in like manner.* This done, the multitude so united in one person is called a COMMONWEALTH, in Latin CIVITAS. This is **100** the generation of that great LEVIATHAN (or rather, to speak more reverently, of that *mortal god*) to which we owe, under the *immortal God*, our peace and defense. For by this authority, given him by every particular man in the commonwealth, he has the use of so much power and strength conferred on him that, by terror thereof, he is enabled to form the wills of them all to peace at home and mutual aid against their enemies abroad. And in him consists the essence of the commonwealth, which, to define it, is *one person, of whose acts a great multitude, by mutual covenants one with another, have made themselves* **110** *every one the author, to the end he may use the strength and means of them all as he shall think expedient for their peace and common defense.* And he that carries this person is called SOVEREIGN and said to have sovereign power: and everyone besides, his SUBJECT.

The attaining to this sovereign power is by two ways. One, by natural force. . . . The other is when men agree among themselves to submit to some man or assembly of men voluntarily, on confidence to be protected by him against all others. This latter may be called a political commonwealth, or **120** commonwealth by *institution*, and the former a commonwealth by *acquisition.* . . .

Part II   Chapter 30: Of the Office of the Sovereign Representative

The office of the sovereign, be it a monarch or an assembly, consists in the end for which he was trusted with the sovereign power, namely, the procuration of the *safety of the people*; to which he is obliged by the law of nature, and to render an account thereof to God, the author of that law, and to none but him. But by safety here is not meant a bare preservation but also all other contentments of life which every man by lawful industry, without danger or hurt to the **130** commonwealth, shall acquire to himself.

And this is intended should be done, not by care applied to individuals further than their protection from injuries when they shall complain, but by a general providence contained in public instruction, both of doctrine and example, and in the making and executing of good laws, to which individual persons may apply their own cases.

And because, if the essential rights of sovereignty . . . be taken away, the commonwealth is thereby dissolved and every man returns into the condition and calamity of a war with **140**

every other man, which is the greatest evil that can happen in this life, it is the office of the sovereign to maintain those rights entire, and consequently against his duty, first, to transfer to another or to lay from himself any of them. For he that deserts the means deserts the ends. . . .

Q What is Hobbes' view of human nature?

Q What is the function of a "Leviathan?"

Locke's Government of the People

Locke (Figure **24.1**) disagreed with Hobbes' view of humankind as self-serving and aggressive. He held that since human beings were born without any preexisting qualities, their natural state was one of perfect freedom. Whether people became brutish or otherwise depended solely upon their experiences and their environment. People have, by their very nature as human beings, said Locke, the right to life, liberty, and estate (or "property"). Government must arbitrate between the exercise of one person's liberty and that of the next. The social contract thus preserves the natural rights of the governed. While individuals may willingly consent to give up some of their liberty in return for the ruler's protection, they may never relinquish their ultimate authority. If a ruler is tyrannical or oppressive, the people have not only the right but the obligation to rebel and seek a new ruler. Locke's defense of political rebellion in the face of tyranny served as justification for the "Glorious Revolution" of 1688. It also

Figure 24.1 JOHN GREENHILL, *Portrait of John Locke*, ca. 1672–1676. Oil on canvas, 22⅛ × 18½ in. © National Portrait Gallery, London.

inspired the revolutions that took place in America and in France toward the end of the eighteenth century.

If for Hobbes the state was sovereign, for Locke sovereignty rested with the people, and government existed only to protect the natural rights of its citizens. In his first treatise, *On Government* (1689), Locke argued that individuals might attain their maximum development only in a society free from the unnatural restrictions imposed by absolute rulers. In his second treatise, *Of Civil Government* (an excerpt from which follows), Locke expounded the idea that government must rest upon the consent of the governed. While Locke's views were basic to the development of modern liberal thought, Hobbes' views provided the justification for all forms of tyranny, including the enlightened despotism of such eighteenth-century rulers as Frederick of Prussia and Catherine II of Russia, who claimed that their authority was founded in the general consent of the people. Nevertheless, the notion of government as the product of a social contract between the ruler and the ruled has become one of the dominating ideas of modern Western—and more recently of Eastern European and Asian—political life.

READING 4.15 From Locke's *Of Civil Government* (1690)

Book II   Chapter II: Of the State of Nature

To understand political power right and derive it from its **1** original, we must consider what state all men are naturally in, and that is a state of perfect freedom to order their actions and dispose of their possessions and persons as they think fit, within the bounds of the law of nature without asking leave or depending upon the will of any other man.

A state also of equality, wherein all the power and jurisdiction is reciprocal, no one having more than another; there being nothing more evident than that creatures of the same species and rank, promiscuously born to all the same **10** advantages of nature and the use of the same faculties, should also be equal one amongst another without subordination or subjection; unless the Lord and Master of them all should, by any manifest declaration of his will, set one above another and confer on him, by an evident and clear appointment, an undoubted right to dominion and sovereignty....

Chapter V: Of Property

God, who hath given the world to men in common, hath also given them reason to make use of it to the best advantage of life and convenience. The earth and all that is therein is given to men for the support and comfort of their being. And though **20** all the fruits it naturally produces and beasts it feeds belong to mankind in common . . ., there must of necessity be a means to appropriate them some way or other before they can be of any use, or at all beneficial to any particular man....

Though the earth and all inferior creatures be common to all men, yet every man has a property in his own person: this nobody has any right to but himself. The labor of his body, and the work of his hands we may say, are properly his.

Whatsoever then he removes out of the state that nature has provided and left it in, he has mixed his labor with and joined **30** to it something that is his own, and thereby makes it his property....

Chapter VIII: The Beginning of Political Societies

Men being, as has been said, by nature all free, equal, and independent, no one can be put out of this estate and subjected to the political power of another without his own consent. The only way whereby any one divests himself of his natural liberty and puts on the bonds of civil society is by agreeing with other men to join and unite into a community for their comfortable, safe, and peaceable living one amongst another, in a secure enjoyment of their properties, and a **40** greater security against any that are not of it. This any number of men may do, because it injures not the freedom of the rest; they are left as they were in the liberty of the state of nature. When any number of men have so consented to make one community or government, they are thereby presently incorporated and make one body politic, wherein the majority have a right to act and conclude the rest.

For when any number of men have, by the consent of every individual, made a community, they have thereby made that community one body, with a power to act as one body, which is **50** only by the will and determination of the majority: . . . And therefore we see that in assemblies empowered to act by positive laws, where no number is set by that positive law which empowers them, the act of the majority passes for the act of the whole and of course determines; as having, by the law of nature and reason, the power of the whole.

And thus every man, by consenting with others to make one body politic under one government, puts himself under an obligation to every one of that society to submit to the determination of the majority and to be concluded by it; or else **60** this original compact whereby he with others incorporate into one society, would signify nothing and be no compact if he be left free and under no other ties than he was in before in the state of nature....

Chapter IX: Of the Ends of Political Society and Government

If man in the state of nature be so free as has been said; if he be absolute lord of his own person and possessions, equal to the greatest, and subject to nobody, why will he part with his freedom, why will he give up this empire and subject himself to the dominion and control of any other power? To which it is obvious to answer that though in the state of nature he has **70** such a right, yet the enjoyment of it is very uncertain and constantly exposed to the invasion of others; for all being kings as much as he, every man his equal and the greater part no strict observers of equity and justice, the enjoyment of the property he has in this state is very unsafe, very unsecure. This makes him willing to quit a condition, which, however free, is full of fears and continual dangers: and it is not without reason that he seeks out and is willing to join in society with others who are already united or have a mind to unite for the mutual preservation of their lives, liberties, and estates, which I call by **80** the general name property.

The great and chief end, therefore, of men's uniting into commonwealths, and putting themselves under government, is the preservation of their property. . . .

Chapter XVIII: Of Tyranny

As usurpation is the exercise of power, which another hath a right to, so tyranny is the exercise of power beyond right, which nobody can have a right to. And this is making use of the power any one has in his hands, not for the good of those who are under it, but for his own private, separate advantage—when the governor, however entitled, makes not the law, but **90** his will, the rule; and his commands and actions are not directed to the preservation of the properties of his people, but [to] the satisfaction of his own ambition, revenge, covetousness, or any other irregular passion. . . .

Wherever law ends, tyranny begins, if the law be transgressed to another's harm; and whosoever in authority exceeds the power given him by the law, and makes use of the force he has under his command, . . . ceases in that to be a [magistrate]; and, acting without authority, may be opposed as any other man who by force invades the right of another. . . . **100**

"May the commands then of a prince be opposed? may he be resisted as often as any one shall find himself aggrieved, and but imagine he has not right done him? This will unhinge and overturn all politics, and, instead of government and order, leave nothing but anarchy and confusion."

To this I answer that force is to be opposed to nothing but to unjust and unlawful force; whoever makes any opposition in any other case, draws on himself a just condemnation both from God and man. . . .

Q Why, according to Locke, are people willing to give up their freedom?

Q What, in Locke's view, is the function of law?

The Influence of Locke on Montesquieu and Jefferson

Locke's political treatises were read widely. So too, his defense of religious toleration (issued even as Louis XIV forced all Calvinists to leave France), his plea for equality of education among men and women, and his arguments for the use of modern languages in place of Latin won the attention of many intellectuals. Published during the last decade of the seventeenth century, Locke's treatises became the wellspring of the Enlightenment in both Europe and America.

In France, the keen-minded aristocrat Charles Louis de Secondat Montesquieu (1689–1755) championed Locke's views on political freedom and expanded on his theories. Intrigued by the ways in which nature seemed to govern social behavior, the Baron de Montesquieu investigated the effects of climate and custom on human conduct, thus pioneering the field of sociology. In his elegantly written thousand-page treatise *The Spirit of the Laws* (1748), Montesquieu defended liberty as the free exercise of the

will. He condemned slavery as fundamentally "unnatural and evil." A proponent of constitutional monarchy, he advanced the idea of a separation of powers among the executive, legislative, and judicial agencies of government, advising that each monitor the activities of the others in order to ensure a balanced system of government. He warned that when legislative and executive powers were united in the same person (or body of magistrates), or when judicial power was inseparable from legislative and executive powers, human liberty might be gravely threatened. Montesquieu's system of checks and balances was later enshrined in the Constitution of the United States of America (1787).

Across the Atlantic, the most eloquent expression of Locke's ideas appeared in the preamble to the statement declaring the independence of the North American colonies from the rule of the British king George III. Written by the leading American apostle of the Enlightenment, Thomas Jefferson (1743–1826; Figure **24.2**), and adopted by the Continental Congress on July 4, 1776, the American Declaration of Independence echoes Locke's ideology of revolt as well as his view that governments derive their just powers from the consent of the governed. Following Locke and Montesquieu, Jefferson advocated the establishment of a social contract between ruler and ruled as the principal means of fulfilling natural law—the "unalienable right" to life, liberty, and the pursuit of happiness.

Figure 24.2 JEAN-ANTOINE HOUDON, *Thomas Jefferson*, 1789. Marble, height 21½ in. Library of Congress, Washington, D.C.

While Jefferson did not include "property" among the unalienable rights, he was, as well, fully committed to the individual's natural right to property.

READING 4.16 From Jefferson's Declaration of Independence (1776)

When, in the course of human events, it becomes necessary   1
for one people to dissolve the political bands which have
connected them with another, and to assume among the
powers of the earth, the separate and equal station to which
the laws of nature and of nature's God entitle them, a decent
respect to the opinions of mankind requires that they should
declare the causes which impel them to separation.

   We hold these truths to be self-evident: That all men are
created equal; that they are endowed by their Creator with
certain unalienable rights; that among these are life, liberty   10
and the pursuit of happiness; that to secure these rights
governments are instituted among men, deriving their just
powers from the consent of the governed; that whenever any
form of government becomes destructive of these ends, it is
the right of the people to alter or to abolish it, and to institute
new government, laying its foundation on such principles and
organizing its powers in such form, as to them shall seem most
likely to effect their safety and happiness....

Q What is meant by "unalienable rights?"
Q How does Jefferson justify revolution?

The Declaration of Independence made clear the belief of America's founding fathers in equality among men. Equality between the sexes was, however, another matter: although both Locke and Jefferson acknowledged that women held the same natural rights as men, they did not consider women—or slaves, or children, for that matter—capable of exercising such rights. Recognizing this bias, Abigail Adams (d. 1818) wrote to her husband, John, who was serving as a delegate to the Second Continental Congress (1777), as follows:

> I . . . hear that you have declared an
> independency, and, by the way, in the new code
> of laws which I suppose it will be necessary for you
> to make, I desire you would remember the ladies
> and be more generous and favorable to them than
> were your ancestors. Do not put such unlimited
> power into the hands of husbands. Remember all
> men would be tyrants if they could. If particular
> care and attention are not paid to the ladies we
> are determined to foment a rebellion, and will
> not hold ourselves bound to obey any laws in
> which we have no voice or representation.*

*Letter of March 31, 1776, in *Familiar Letters of John Adams and His Wife Abigail Adams During the Revolution*, ed. Charles Francis Adams (New York: Hurd and Houghton, 1876. Reprint: Freeport, N.Y.: Books for Library Press, 1970), p. 148.

Despite the future First Lady's spirited admonitions, however, American women did not secure the legal right to vote or to hold political office until well into the twentieth century.

If the Declaration of Independence constituted a clear expression of Enlightenment theory in justifying revolution against tyrannical rule, the Constitution of the new United States of America represented the practical outcome of the Revolution: the creation of a viable new nation with its government based ultimately on Enlightenment principles. The U.S. Constitution, framed in 1787 and ratified by popular vote in 1788–1789, articulated the mechanics of self-rule. First, it created a form of government new to the modern world: a system of representative government embodying the principle of "Republicanism," that is, government run by the elected representatives of the people. Second, following the precepts of Montesquieu, the framers of the Constitution divided the new government into three branches—legislative, executive, and judicial—each to be "checked and balanced" by the others to prevent the possible tyranny of any one branch. Third, the new republic was granted sufficient power to govern primarily through the authority granted the president to execute national laws and constitutional provisions. Withal, the U.S. Constitution would prove effective for over two centuries, and would serve as the model for the constitutions of all the newborn republics created throughout the world.

Adam Smith and the Birth of Economic Theory

While Enlightenment thinkers were primarily concerned with matters of political equality, they also addressed questions related to the economy of the modern European state. The Scottish philosopher Adam Smith (1723–1790) applied the idea of natural law to the domains of human labor, productivity, and the exchange of goods. In his epoch-making synthesis of ethics and economics, *An Inquiry into the Nature and Causes of the Wealth of Nations*, published in 1776, Smith set forth the "laws" of labor, production, and trade with an exhaustiveness reminiscent of Newton's *Principia Mathematica* (see chapter 23). Smith contended that labor, a condition natural to humankind (as Locke had observed), was the foundation for prosperity. A nation's wealth is not its land or its money, said Smith, but its labor force. In the "natural" economic order, individual self-interest guides the progress of economic life, and certain natural forces, such as the "law of supply and demand," motivate a market economy. Since government interference would infringe on this order, reasoned Smith, such interference is undesirable. He thus opposed all artificial restraints on economic progress and all forms of government regulation and control. The modern concepts of free enterprise and ***laissez-faire*** (literally, "allow to act") economics spring from Smith's incisive formulations. In the following excerpt, Smith examines the origin of the division of labor among human beings and defends the natural and unimpeded operation of trade and competition among nations.

READING 4.17 From Smith's *An Inquiry into the Nature and Causes of the Wealth of Nations* (1776)

Book I Chapter II: The Principle which Occasions the Division of Labor

[The] division of labor, from which so many advantages are derived, is not originally the effect of any human wisdom, which foresees and intends that general opulence to which it gives occasion. It is the necessary, though very slow and gradual, consequence of a certain propensity in human nature which has in view no such extensive utility; the propensity to truck, barter, and exchange one thing for another. 1

. . . . [This propensity] is common to all men, and to be found in no other race of animals, which seem to know neither this nor any other species of contracts. Two greyhounds, in running 10 down the same hare, have sometimes the appearance of acting in some sort of concert. Each turns her towards his companion, or endeavors to intercept her when his companion turns her towards himself. This, however, is not the effect of any contract, but of the accidental concurrence of their passions in the same object at that particular time. Nobody ever saw a dog make a fair and deliberate exchange of one bone for another with another dog. . . . In almost every other race of animals each individual, when it is grown up to maturity, is entirely independent, and in its natural state has occasion for the 20 assistance of no other living creature. But man has almost constant occasion for the help of his brethren, and it is in vain for him to expect it from their benevolence only. He will be more likely to prevail if he can interest their self-love in his favor, and show them that it is for their own advantage to do for him what he requires of them. Whoever offers to another a bargain of any kind, proposes to do this. Give me that which I want, and you shall have this which you want, is the meaning of every such offer; and it is in this manner that we obtain from one another the far greater part of those good offices which we stand in 30 need of. It is not from the benevolence of the butcher, the brewer, or the baker, that we expect our dinner, but from their regard to their own interest. We address ourselves, not to their humanity, but to their self-love; and never talk to them of our own necessities, but of their advantages. . . .

As it is by treaty, by barter, and by purchase, that we obtain from one another the greater part of those mutual good offices which we stand in need of, so it is this same trucking disposition which originally gives occasion to the division of labor. In a tribe of hunters or shepherds a particular person 40 makes bows and arrows, for example, with more readiness and dexterity than any other. He frequently exchanges them for cattle or for venison with his companions; and he finds at last that he can in this manner get more cattle and venison, than if he himself went to the field to catch them. From a regard to his own interest, therefore, the making of bows and arrows grows to be his chief business. . . .

Book IV Chapter III, Part II: Of the Unreasonableness of Restraints [on Trade]

Nations have been taught that their interest consisted in beggaring all their neighbors. Each nation has been made to look with an invidious eye upon the prosperity of all the 50 nations with which it trades, and to consider their gain as its own loss. Commerce, which ought naturally to be, among nations as among individuals, a bond of union and friendship, has become the most fertile source of discord and animosity. The capricious ambition of kings and ministers has not, during the present and the preceding century, been more fatal to the repose of Europe, than the impertinent jealousy of merchants and manufacturers. The violence and injustice of the rulers of mankind is an ancient evil, for which, I am afraid, the nature of human affairs can scarce admit of a remedy. But the mean 60 rapacity, the monopolizing spirit of merchants and manufacturers, who neither are, nor ought to be, the rulers of mankind, though it cannot perhaps be corrected, may very easily be prevented from disturbing the tranquility of anybody but themselves.

That it was the spirit of monopoly which originally both invented and propagated this doctrine, cannot be doubted; and they who first taught it were by no means such fools as they who believed it. In every country it always is and must be the interest of the great body of the people to buy whatever they 70 want of those who sell it cheapest. The proposition is so very manifest, that it seems ridiculous to take any pains to prove it; nor could it ever have been called in question had not the interested sophistry of merchants and manufacturers confounded the common sense of mankind. Their interest is, in this respect, directly opposed to that of the great body of the people. . . .

The wealth of a neighboring nation, though dangerous in war and politics, is certainly advantageous in trade. In a state of hostility it may enable our enemies to maintain fleets and 80 armies superior to our own; but in a state of peace and commerce it must likewise enable them to exchange with us to a greater value and to afford a better market, either for the immediate produce of our own industry or for whatever is purchased with that produce. As a rich man is likely to be a better customer to the industrious people in his neighborhood, than a poor, so is likewise a rich nation. . . .

Q What natural forces dominate the economic life of the nation, according to Smith?

Q Would you consider Smith a realist or an idealist?

The *Philosophes*

When Louis XIV died in 1715, the French nobility fled the Palace of Versailles and settled in Paris townhouses, often decorated in the latest fashion. Socially ambitious noblewomen, many of whom championed a freer and more public role for their gender, organized gatherings in the *salons* of these townhouses, where nobility and middle-class thinkers met to exchange views on morality, politics, science, and religion and to voice opinions on everything ranging from diet to the latest fashions in theater and dress. Inevitably, new ideas began to circulate in these meetings,

Figure 24.3 FRANÇOIS DEQUEVAUVILLER after **N. LAVRÉINCE**, *Assembly in a Salon*, 1745–1807. Engraving, 15¹³⁄₁₆ × 19⅝ in. The Metropolitan Museum of Art, New York. Harris Brisbane Dick Fund, 1935 (35.100.17).

and Paris became the hub of intellectual activity (Figure 24.3). The well-educated individuals who graced the *salons* came to be known as **philosophes** (the French word for "philosophers"). Intellectuals rather than philosophers in the strictest sense of the term, the *philosophes* dominated the intellectual activity of the Enlightenment. Like the humanists of fifteenth-century Florence, their interests were mainly secular and social. Unlike their Renaissance counterparts, however, the *philosophes* scorned all forms of authority—they believed that they had surpassed the ancients, and they looked beyond the present state of knowledge to the establishment of a superior moral and social order.

Most *philosophes* held to the deist view of God as Creator and providential force behind nature and natural law, rather than as personal Redeemer. They believed in the immortality of the soul, not out of commitment to any religious doctrine, but because they saw human beings as fundamentally different from other living creatures. They viewed the Bible as mythology rather than as revealed truth, and scorned Church hierarchy and ritual. Their antipathy to irrationality, superstition, and religious dogma (as reflected, for instance, in the Catholic doctrine of original sin) alienated them from the Church and set them at odds with the established authorities—a position memo-

Science and Technology

1702 the world's first daily newspaper is published in England

1704 the first alphabetical encyclopedia in English is printed

1714 a London engineer patents the first known typewriter

1765 Diderot's *Encyclopédie* is issued in seventeen volumes

rably expressed in Voltaire's acerbic pronouncement that "men will not be free until the last king is strangled with the entrails of the last priest." The quest for a nonauthoritarian, secular morality led the *philosophes* to challenge all existing forms of intolerance, inequality, and injustice. The banner cry of the *philosophes*, "Ecrasez l'infame" ("Wipe out all evils"), sparked a commitment to social reforms that led to the French Revolution (see chapter 25).

Diderot and the *Encyclopédie*

The basic ideals of the Enlightenment were summed up in a monumental literary endeavor to which many of the *philosophes* contributed: the thirty-five-volume *Encyclopédie* (including eleven volumes of engraved plates), published between 1751 and 1772 and edited by Denis Diderot (1713–1784; Figure **24.4**). Modeled on the two-volume Chambers' Encyclopedia printed in England in 1751, Diderot's *Encyclopédie*—also known as *The Analytical Dictionary of the Sciences, Arts, and Crafts*—was the largest compendium of contemporary social, philosophic, artistic, scientific, and technological knowledge ever produced in the West. A collection of "all the knowledge scattered over the face of the earth," as Diderot explained, it manifested the zealous desire of the *philosophes* to dispel human ignorance and transform society. It was also, in part, a response to rising literacy and to the widespread public interest in the facts of everyday life. Not all members of society welcomed the enterprise, however: King Louis XV claimed that the *Encyclopédie* was doing "irreparable damage to morality and religion." Although the crown twice banned its printing, some volumes were published and distributed secretly.

Diderot's *Encyclopédie* was the most ambitious and influential literary undertaking of the eighteenth century. Almost two hundred individuals contributed seventy-two thousand entries on subjects ranging from political theory, cultural history, and art criticism to the technology of theater machinery, the making of silk stockings, and the varieties of wigs (Figure **24.5**). Articles on Islam, India, and China indicate a more than idle curiosity about civilizations that remained to most Westerners remote and exotic. Diderot enlisted as contributors to the *Encyclopédie* the

Figure 24.4 JEAN-ANTOINE HOUDON, *Diderot*, 1773. Marble, height 20⁷⁄₁₆ in. The Metropolitan Museum of Art, New York. Gift of Mr. and Mrs. Charles Wrightsman, 1974 (1974.291).

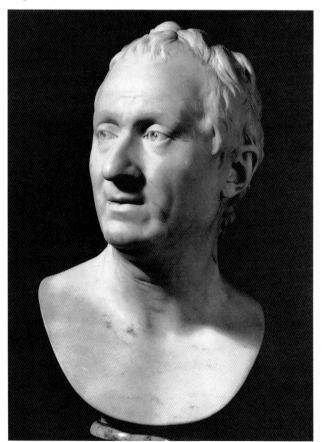

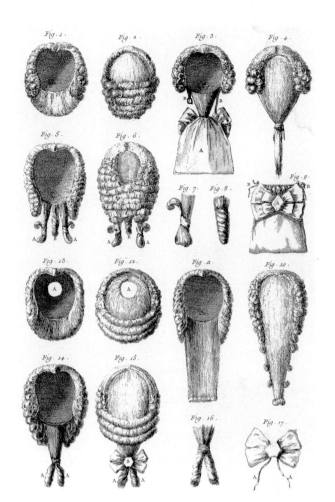

Figure 24.5 *Wigs*, a plate from the *Encylopédie* illustrating the varieties of men's wigs that were fashionable in Europe in the 1750s. Thomas J. Watson Library, The Metropolitan Museum of Art, New York.

most progressive minds of the Enlightenment: François Marie Arouet (1694–1778), known as Voltaire, wrote on "matters of nature and art"; the French philosopher and educator Jean-Jacques Rousseau (1712–1778; see chapter 25) provided articles on music; François Quesnay wrote on political economy; Montesquieu (whose articles were published posthumously) examined the different types of governments; Jean Le Rond d'Alembert (1717–1783) treated the subject of higher education; and Diderot himself prepared numerous entries on art and politics.

Although women contributed moral and financial support to the *Encyclopédie*, none was invited to participate in its production. Moreover, not one of the thirty-one entries on women makes reference to the contributions of exceptional eighteenth-century women such as Gabrielle-Emilie Le Tonnelier de Breteuil, the Marquise du Châtelet (1706–1749). An impeccable scholar and a brilliant mathematician, Madame du Châtelet produced an annotated French translation of Newton's *Principia*—a monumental achievement that was almost finished when she died, a few days after giving birth to her fourth child. Proficient in Latin, Italian, and English, the Marquise also translated the works of Virgil, Horace, and Ovid into eloquent French; she wrote original poetry and conducted experiments in physics and chemistry. She was a reckless gambler, a

Figure 24.6 NICOLAS DE LARGILLIÈRE, *Gabrielle-Emilie Le Tonnelier de Breteuil, Marquise du Châtelet*, ca. 1740. Oil on canvas, 4 ft. 3½ in. × 3 ft. 4¼ in. Columbus Museum of Art, Ohio. Bequest of Frederick W. Schumacher.

feminist, a champion of the fashionably low-cut neckline (Figure 24.6), and the mistress of Voltaire, who lived at her *château* until her death in 1749. Voltaire confessed that he could hardly live without the Marquise, whom he regarded as "a great man." In their assessment of the abilities and the rights of women, the *philosophes* were ambivalent at best, their personal sentiments characterized by Rousseau's self-scorning complaint that one of his greatest misfortunes was "always to be connected with some literary woman." Nevertheless, the *Encyclopédie* remains a monument to secular knowledge and to the Enlightenment faith in the promise of reason—a spirit summed up in Voltaire's proclamation, "Let the facts prevail." The following excerpts come from the entry on natural law written by the French lawyer Antoine-Gaspart Boucher d'Argis and from the long article on black Africans written by Le Romain (first name and dates unknown).

READING 4.18 From the *Encyclopédie* (1751–1772)

Law of Nature or Natural Law

In its broadest sense the term is taken to designate certain principles which nature alone inspires and which all animals as well as all men have in common. On this law are based the union of male and female, the begetting of children as well as their education, love of liberty, self-preservation, concern for self-defense. [1]

It is improper to call the behavior of animals natural law, for, not being endowed with reason, they can know neither law nor justice.

More commonly we understand by natural law certain laws [10] of justice and equity which only natural reason has established among men, or better, which God has engraved in our hearts.

The fundamental principles of law and all justice are: to live honestly, not to give offense to anyone, and to render unto each whatever is his. From these general principles derive a great many particular rules which nature alone, that is, reason and equity, suggest to mankind.

Since this natural law is based on such fundamental principles, it is perpetual and unchangeable: no agreement can debase it, no law can alter it or exempt anyone from the [20] obligation it imposes. . . .

The principles of natural law, therefore, form part of the law of nations, particularly the primitive law of nations; they also form part of public and of private law: for the principles of natural law, which we have stated, are the purest source of the foundation of most of private and public law. . . .

The authority of natural laws stems from the fact that they owe their existence to God. Men submit to them because to observe them leads to the happiness of men and society. This is a truth demonstrated by reason. It is equally true that virtue [30] by itself is a principle of inner satisfaction whereas vice is a principle of unrest and trouble. It is equally certain that virtue produces great external advantage, while vice produces great ills. . . .

Negroes[1]

For the last few centuries the Europeans have carried on a trade in Negroes whom they obtain from Guinea and other coasts of Africa and whom they use to maintain the colonies established in various parts of America and in the West Indies. To justify this loathsome commerce, which is contrary to natural law, it is argued that ordinarily these slaves find the [40] salvation of their souls in the loss of their liberty, and that the Christian teaching they receive, together with their indispensable role in the cultivation of sugar cane, tobacco, indigo, etc., softens the apparent inhumanity of a commerce where men buy and sell their fellow men as they would animals used in the cultivation of the land.

Trade in Negroes is carried on by all the nations which have settlements in the West Indies, and especially by the French, the English, the Portuguese, the Dutch, the Swedes, and the Danes. The Spaniards, in spite of the fact that they possess the [50] greatest part of the Americas, have no direct way of acquiring slaves but have concluded treaties with other nations to furnish them with Negroes. . . .

As soon as the trade is completed no time must be lost in setting sail. Experience has shown that as long as these unfortunates are still within sight of their homeland, they are overcome by sorrow and gripped by despair. The former is the cause of many illnesses from which a large number perish during the crossing; the latter inclines them to suicide, which they effect either by refusing nourishment or by shutting off [60]

---

[1]A term originally used by the Spanish and Portuguese to identify black Africans.

their breathing. This they do in a way they know of turning and twisting their tongues which unfailingly suffocates them. Others again shatter their head against the sides of the ship or throw themselves into the sea if the occasion presents itself. . . .

Punishment of the Negroes, policing, and regulations concerning these matters:

If the Negro commits a slight offense the overseer may on his own responsibility punish him with a few strokes of the whip. If, however, it is a serious matter, the master has the culprit clapped in irons and then decides the number of strokes with which he will be punished. If all men were equally just, these **70** necessary punishments would be kept within limits, but it often happens that certain masters abuse the authority which they claim over their slaves and chastise these unfortunates too harshly. Yet the masters themselves may be responsible for the situation which led to the offense. To put an end to the cruelties of these barbarous men who would be capable of leaving their slaves without the basic necessities of life while driving them to forced labor, the officers of His Majesty, who are resident in the colonies, have the responsibility of enforcing the edict of the king, which is called the Black Code. **80** In the French islands of America this code regulates the governing and the administration of justice and of the police, as well as the discipline of the slaves and the slave-trade. . . .

 Q What is the relationship between natural law and reason?
Q How is slavery assessed in this reading?

The Encyclopedic Cast of Mind

The *Encyclopédie* had an enormous impact on eighteenth-century culture. Although it was read and understood by few, it fostered an encyclopedic cast of mind. Indeed, the emphasis on the accumulation, codification, and systematic preservation of knowledge linked the eighteenth century to the Scientific Revolution and to that other Enlightenment "bible," Newton's *Principia*.

Eighteenth-century scientists made notable advances in the fields of chemistry, electricity, biology, and the medical sciences. They produced the mercury thermometer and the stethoscope and introduced the science of immunology to the West—some seven centuries after the Chinese had invented the first inoculations against smallpox. Antoine Lavoisier (1743–1794) published the *Elementary Treatise of Chemistry* (1789) and launched chemistry as an exact science. The Swede Carolus Linnaeus (1707–1778) produced a systematic method for classifying plants, and the French naturalist Georges Louis Leclerc, Comte de Buffon (1707–1788), made landmark advances in zoology.

Valuable efforts to accumulate and classify knowledge took place in the arts as well. The English critic and poet Samuel Johnson (1709–1784) published the first dictionary of the English language and Rousseau produced the first Western dictionary of music. In the social sciences, Voltaire's seven-volume general history (published in

1756), which included a monumental account of the age of Louis XIV, provided a model for a new universal and rationalist kind of history-writing. Voltaire was among the first to recognize Europe's debt to Arab science and Asian thought. He rejected faith-based explanations of the past and was generally critical of the role played by the Catholic Church in Western history. But it fell to the English historian Edward Gibbon (1737–1794) to provide the rationale that blamed Christianity for contributing to the collapse of Rome. *The Decline and Fall of the Roman Empire* (1776) was the product of Gibbon's unique interpretation of the sociological forces that shaped ancient cultures.

Eighteenth-century China lay beyond the immediate influence of the European Enlightenment; nevertheless, in the East an encyclopedic impulse similar to that prevailing in the West came to a climax at this time. Qing rulers followed their Ming predecessors in directing groups of scholars to assemble exhaustive collections of information, some filling as many as 36,000 manuscript volumes. These "encyclopedias" were actually anthologies of the writings of former Chinese artists and scholars, rather than comprehensive collections of contemporary knowledge. Nevertheless, as in France, some of China's rulers deemed the indiscriminate accumulation of information itself dangerous, and at least one eighteenth-century Qing emperor authorized the official burning of thousands of books.

The Crusade for Progress

Among European intellectuals, the belief in the reforming powers of reason became the basis for a progressive view of human history. The German mathematician and philosopher Gottfried Wilhelm Leibniz (1646–1716) systematically defended the view that human beings live in perfect harmony with God and nature. Leibniz linked optimism to the logic of probability: his *principle of sufficient reason* held, simply, that there must be a reason or purpose for everything in nature. In response to the question, Why does evil exist in a world created by a good God? Leibniz answered that all events conformed to the preestablished harmony of the universe. Even evil, according to Leibniz, was necessary in a world that was "better than any other possible world"—a position that came to be called "philosophic optimism."

For the *philosophes*, the key to social reform lay in a true understanding of human nature, which, they argued, might best be acquired by examining human history. They viewed, for instance, the transition from Paleolithic hunting and gathering to the birth of civilization as clear evidence of the steady march toward social improvement. Faith in that march motivated the Enlightenment crusade for progress. The Italian lawyer and social reformer Cesare de Beccaria (1738–1794) enlisted in this crusade when he wrote his treatise *On Crimes and Punishments*, in which he suggested that torturing criminals did not work to deter crime. Rather, argued Beccaria, society should seek methods by which to rehabilitate those who commit crimes. Although Beccaria's book generated no immediate changes, it went through six editions in eighteen months and ultimately contributed to movements for prison reform in Europe and the United States. The questions that Beccaria raised concerning the value of punishment are still being debated today.

The most passionate warrior in the Enlightenment crusade for progress was the French aristocrat Antoine Nicolas de Condorcet (1743–1794). Condorcet was a mathematician, a social theorist, and a political moderate amidst revolutionary extremists. His *Sketch for a Historical Picture of the Progress of the Human Mind*, written during the early days of the French Revolution, was the preface to a longer work he never completed, for he committed suicide shortly after being imprisoned as an "enemy" of the Revolution. Condorcet believed that human nature could be perfected through reason. All errors in politics and morals, he argued, were based in philosophic and scientific errors. "There is not a religious system nor a supernatural extravagance," wrote Condorcet, "that is not founded on ignorance of the laws of nature." Fiercely optimistic about the future of humankind, Condorcet was one of the first modern champions of sexual equality. He called for the "complete annihilation of the prejudices that have brought about an inequality of rights between the sexes, an inequality fatal even to the party in whose favor it works." Such inequality, he protested, "has its origin solely in an abuse of strength, and all the later sophistical attempts that have been made to excuse it are vain."

In his *Sketch*, the visionary Condorcet traced the "progress" of humankind through ten stages, from ignorance and tyranny to the threshold of enlightenment and equality. The utopian tenth stage, subtitled "The Future Progress of the Human Mind" (an excerpt of which follows), sets forth ideas that were well ahead of their time, such as a guaranteed livelihood for the aged, a universal system of education, fewer work hours, and the refinement of a technology for the accumulation of knowledge. (How digital computers would have delighted this prophet of the Information Age!) The educational goals that Condorcet outlines toward the end of the excerpt still carry the force of sound judgment.

READING 4.19 From Condorcet's *Sketch for a Historical Picture of the Progress of the Human Mind*

(1793)

If man can, with almost complete assurance, predict   1
phenomena when he knows their laws, and if, even when he
does not, he can still, with great expectation of success,
forecast the future on the basis of his experience of the past,
why, then, should it be regarded as a fantastic undertaking to
sketch, with some pretense to truth, the future destiny of man
on the basis of his history? The sole foundation for belief in the
natural sciences is this idea that the general laws directing the
phenomena of the universe, known or unknown, are necessary
and constant. Why should this principle be any less true for the   10
development of the intellectual and moral faculties of man

Science and Technology

1714 the mercury thermometer and the Fahrenheit scale
are invented in Germany

1726 the first measurement of blood pressure is taken
in England

1751 the first mental hospital opens in London

1774 Franz Mesmer (Austrian) uses hypnotism to aid in curing
disease

---

than for the other operations of nature? Since beliefs founded
on past experience of like conditions provide the only rule of
conduct for the wisest of men, why should the philosopher be
forbidden to base his conjectures on these same foundations,
so long as he does not attribute to them a certainty superior to
that warranted by the number, the constancy, and the accuracy
of his observations? . . .

The time will therefore come when the sun will shine only
on free men who know no other master but their reason; when   20
tyrants and slaves, priests and their stupid or hypocritical
instruments will exist only in works of history and on the stage;
and when we shall think of them only to pity their victims and
their dupes; to maintain ourselves in a state of vigilance by
thinking on their excesses; and to learn how to recognize and
so to destroy, by force of reason, the first seeds of tyranny and
superstition, should they ever dare to reappear among us.

In looking at the history of societies we shall have had
occasion to observe that there is often a great difference
between the rights that the law allows its citizens and the   30
rights that they actually enjoy, and, again, between the
equality established by political codes and that which in fact
exists among individuals. . . .

These differences have three main causes: inequality in
wealth, inequality in status between the man whose means of
subsistence are hereditary and the man whose means are
dependent on the length of his life, or, rather, on that part of
his life in which he is capable of work; and, finally, inequality
in education.

We therefore need to show that these three sorts of real   40
inequality must constantly diminish without however
disappearing altogether: for they are the result of natural and
necessary causes which it would be foolish and dangerous to
wish to eradicate. . . .

[As to education] we can teach the citizen everything that he
needs to know in order to be able to manage his household,
administer his affairs, and employ his labor and his faculties in
freedom; to know his rights and to be able to exercise them; to
be acquainted with his duties and fulfill them satisfactorily; to
judge his own and other men's actions according to his own   50
lights and to be a stranger to none of the high and delicate
feelings which honor human nature; not to be in a state of blind
dependence upon those to whom he must entrust his affairs or
the exercise of his rights; to be in a proper condition to choose
and supervise them; to be no longer the dupe of those popular
errors which torment man with superstitious fears and
chimerical hopes; to defend himself against prejudice by the

strength of his reason alone; and, finally, to escape the deceits of charlatans who would lay snares for his fortune, his health, his freedom of thought, and his conscience under the pretext of granting him health, wealth, and salvation. . . .   **60**

The real advantages that should result from this progress, of which we can entertain a hope that is almost a certainty, can have no other term than that of the absolute perfection of the human race; since, as the various kinds of equality come to work in its favor by producing ampler sources of supply, more extensive education, more complete liberty, so equality will be more real and will embrace everything which is really of importance for the happiness of human beings. . . .

Q In what ways does this reading illustrate the optimism of Enlightenment thought?

Q What, according to Condorcet, are the three main causes of social discord?

Enlightenment and the Rights of Women

While Condorcet was among the first moderns to champion the equality of the sexes, his efforts pale before the impassioned defense of women launched by Mary Wollstonecraft (1759–1797; Figure **24.7**). This self-educated British intellectual applied Enlightenment principles of natural law, liberty, and equality to forge a radical rethinking of the roles and responsibilities of women in Western society. In *A Vindication of the Rights of Woman*, Wollstonecraft attacked the persistence of the female stereotype (docile, domestic, and childlike) as

Figure 24.7 JOHN OPIE, *Mary Wollstonecraft*, ca. 1797. Oil on canvas, 29½ in. × 24½ in. © National Portrait Gallery, London.

formulated by misguided, misogynistic, and tyrannical males, who, as she complained, "try to secure the good conduct of women by attempting to keep them in a state of childhood." Calling for a "revolution of female manners," she criticized the "disorderly kind of education" received by women, who, owing to their domestic roles, learn "rather by snatches."

Wollstonecraft emphasized the importance of reason in the cultivation of virtue, observing that, "it is a farce to call any being virtuous whose virtues do not result from the exercise of its own reason." She condemned women for embracing their roles in "the great art of pleasing [men]"; nevertheless, she seems to have been deeply conflicted by her own personal efforts to reconcile her sexual passions, her need for independence, and her free-spirited will. Her affair with an American speculator and timber-merchant produced an illegitimate child and at least two attempts at suicide; and her marriage to the novelist William Godwin (subsequent to her becoming pregnant by him) proved no less turbulent. She died at the age of thirty-eight, following the birth of their daughter, the future Mary Shelley (see chapter 28). In contrast with her short and troubled life, Wollstonecraft's treatise has enjoyed sustained and significant influence; it stands at the threshold of the modern movement for female equality.

READING 4.20 From Wollstonecraft's *A Vindication of the Rights of Woman* (1792)

After considering the historic page, and viewing the living **1**
world with anxious solicitude, the most melancholy emotions
of sorrowful indignation have depressed my spirits, and I have
sighed when obliged to confess, that either nature has made a
great difference between man and man, or that the civilization
which has hitherto taken place in the world has been very
partial. I have turned over various books written on the subject
of education, and patiently observed the conduct of parents
and the management of schools; but what has been the
result?—a profound conviction that the neglected education of **10**
my fellow-creatures is the grand source of the misery I deplore;
and that women, in particular, are rendered weak and
wretched by a variety of concurring causes, originating from
one hasty conclusion. The conduct and manners of women, in
fact, evidently prove that their minds are not in a healthy state;
for, like the flowers which are planted in too rich a soil,
strength and usefulness are sacrificed to beauty; and the
flaunting leaves, after having pleased a fastidious eye, fade,
disregarded on the stalk, long before the season when they
ought to have arrived at maturity.—One cause of this barren **20**
blooming I attribute to a false system of education, gathered
from the books written on this subject by men who,
considering females rather as women than human creatures,
have been more anxious to make them alluring mistresses than
affectionate wives and rational mothers and the understanding
of the sex has been so bubbled by this specious homage, that
the civilized women of the present century, with a few

exceptions, are only anxious to inspire love, when they ought to cherish a nobler ambition, and by their abilities and virtues exact respect. **30**

In a treatise, therefore, on female rights and manners, the works which have been particularly written for their improvement must not be overlooked; especially when it is asserted, in direct terms, that the minds of women are enfeebled by false refinement; that the books of instruction, written by men of genius, have had the same tendency as more frivolous productions; and that, in the true style of Mahometanism,[1] they are treated as a kind of subordinate beings, and not as a part of the human species, when improveable reason is allowed to be the dignified distinction **40** which raises men above the brute creation, and puts a natural sceptre in a feeble hand.

Yet, because I am a woman, I would not lead my readers to suppose that I mean violently to agitate the contested question respecting the equality or inferiority of the sex; but as the subject lies in my way, and I cannot pass it over without subjecting the main tendency of my reasoning to misconstruction, I shall stop a moment to deliver, in a few words, my opinion.—In the government of the physical world it is observable that the female in point of strength is, **50** in general, inferior to the male. This is the law of nature; and it does not appear to be suspended or abrogated in favour of woman. A degree of physical superiority cannot, therefore, be denied—and it is a noble prerogative! But not content with this natural preeminence, men endeavour to sink us still lower, merely to render us alluring objects for a moment; and women, intoxicated by the adoration which men, under the influence of their senses, pay to them, do not seek to obtain a durable interest in their hearts, or to become the friends of the fellow creatures who find **60** amusement in their society. . . .

My own sex, I hope, will excuse me, if I treat them like rational creatures, instead of flattering their *fascinating* graces, and viewing them as if they were in a state of perpetual childhood, unable to stand alone. I earnestly wish to point out in what true dignity and human happiness consists—I wish to persuade women to endeavour to acquire strength, both of mind and body, and to convince them that the soft phrases, susceptibility of heart, delicacy of sentiment, and refinement of taste, are almost **70** synonymous with epithets of weakness, and that those beings who are only the objects of pity and that kind of love, which has been termed its sister, will soon become objects of contempt.

Dismissing then those pretty feminine phrases, which the men condescendingly use to soften our slavish dependence, and despising that weak elegancy of mind, exquisite sensibility, and sweet docility of manners, supposed to be the sexual characteristics of the weaker vessel, I wish to shew that elegance is inferior to virtue, that the first object of **80** laudable ambition is to obtain a character as a human being, regardless of the distinction of sex; and that secondary views should be brought to this simple touchstone. . . .

The education of women has, of late, been more attended to than formerly; yet they are still reckoned a frivolous sex, and ridiculed or pitied by the writers who endeavour by satire or instruction to improve them. It is acknowledged that they spend many of the first years of their lives in acquiring a smattering of accomplishments; meanwhile strength of body and mind are sacrificed to libertine notions of beauty, to the **90** desire of establishing themselves,—the only way women can rise in the world,—by marriage. And this desire making mere animals of them, when they marry they act as such children may be expected to act:—they dress; they paint, and nickname God's creatures.—Surely these weak beings are only fit for a seraglio! Can they be expected to govern a family with judgment, or take care of the poor babes whom they bring into the world?

If then it can be fairly deduced from the present conduct of the sex, from the prevalent fondness for pleasure which takes **100** place of ambition and those nobler passions that open and enlarge the soul; that the instruction which women have hitherto received has only tended, with the constitution of civil society, to render them insignificant objects of desire—mere propagators of fools!—if it can be proved that in aiming to accomplish them, without cultivating their understandings, they are taken out of their sphere of duties, and made ridiculous and useless when the short-lived bloom of beauty is over, I presume that *rational* men will excuse me for endeavouring to persuade them to become more masculine **110** and respectable. . . .

In the present state of society it appears necessary to go back to first principles in search of the most simple truths, and to dispute with some prevailing prejudice every inch of ground. To clear my way, I must be allowed to ask some plain questions, and the answers will probably appear as unequivocal as the axioms on which reasoning is built; though, when entangled with various motives of action, they are formally contradicted, either by the words or conduct of men.

In what does man's pre-eminence over the brute creation **120** consist? The answer is as clear as that a half is less than the whole; in Reason.

What acquirement exalts one being above another? Virtue; we spontaneously reply.

For what purpose were the passions implanted? That man by struggling with them might attain a degree of knowledge denied to the brutes; whispers Experience.

Consequently the perfection of our nature and capability of happiness, must be estimated by the degree of reason, virtue, and knowledge, that distinguish the individual, and direct the **130** laws which bind society: and that from the exercise of reason, knowledge and virtue naturally flow, is equally undeniable, if mankind be viewed collectively.

The rights and duties of man thus simplified, it seems almost impertinent to attempt to illustrate truths that appear so incontrovertible; yet such deeply rooted prejudices have clouded reason, and such spurious qualities have assumed the name of virtues, that it is necessary to pursue the course of reason as it has been perplexed and involved in error, by various adventitious circumstances, comparing the simple **140** axiom with casual deviations. Men, in general, seem to employ their reason to justify prejudices, which they have imbibed,

---

[1] A reference to the widespread Christian misconception that Islam denied that women had souls.

they can scarcely trace how, rather than to root them out. The mind must be strong that resolutely forms its own principles; for a kind of intellectual cowardice prevails which makes many men shrink from the task, or only do it by halves. . . .

Many are the causes that, in the present corrupt state of society, contribute to enslave women by cramping their understandings and sharpening their senses. One, perhaps, that silently does more mischief than all the rest, is their disregard of order.   150

To do every thing in an orderly manner, is a most important precept, which women, who, generally speaking, receive only a disorderly kind of education, seldom attend to with that degree of exactness that men, who from their infancy are broken into method, observe. This negligent kind of guesswork, for what other epithet can be used to point out the random exertions of a sort of instinctive common sense, never brought to the test of reason? prevents their generalizing matters of fact—so they do to-day, what they did yesterday, merely because they did it   160 yesterday.

This contempt of the understanding in early life has more baneful consequences that is commonly supposed; for the little knowledge which women of strong minds attain, is, from various circumstances, of a more desultory kind than the knowledge of men, and it is acquired more by sheer observations on real life, than from comparing what has been individually observed with the results of experience generalized by speculation. Led by their dependent situation and domestic employments more into society, what they learn   170 is rather by snatches; and as learning is with them, in general, only a secondary thing, they do not pursue any one branch with that persevering ardour necessary to give vigour to the faculties, and clearness to the judgment. In the present state of society, a little learning is required to support the character of a gentleman; and boys are obliged to submit to a few years of discipline. But in the education of women, the cultivation of the understanding is always subordinate to the acquirement of some corporeal accomplishment; even while enervated by confinement and false notions of modesty, the body is   180 prevented from attaining that grace and beauty which relaxed half-formed limbs never exhibit. Besides, in youth their faculties are not brought forward by emulation; and having no serious scientific study, if they have natural sagacity it is turned too soon on life and manners. . . .

Strengthen the female mind by enlarging it, and there will be an end to blind obedience; but, as blind obedience is ever sought for by power, tyrants and sensualists are in the right when they endeavour to keep women in the dark, because the former only want slaves, and the latter a play-thing. The   190 sensualist, indeed, has been the most dangerous of tyrants, and women have been duped by their lovers, as princes by their ministers, whilst dreaming that they reigned over them. . . .

It appears to me necessary to dwell on these obvious truths, because females have been insulated, as it were; and, while they have been stripped of the virtues that should clothe humanity, they have been decked with artificial graces that enable them to exercise a short-lived tyranny. Love, in their bosoms, taking place of every nobler passion, their sole ambition is to be fair, to raise emotion instead of inspiring   200 respect; and this ignoble desire, like the servility in absolute monarchies, destroys all strength of character. Liberty is the mother of virtue, and if women be, by their very constitution, slaves, and not allowed to breathe the sharp invigorating air of freedom, they must ever languish like exotics, and be reckoned beautiful flaws in nature. . . .

Make [women] free, and they will quickly become wise and virtuous, as men become more so; for the improvements must be mutual, or the injustice which one half of the human race are obliged to submit to, retorting on their oppressors, the   210 virtue of men will be worm-eaten by the insects whom he keeps under his feet.

Let men take their choice, man and woman were made for each other, though not to become one being; and if they will not improve women, they will deprave them!

Q What does Wollstonecraft mean by "a false system of education?"

Q How does this system contribute to the plight of women?

The Journalistic Essay and the Birth of the Modern Novel

As the writings of Condorcet and Wollstonecraft suggest, social criticism assumed an important place in Enlightenment thought. Such criticism now also manifested itself in a new literary genre: the journalistic essay. Designed to address the middle-class reading public, prose essays and editorials were the stuff of magazines and daily newspapers. The first daily emerged in London during the eighteenth century, although a weekly had been published since 1642. At this time, London, with a population of some three-quarters of a million people, was the largest European city, and England claimed the highest rate of literacy in Western Europe. With the rise of newspapers and periodicals, the "poetic" prose of the seventeenth century—characterized by long sentences and magisterial phrases (see Bacon's *Of Studies*, Reading 4.11)—gave way to a more informal prose style, one that reflected the conversational chatter of the *salons* and the cafés. Journalistic essays brought "philosophy out of the closets and libraries, schools and colleges, to dwell in clubs and assemblies, at tea-tables and in coffee houses," explained Joseph Addison (1672–1719), the leading British prose stylist of his day. In collaboration with his lifelong friend, Richard Steele (1672–1729), Addison published two London periodicals, the *Tatler* and the *Spectator*, which featured penetrating commentaries on current events and social behavior. The *Spectator* had a circulation of some twenty-five thousand readers. Anticipating modern news magazines, eighteenth-century broadsheets and periodicals offered the literate public timely reports and diverse views on all aspects of popular culture. They provided entertainment even as they shaped popular opinion and cultivated an urban chauvinism best expressed by the English pundit Samuel Johnson (1709–1784): "When a man is tired of London, he is tired of life: for there is in London all that life can afford."

The most important new form of eighteenth-century literary entertainment, however, was the *novel*. The novel first appeared in world literature in China and Japan (see chapters 14 and 21). The most famous of the early Japanese novels, *The Tale of Genji*, was written by an unknown eleventh-century author known as Lady Shikibu Murasaki. In China, where the history of the novel reached back to the twelfth century, prose tales of travel, love, and adventure were popular sources for operas and plays. Neither Japanese nor Chinese prose fiction had any direct influence on Western writers. Nevertheless, during the eighteenth century the vernacular novel rose to prominence in East Asia and the West. In both East and West, the advance of the novel occurred at a moment of increasing urbanization. Its popularity reflected the demands of a larger reading public, although, in China, literacy was still confined to the educated elite—only ten percent of Chinese women, for instance, could read and write.

The modern novel made its appearance in England at the beginning of the eighteenth century with the publication of the popular adventure story *Robinson Crusoe* (1719), by Daniel Defoe (1660–1731). Defoe's novel, based on actual experience, was sharply realistic and thus quite different from the fantasy-laden prose of his sixteenth-century predecessors, Cervantes and Rabelais (see chapter 19). The novels of Defoe and his somewhat later contemporaries Samuel Richardson (1689–1761) and Henry Fielding (1707–1754) featured graphic accounts of the personalities and daily lives of the lower and middle classes. With an exuberance reminiscent of Chaucer, these prose narratives brought to life tales of criminals, pirates, and prostitutes. Not surprisingly, such books appealed to the tastes of the same individuals who enjoyed the spicy realism and journalistic prose of contemporary broadsheets.

Pope: Poet of the Age of Reason

If any single poet typified the spirit of the Enlightenment, it was surely Alexander Pope (1688–1744), the greatest English poet of the eighteenth century. Pope, a semi-invalid from the age of twelve, was a great admirer of Newton and a champion of the scientific method. He was also a staunch neoclassicist who devotedly revived the wit and polish of the Golden-Age Roman poets Virgil and Horace. Largely self-taught (in his time Roman Catholics were barred from attending English universities), Pope defended the value of education in Greek and Latin, and his own love of the classics inspired him to produce new translations of Homer's *Iliad* and *Odyssey*. "A *little learning* is a dangerous thing," warned Pope in pleading for a broader and more thorough survey of the past.

Pope's poems are as controlled and refined as a Poussin painting or a Bach fugue. His epigrammatic verses, written in **heroic couplets**, ring with concentrated brilliance. Pope's choice of the heroic couplet for most of his numerous satires, as well as for his translations of Homer, reflects his commitment to the qualities of balance and order. His mastery of the polished two-rhymed line bears out

his claim that "True ease in writing comes from art, not chance,/As those move easiest who have learned to dance."

Pope's most famous poem was his *Essay on Man*. Like Milton's *Paradise Lost*, but on a smaller scale, the *Essay* tries to assess humankind's place in the universal scheme. But whereas Milton explained evil in terms of human will, Pope—a Catholic turned deist—asserted that evil was simply part of God's design for the universe, a universe that Pope describes as "A mighty maze! but not without a plan." According to Pope (and to Leibniz, whom he admired), whatever occurs in nature has been "programmed" by God and is part of God's benign and rational order. Pope lacked the reforming zeal of the *philosophes*, but he caught the optimism of the Enlightenment in a single statement: "Whatever is, is right." In the *Essay on Man*, Pope warns that we must not presume to understand the whole of nature. Nor should we aspire to a higher place in the great "chain of being." Rather, he counsels the reader, "Know then thyself, presume not God to scan;/The proper study of Mankind is Man."

READING 4.21 From Pope's *Essay on Man* (1773–1774)

Epistle I

IX What if the foot, ordain'd the dust to tread,   1
Or hand, to toil, aspir'd to be the head?
What if the head, the eye, or ear repin'd[1]
To serve mere engines to the ruling Mind?
Just as absurd for any part to claim
To be another, in his gen'ral frame:
Just as absurd, to mourn the tasks or pains.
The great directing Mind of All ordains.

　All are but parts of one stupendous whole,
Whose body Nature is, and God the soul;   10
That, chang'd thro' all, and yet in all the same;
Great in the earth, as in th' ethereal frame;
Warms in the sun, refreshes in the breeze,
Glows in the stars, and blossoms in the trees,
Lives thro' all life, extends thro' all extent,
Spreads undivided, operates unspent;
Breathes in our soul, informs our mortal part,
As full, as perfect, in a hair as heart:
As full, as perfect, in vile Man that mourns,
As the rapt Seraph[2] that adores and burns: 20
To him no high, no low, no great, no small;
He fills, he bounds, connects, and equals all.

X Cease then, nor Order Imperfection name:
Our proper bliss depends on what we blame.
Know thy own point: This kind, this due degree
Of blindness, weakness, Heav'n bestows on thee.
Submit—In this, or any other sphere,

―――――
[1]Complained
[2]A member of the highest order of angels.

Secure to be as blest as thou canst bear:
Safe in the hand of one disposing Pow'r,
Or in the natal, or the mortal hour.   **30**
All Nature is but Art,[3] unknown to thee;
All Chance, Direction, which thou canst not see;
All Discord, Harmony not understood;
All partial Evil, universal Good:
And, spite of Pride, in erring Reason's spite,
One truth is clear, WHATEVER IS, IS RIGHT.

Epistle II
I   Know then thyself, presume not God to scan;[4]
The proper study of Mankind is Man.
Plac'd on this isthmus of a middle state,[5]
A Being darkly wise, and rudely great: **40**
With too much knowledge for the Sceptic side,
With too much weakness for the Stoic's pride,
He hangs between; in doubt to act, or rest;
In doubt to deem himself a God, or Beast;
In doubt his Mind or Body to prefer,
Born but to die, and reas'ning but to err;
Alike in ignorance, his reason such.
Whether he thinks too little, or too much:
Chaos of Thought and Passion, all confus'd;
Still by himself abus'd, or disabus'd;   **50**
Created half to rise, and half to fall;[6]
Great lord of all things, yet a prey to all;
Sole judge of Truth, in endless Error hurl'd:[7]
The glory, jest, and riddle of the world!

Q What aspects of this poem typify the spirit of the enlightenment?
Q What does Pope see as Man's limitations?

SUMMARY

The Age of the European Enlightenment marks the beginning of the Western notion of social progress and human perfectibility. In political thought, Thomas Hobbes and John Locke advanced the idea of government based on a social contract between ruler and ruled. While Hobbes envisioned this contract as a bond between individuals who surrendered some portion of their freedom to a sovereign authority, Locke saw government as an agent of the people—bound to exercise the will of the majority. According to Locke, government must operate according to the consent of the governed.

Locke's writings provided the intellectual foundation for the Enlightenment faith in reason as the sure guide to social progress. Jefferson, Montesquieu, and Adam Smith adapted Locke's views on natural law to political and economic life. The idea that human beings, free from the bonds of ignorance and superstition and operating according to the principles of reason, might achieve the good life here on earth inspired the philosophic optimism of Leibniz in Germany, the progressive theories of Beccaria in Italy and Condorcet in France, and the eloquent defense of womankind by Wollstonecraft in England.

The prime symbol of the Enlightenment zeal for knowledge was the *Encyclopédie*, produced by Diderot with the assistance of the *philosophes*. A similar zeal for the ordering of socially useful information inspired the writing of dictionaries, biographies, and histories. The journalistic essay and the early modern novel entertained the new reading public; they offered an intimate examination of everyday, secular life. In poetry, the elegant verses of Alexander Pope optimistically pictured human beings as the enlightened inhabitants of an orderly and harmonious universe.

The promise of reason and the gospel of progress—two fundamental ideas of the Enlightenment—have shaped the course of modern Western culture. Imported to America during the eighteenth century, they became the informing ideals of a new order of society. They served a "cult of utility," which promoted the idea that rational thought and its application in science and technology would advance and improve the quality of life for all members of society. More recently, the promise of reason and the gospel of progress have worked to challenge tyranny and injustice in many other parts of the world, including Africa, East Asia, and the Middle East—a sign of the durability of Enlightenment thought within the humanistic tradition.

GLOSSARY

heroic couplet a pair of rhymed iambic pentameter lines that reach completion in structure and in sense at the end of the second line

laissez-faire (French, "allow to act") a general policy of noninterference in the economy, defended by such classical economists as Adam Smith

philosophes (French, "philosophers") the intellectuals of the European Enlightenment

social contract an agreement made between citizens leading to the establishment of the state

---

[3]Compare Hobbes: "Nature is the art whereby God governs the world."
[4]Investigate.
[5] Between the angels (above) and the animal kingdom (below). Compare Pico della Mirandola's view of human beings as creatures who partake of both earthly and celestial qualities and can therefore ascend or descend the great "chain of being" (chapter 16).
[6]See note 5.
[7]Cast back and forth.

CHAPTER 25

The Limits of Reason

"'What does it matter,' said the dervish, 'whether there be good or evil [in the world]?'"
Voltaire

Even that most enthusiastic optimist, Alexander Pope, acknowledged in his *Essay on Man* that human beings were "Born but to die and reas'ning but to err"—that is, that people were finite and fallible. Pope and other champions of reason were, in fact, ambivalent: while generally committed to the belief in human perfectibility and the rational potential of humankind, they observed that people often acted in ways that were wholly irrational. Reason was all too frequently ignored or abandoned altogether. Moreover, the critical exercise of reason, when taken to an extreme, often deteriorated into bitter skepticism and cynicism.

Perhaps the greatest obstacle to the belief in the promise of reason lay, however, in the hard realities of everyday life. In eighteenth-century Europe, where Enlightenment intellectuals were exalting the ideals of human progress, there was clear evidence of human ignorance, depravity, and despair. Upon visiting the much-acclaimed city of Paris, Rousseau lamented its "dirty, stinking streets, filthy black houses, an air of slovenliness" and alleys filled with beggars. Indeed, outside the elegant drawing rooms of Paris and London lay clear signs of poverty, violence, and degradation.

Science and technology spawned a new barbarism in the form of machines that were potentially as destructive as they were beneficial. In England, the invention of the "flying shuttle" (1733), the "spinning jenny" (1765), and the power loom (1785)—machines for the manufacture of textile goods—facilitated the rise of the factory system and the Industrial Revolution. James Watt's steam engine (1775) provided a new power source for textiles and other industries. But such technological achievements, allied with unregulated capitalism, gave rise to dangerous working conditions and the exploitation of labor. In many of London's factories, children tended the new machines for twelve- to fourteen-hour shifts, following which they were boarded in shabby barracks. And in the mines of Cornwall and County Durham, women and children were paid a pittance to labor like animals,

pulling carts laden with coal. Some miners worked such long hours that they never saw the light of day.

The Transatlantic Slave Trade

In human terms, however, the most glaring evidence of the failure of the Enlightenment to achieve immediate social reforms was the perpetuation of the slave trade, which, despite the condemnation of many of the *philosophes*, flourished until the mid-nineteenth century. Begun by the Portuguese in the fifteenth century (see chapter 18), the transatlantic slave trade, by which millions of Africans were bought and shipped against their will to colonies in the "New World," reached its peak in the eighteenth century (Figure **25.1**). As England—lured by the lucrative sugar trade—became the leading player in the transatlantic traffic, some six to seven million slaves were transported to work on sugar plantations in the West Indies and elsewhere in the Americas. To supply this market, Africans—including African children—were frequently kidnapped by their unscrupulous countrymen, who profited handsomely by selling their captives to white slave traders. The fate of the African slave who survived the perilous "Middle Passage" between Africa and the Americas (it is estimated that roughly one-third perished in transit) was a life of unspeakable suffering.

A first-hand account of this inhumane system is central to the autobiographical narrative of Olaudah Equiano (1745–1797), who was born in the West African kingdom of Benin and kidnapped and enslaved at the age of eleven. Both as a slave and after his release from slavery in 1766, Equiano traveled widely; during his stay in England (as one of only thirty thousand blacks in mid-eighteenth-century England), he mastered the English language and became an outspoken abolitionist (Figure **25.2**). The following excerpt from Equiano's autobiographic narrative

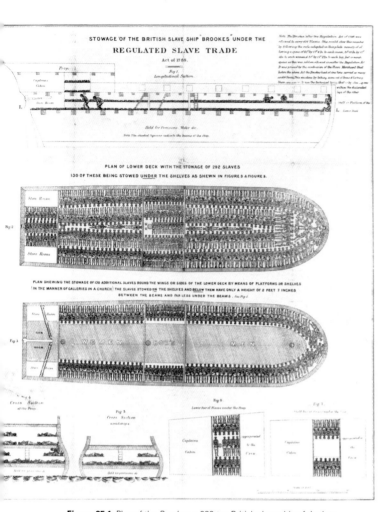

Figure 25.1 Plan of the *Brookes*, a 320-ton British slave ship of the late eighteenth century.
Fig. 1 lengthwise cross-section of the ship;
Fig. 2 lower deck with stowage of 292 slaves, 130 of these being stowed under platforms as seen in Figs. 4 and 5;
Fig. 3 lower deck with platforms stowing an additional 130 slaves;
Figs. 6 and 7 half-deck with and with platforms. The *Brookes* was one of eighteen vessels examined in 1788 by a committee making recommendations to Parliament for the regulation of slave ships. Library of Congress

recounts with dramatic simplicity the traumatic experience of an eleven-year-old child who was cruelly sold into bondage.

READING 4.22 From Equiano's *Travels* (1789)

That part of Africa known by the name of Guinea to which the trade for slaves is carried on extends along the coast above 3,400 miles, from the Senegal to Angola, and includes a variety of kingdoms. Of these the most considerable is the kingdom of Benin, both as to extent and wealth, the richness and cultivation of the soil, the power of its king, and the number and warlike disposition of the inhabitants. . . . This kingdom is divided into many provinces or districts, in one of the most remote and fertile of which, called Eboe, I was born in the year 1745, situated in a charming fruitful vale, named Essaka. The distance of this province from the capital of Benin and the sea coast must be very considerable, for I had never heard of white men or Europeans, nor of the sea, and our subjection to the king

of Benin was little more than nominal; for every transaction of the government, as far as my slender observation extended, was conducted by the chiefs or elders of the place. . . .

My father, besides many slaves, had a numerous family of which seven lived to grow up, including myself and a sister who was the only daughter. As I was the youngest of the sons I became, of course, the greatest favourite with my mother and was always with her; and she used to take particular pains to form my mind. I was trained up from my earliest years in the art of war, my daily exercise was shooting and throwing javelins, and my mother adorned me with emblems[1] after the manner of our greatest warriors. In this way I grew up till I was turned the age of 11, when an end was put to my happiness in the following manner. Generally when the grown people in the neighbourhood were gone far in the fields to labour, the children assembled together in some of the neighbours' premises to play, and commonly some of us used to get up a tree to look out for any assailant or kidnapper that might come upon us, for they sometimes took those opportunities of our parents' absence to attack and carry off as many as they could seize. One day, as I was watching at the top of a tree in our yard, I saw one of those people come into the yard of our next neighbour but one to kidnap, there being many stout young people in it. Immediately on this I gave the alarm of the rogue and he was surrounded by the stoutest of them, who entangled him with cords so that he could not escape till some of the grown people came and secured him. But alas! ere long it was my fate to be thus attacked and to be carried off when none of the grown people were nigh. One day, when all our people were gone out to their works as usual and only I and my dear sister were left to mind the house, two men and a woman got over our walls, and in a moment seized us both, and without giving us time to cry out or make resistance they stopped our mouths and ran off with us into the nearest wood. Here they tied our hands and continued to carry us as far as they could till night came on, when we reached a small house where the robbers halted for refreshment and spent the night. We were then unbound but were unable to take any food, and being quite overpowered by fatigue and grief, our only relief was some sleep, which allayed our misfortune for a short time. The next morning we left the house and continued travelling all the day. For a long time we had kept to the woods, but at last we came into a road which I believed I knew. I had now some hopes of being delivered, for we had advanced but a little way before I discovered some people at a distance, on which I began to cry out for their assistance: but my cries had no other effect than to make them tie me faster and stop my mouth, and then they put me into a large sack. They also stopped my sister's mouth and tied her hands, and in this manner we proceeded till we were out of the sight of these people. . . . It was in vain that we besought them not to part us; she was torn from me and immediately carried away, while I was left in a state of distraction not to be described. I cried and grieved continually, and for several days I did not eat anything but what they forced into my mouth. At length, after many days' travelling, during which I had often changed masters, I got into the hands of a chieftain in a very pleasant country. . . .

[1] Body decorations, such as scarification.

[Equiano describes his tenure with African masters; he is sold a number of times (during a period of six to seven months) before he is taken to the sea coast.]

The first object which saluted my eyes when I arrived on the coast was the sea, and a slave ship which was then riding at anchor and waiting for its cargo. These filled me with astonishment, which was soon converted into terror when I was carried on board. I was immediately handled and tossed up to see if I were sound by some of the crew, and I was now persuaded that I had gotten into a world of bad spirits and that they were going to kill me. Their complexions too differing so much from ours, their long hair and the language they spoke (which was very different from any I had ever heard) united to 80 confirm me in this belief. Indeed such were the horrors of my views and fears at the moment that, if ten thousand worlds had been my own, I would have freely parted with them all to have exchanged my condition with that of the meanest slave in my own country. When I looked round the ship too and saw a large furnace or copper boiling and a multitude of black people of every description chained together, every one of their countenances expressing dejection and sorrow, I no longer doubted of my fate; and quite overpowered with horror and anguish, I fell motionless on the deck and fainted. When I 90 recovered a little I found some black people about me, who I believed were some of those who had brought me on board and had been receiving their pay; they talked to me in order to cheer me, but all in vain. I asked them if we were not to be eaten by those white men with horrible looks, red faces, and loose hair. They told me I was not, and one of the crew brought me a small portion of spirituous liquor in a wine glass, but being afraid of him I would not take it out of his hand. One of the blacks therefore took it from him and gave it to me, and I took a little down my palate, which instead of reviving me, as they thought 100 it would, threw me into the greatest consternation at the strange feeling it produced, having never tasted any such liquor before. Soon after this the blacks who brought me on board went off, and left me abandoned to despair.

I now saw myself deprived of all chance of returning to my native country or even the least glimpse of hope of gaining the shore, which I now considered as friendly; and I even wished for my former slavery in preference to my present situation, which was filled with horrors of every kind, still heightened by my ignorance of what I was to undergo. I was not long suffered to 110 indulge my grief; I was soon put down under the decks, and there I received such a salutation in my nostrils as I had never experienced in my life: so that with the loathsomeness of the stench and crying together, I became so sick and low that I was not able to eat, nor had I the least desire to taste anything. I now wished for the last friend, death, to relieve me; but soon, to my grief, two of the white men offered me eatables, and on my refusing to eat, one of them held me fast by the hands and laid me across I think the windlass,[2] and tied my feet while the other flogged me severely. I had never experienced anything of 120 this kind before, and although, not being used to the water, I naturally feared that element the first time I saw it, yet nevertheless could I have got over the nettings I would have jumped over the side, but I could not; and besides, the crew

used to watch us very closely who were not chained down to the decks, lest we should leap into the water: and I have seen some of these poor African prisoners most severely cut for attempting to do so, and hourly whipped for not eating. This indeed was often the case with myself. In a little time after, amongst the poor chained men I found some of my own nation,[3] 130 which in a small degree gave ease to my mind. I inquired of these what was to be done with us; they gave me to understand we were to be carried to these white people's country to work for them. I then was a little revived, and thought if it were no worse than working, my situation was not so desperate: but still I feared I should be put to death, the white people looked and acted, as I thought, in so savage a manner; for I had never seen among my people such instances of brutal cruelty, and this not only shewn towards us blacks but also to some of the whites themselves. One white man in particular I saw, when we were 140 permitted to be on deck, flogged so unmercifully with a large rope near the foremast that he died in consequence of it; and they tossed him over the side as they would have done a brute. This made me fear these people the more, and I expected nothing less than to be treated in the same manner. I could not help expressing my fears and apprehensions to some of my countrymen: I asked them if these people had no country but lived in this hollow place (the ship): they told me they did not, but came from a distant one. "Then," said I, "how comes it in all our country we never heard of them?" They told me because 150 they lived so very far off. I then asked where were their women? had they any like themselves? I was told they had: "and why," said I, "do we not see them?" They answered, because they were left behind. . . . The stench of the hold while we were on the coast was so intolerably loathsome that it was dangerous to remain there for any time, and some of us had been permitted to stay on the deck for the fresh air; but now that the whole ship's cargo were confined together it became absolutely pestilential. The closeness of the place and the heat of the climate, added to the number in the ship, which was so 160 crowded that each had scarcely room to turn himself, almost suffocated us. This produced copious perspirations, so that the air soon became unfit for respiration from a variety of loathsome smells, and brought on a sickness among the slaves, of which many died, thus falling victims to the improvident avarice, as I may call it, of their purchasers. This wretched situation was again aggravated by the galling of the chains, now become insupportable, and the filth of the necessary tubs, into which the children often fell and were almost suffocated. The shrieks of the women and the groans of the dying rendered 170 the whole a scene of horror almost inconceivable. Happily perhaps for myself I was soon reduced so low here that it was thought necessary to keep me almost always on deck, and from my extreme youth I was not put in fetters. In this situation I expected every hour to share the fate of my companions, some of whom were almost daily brought upon deck at the point of death, which I began to hope would soon put an end to my miseries. Often did I think many of the inhabitants of the deep much more happy than myself. I envied them the freedom they enjoyed, and as often wished I could change my condition for 180 theirs. Every circumstance I met with served only to render my

---

[2]The device that works the ship's anchor.

[3]Ethnic group.

state more painful, and heighten my apprehensions and my opinion of the cruelty of the whites. One day they had taken a number of fishes, and when they had killed and satisfied themselves with as many as they thought fit, to our astonishment who were on the deck, rather than give any of them to us to eat as we expected, they tossed the remaining fish into the sea again, although we begged and prayed for some as well as we could, but in vain; and some of my countrymen, being pressed by hunger, took an opportunity when 190 they thought no one saw them of trying to get a little privately; but they were discovered, and the attempt procured them some very severe floggings. One day, when we had a smooth sea and moderate wind, two of my wearied countrymen who were chained together (I was near them at the time), preferring death to such a life of misery, somehow made through the nettings and jumped into the sea: immediately another quite dejected fellow, who on account of his illness was suffered to be out of irons, also followed their example; and I believe many more would very soon have done the same if they had not been 200 prevented by the ship's crew, who were instantly alarmed. Those of us that were the most active were in a moment put down under the deck, and there was such a noise and confusion amongst the people of the ship as I never heard before, to stop her and get the boat out to go after the slaves. However two of the wretches were drowned, but they got the other and afterwards flogged him unmercifully for thus attempting to prefer death to slavery. In this manner we continued to undergo more hardships than I can now relate, hardships which are inseparable from this accursed trade. . . . At last we came in 210 sight of the island of Barbados, at which the whites on board gave a great shout and made many signs of joy to us. We did not know what to think of this, but as the vessel drew nearer we plainly saw the harbour and other ships of different kinds and sizes, and we soon anchored amongst them off Bridgetown. Many merchants and planters now came on board, though it was in the evening. They put us in separate parcels[4] and examined us attentively. They also made us jump,[5] and pointed to the land, signifying we were to go there. We thought by this we should be eaten by these ugly men, as they appeared to us; 220 and when soon after we were all put down under the deck again, there was much dread and trembling among us, and nothing but bitter cries to be heard all the night from these apprehensions, insomuch that at last the white people got some old slaves from the land to pacify us. They told us we were not to be eaten but to work, and were soon to go on land where we should see many of our countrypeople. This report eased us much; and sure enough soon after we were landed there came to us Africans of all languages. We were conducted immediately to the merchant's yard, where we 230 were all pent up together like so many sheep in a fold without regard to sex or age. . . . We were not many days in the merchant's custody before we were sold after their usual manner, which is this: On a signal given, (as the beat of a drum) the buyers rush at once into the yard where the slaves are confined, and make choice of that parcel they like best. The noise and clamour with which this is attended and the

Figure 25.2 *Olaudah Equiano*, 1789. Engraving.

eagerness visible in the countenances of the buyers serve not a little to increase the apprehensions of the terrified Africans, who may well be supposed to consider them as the 240 ministers of that destruction to which they think themselves devoted. In this manner, without scruple, are relations and friends separated, most of them never to see each other again. I remember in the vessel in which I was brought over, in the men's apartment there were several brothers who, in the sale, were sold in different lots; and it was very moving on this occasion to see and hear their cries at parting. O, ye nominal Christians! might not an African ask you, Learned you this from your God who says unto you, Do unto all men as you would men should do unto you? Is it not enough that 250 we are torn from our country and friends to toil for your luxury and lust of gain? Must every tender feeling be likewise sacrificed to your avarice? Are the dearest friends and relations, now rendered more dear by their separation from their kindred, still to be parted from each other and thus prevented from cheering the gloom of slavery with the small comfort of being together and mingling their sufferings and sorrows? Why are parents to lose their children, brothers their sisters, or husbands their wives? Surely this is a new refinement in cruelty which, while it has no advantage to atone for it, thus aggravates 260 distress and adds fresh horrors even to the wretchedness of slavery. . . .

Q Which of the circumstances and conditions described by Equiano strike you as most removed from the ideals of the *philosophes*?

---

[4]Groups.
[5]In order to determine whether they were healthy.

As Equiano suggests, the "gloom of slavery" itself left slaves little opportunity for self-expression. It is therefore notable that one particular slave would become America's first black woman poet. Phillis Wheatley (1754?–1784) was kidnapped from Senegal and sold at auction in Boston at the age of seven. She was educated along with the children of her master, John Wheatley, and learned to read and write English, as well as Greek and Latin. Producing her first poem at the age of thirteen, Wheatley had difficulty publishing her collection of poems in America, where the authenticity of her work was held in doubt. Following interrogation by a panel of eighteen illustrious Bostonians, it was concluded that "Phillis, a young Negro Girl, who was but a few Years since, brought an uncultivated Barbarian from Africa" had indeed written the verses in question. In 1773, her *Poems on Various Subjects; Religious and Moral* was published in England (which was more receptive than America to black authors), and soon won acclaim in both Europe and America. An encouragement to the work of other black writers, it became a landmark in black literary achievement. John Wheatley emancipated Phillis in 1773, giving her the opportunity to travel and continue writing. The poem that follows, written in heroic couplets—the favorite meter of Chaucer and Pope—is a terse and eloquent appeal to the Christian promise of equality before God and the enlightenment promise of reason.

READING 4.23 Wheatley's "On Being Brought from Africa to America" (1772)

'TWAS mercy brought me from my *Pagan* land,
Taught my benighted soul to understand
That there's a God, that there's a *Saviour* too:
Once I redemption neither sought nor knew.
Some view our sable[1] race with scornful eye,
"Their colour is a diabolic die."
Remember, *Christians*, *Negros*, black as *Cain*,
May be refin'd, and join the' angelic train.

 Q How does the tone of Wheatley's poem differ from that of Equiano's narrative?

If slavery and industrialization in the West generated material conditions that were contrary to Enlightenment ideals, other factors served as serious obstacles to their realization. Ignorance, for example, the foundation for bias and (in many cases) unwitting prejudice, clouded the perceptions and judgments of some of the most educated *philosophes*. Diderot himself, who had no first-hand knowledge of the Moslem world, described Arabs (in his *Encyclopédie*) as "thievish and bellicose." Voltaire, who wrote a universal history that charted the customs of nations (including Russia and Africa), brought to his

analysis an anti-Church, anti-Semitic, and anti-black bias. And in America the leading Enlightenment thinker, Thomas Jefferson, believed Africans to be intellectually inferior, and he defended the institution of slavery as a "necessary evil." His perception of African-American slaves was colored by prejudices that are shocking to modern sensibilities. In his *Notes on the State of Virginia*, Jefferson wrote: "Comparing [blacks] by their faculties of memory, reason, and imagination, it appears to me that in memory they are equal to the whites; in reason much inferior . . . I advance it . . . as a suspicion only, that the blacks, whether originally a distinct race, or made distinct by time and circumstances, are inferior to the whites in the endowments both of body and mind . . . This unfortunate difference of color, and perhaps of faculty, is a powerful obstacle to the emancipation of these people."* In such opinions, shared by most of his fellow *philosophes*, Jefferson provided an implicit rationale for enslaving African people. Clearly, such thinkers were all too capable of finding rationalizations for policies in which political or social advantage for the privileged few overrode the abstract ideals of liberty and equality. Thus slavery persisted in the Western hemisphere (and elsewhere) for nearly a century beyond the Age of Enlightenment.

Satire: Weapon of the Enlightenment

The discrepancies between the sordid realities of eighteenth-century life and the progressive ideas of the Enlightenment provoked indignant protests, and none so potent as those couched in humor. The eighteenth century was history's greatest age of satire. The favorite weapon of many Enlightenment intellectuals, satire fused wit and irony to underscore human folly and error. The genre that had served Juvenal in imperial Rome (see chapter 6) and Erasmus in the age of the Reformation (see chapter 19) now became the favorite tool of social reformers, who drew attention to the vast contradictions between morals and manners, intentions and actions, and, more generally, between Enlightenment aspirations and contemporary injustice.

The Satires of Jonathan Swift

 The premier British satirist of the eighteenth century was Jonathan Swift (1667–1745). Unlike the *philosophes*, this Dublin-born Anglican priest took a pessimistic view of human nature. He once confided (in a letter to the poet Alexander Pope) that he hated the human race, whose misuse of reason produced, in his view, an irredeemably corrupt society. Such

---

[1]Black or dark brown.

*David A. Hollinger and Charles Capper, eds. *The American Intellectual Tradition: A Sourcebook: 1630–1865*, vol. 1 (New York, third edition, Oxford University Press, 1997), 177.

negativism accompanied Swift's self-acclaimed "savage indignation." Yet Swift was not a man of despair, for no despairing personality could have produced such a profoundly moralizing body of literature. In 1726, he published his classic satire, *Gulliver's Travels*. At the simplest level, it is a story of travel and adventure that (somewhat like Equiano's true-to-life travels) describes the fortunes of a hero in imaginary lands peopled with midgets, giants, and other fabulous creatures. At a second, symbolic level, however, it is a social statement on the vagaries of human behavior. In one chapter, Gulliver visits the Lilliputians— "little people" whose moral pettiness and inhumanity seem to characterize humankind at its worst. In another, he meets noble horses whose rational behavior contrasts with the bestiality of their human-looking slaves, the Yahoos. An immediate popular sensation, *Gulliver's Travels* has become a landmark in fantasy literature and social satire.

Swift also wrote many pamphlets and letters protesting social and political ills. Among the most famous is an essay publicizing the wretched condition of the Irish peasants, who were exploited unmercifully by the British government. In his satirical treatise *A Modest Proposal*, Swift observed that many Irish peasants were too poor to feed their families; he proposed with deadpan frankness that Irish children should be bred and butchered for the English dining table, thus providing income for the poor and alleviating the miseries of all. While *Gulliver's Travels* attacks conditions that are universal and timeless, *A Modest Proposal* mocks a specific crisis of Swift's own time.

READING 4.24 From Swift's *A Modest Proposal* (1729)

for Preventing the Children of Poor People in Ireland from Being a Burden to Their Parents or Country, and for Making Them Beneficial to the Public

It is a melancholy object to those who walk through this great town[1] or travel in the country, when they see the streets, the roads, and cabin-doors, crowded with beggars of the female sex, followed by three, four, or six children, *all in rags*, and importuning every passenger for an alms[2]. These mothers, instead of being able to work for their honest livelihood, are forced to employ all their time in strolling, to beg sustenance for their helpless infants, who, as they grow up, either turn thieves for want of work, or leave their dear native country to fight. . . in Spain, or sell themselves to the Barbadoes[3]. **10**

I think it is agreed by all parties that this prodigious number of children, in the arms, or on the backs, or at the heels of their mothers, and frequently of their fathers, is in the present deplorable state of the kingdom a very great additional grievance; and therefore whoever could find out a fair, cheap, and easy method of making these children sound, useful members of the commonwealth, would deserve so well of the public as to have his statue set up for a preserver of the nation.

But my intention is very far from being confined to provide only for the children of professed beggars; it is of a much greater extent, and shall take in the whole number of infants at **20** a certain age, who are born of parents in effect as little able to support them as those who demand our charity in the streets.

As to my own part, having turned my thoughts for many years upon this important subject, and maturely weighed the several schemes of other projectors[4], I have always found them grossly mistaken in their computation. It is true, a child, just dropped from its dam[5], may be supported by her milk for a solar year with little other nourishment, at most not above the value of two shillings, which the mother may certainly get, or the value **30** in scraps, by her lawful occupation of begging; and it is exactly at one year old that I propose to provide for them in such a manner as instead of being a charge upon their parents or the parish, or wanting food and raiment[6] for the rest of their lives, they shall, on the contrary, contribute to the feeding and partly to the clothing of many thousands.

There is likewise another great advantage in my scheme, that it will prevent those voluntary abortions, and that horrid practice of women murdering their bastard children, alas too frequent among us, sacrificing the poor innocent babes, I **40** doubt, more to avoid the expense than the shame, which would move tears and pity in the most savage and inhuman breast.

The number of souls in this kingdom being usually reckoned one million and a half, of these I calculate there may be about two hundred thousand couple whose wives are breeders; from which number I subtract thirty thousand couple who are able to maintain their own children, although I apprehend there cannot be so many under the present distresses of the kingdom; but this being granted, there will remain an hundred and seventy thousand breeders. I again subtract fifty thousand **50** for those women who miscarry, or whose children die by accident or disease within the year. There only remain an hundred and twenty thousand children of poor parents annually born. The question therefore is, how this number shall be reared and provided for, which, as I have already said, under the present situation of affairs, is utterly impossible by all the methods hitherto proposed, for we can neither employ them in handicraft or agriculture; we neither build houses (I mean in the country) nor cultivate land; they can very seldom pick up a livelihood by stealing till they arrive at six years old, except **60** where they are of towardly[7] parts, although I confess they learn the rudiments[8] much earlier. . .

I am assured by our merchants that a boy or a girl before twelve years old is no saleable commodity, and even when they come to this age, they will not yield above three pounds, or three pounds and half-a-crown at most on the Exchange, which cannot turn to account either to the parents or kingdom, the charge of nutriment and rags having been at least four times that value.

---

[1]Dublin.
[2]Charity.
[3]As slaves in the West Indies.

[4]Speculators.
[5]Just born.
[6]Clothing.
[7]Handsome.
[8]Fundamentals; first principles.

I shall now therefore humbly propose my own thoughts, which I hope will not be liable to the least objection. 70

I have been assured by a very knowing American of my acquaintance in London, that a young healthy child well nursed is at a year old a most delicious, nourishing, and wholesome food, whether stewed, roasted, baked, or boiled, and I make no doubt that it will serve in a fricassee or a ragout.

I do therefore humbly offer it to public consideration that of the hundred and twenty thousand children already computed, twenty thousand may be reserved for breed, whereof only one fourth part to be males, which is more than we allow to sheep, 80 black cattle, or swine; and my reason is that these children are seldom the fruits of marriage, a circumstance not much regarded by our savages. Therefore one male will be sufficient to serve four females. That the remaining hundred thousand may at a year old be offered in sale to the persons of quality and fortune through the kingdom, always advising the mother to let them suck[9] plentifully in the last month, so as to render them plump and fat for a good table. A child will make two dishes at an entertainment for friends, and when the family dines alone, the fore or hind quarter will make a reasonable dish, and 90 seasoned with a little pepper or salt will be very good boiled on the fourth day, especially in winter.

I have reckoned, upon a medium[10], that a child just born will weigh 12 pounds, and in a solar year if tolerably nursed will increase to 28 pounds.

I grant this food will be somewhat dear, and therefore very proper for landlords, who, as they have already devoured most of the parents, seem to have the best title to the children.

Infants' flesh will be in season throughout the year, but more plentiful in March, and a little before and after, for we are told 100 by a grave author[11], an eminent French physician, that fish being a prolific diet, there are more children born in Roman Catholic countries about nine months after Lent, than at any other season; therefore reckoning a year after Lent, the markets will be more glutted than usual, because the number of Popish infants is at least three to one in this kingdom, and therefore it will have one other collateral advantage, by lessening the number of Papists[12] among us.

I have already computed the charge of nursing a beggar's child (in which list I reckon all cottagers, labourers, and four- 110 fifths of the farmers) to be about two shillings *per annum*, rags included, and I believe no gentleman would repine to give ten shillings for the carcass of a good fat child, which, as I have said, will make four dishes of excellent nutritive meat, when he has only some particular friend or his own family to dine with him. Thus the squire will learn to be a good landlord, and grow popular among his tenants, the mother will have eight shillings for net profit, and be fit for work till she produces another child.

Those who are more thrifty (as I must confess the times require) may flay the carcass; the skin of which, artificially 120 dressed, will make admirable gloves for ladies, and summer boots for fine gentlemen.

As to our city of Dublin, shambles[13] may be appointed for this purpose in the most convenient parts of it, and butchers we may be assured will not be wanting, although I rather recommend buying the children alive, and dressing them hot from the knife, as we do roasting pigs.

A very worthy person, a true lover of his country, and whose virtues I highly esteem, was lately pleased, in discoursing on this matter, to offer a refinement upon my scheme. He said, that 130 many gentlemen of this kingdom having of late destroyed their deer, he conceived that the want of venison might be well supplied by the bodies of young lads and maidens, not exceeding fourteen years of age, nor under twelve, so great a number of both sexes in every country being now ready to starve, for want of work and service, and these to be disposed of by their parents if alive, or otherwise by their nearest relations. But with due deference to so excellent a friend, and so deserving a patriot, I cannot be altogether in his sentiments; for as to the males, my American acquaintance assured me 140 from frequent experience, that their flesh was generally tough and lean, like that of our schoolboys, by continual exercise, and their taste disagreeable, and to fatten them would not answer the charge. Then as to the females, it would, I think with humble submission, be a loss to the public, because they soon would become breeders themselves. And besides, it is not improbable that some scrupulous people might be apt to censure such a practice (although indeed very unjustly), as a little bordering upon cruelty, which, I confess, has always been with me the strongest objection against any project, however 150 so well intended. . . .

I have too long digressed, and therefore shall return to my subject. I think the advantages by the proposal which I have made are obvious and many, as well as of the highest importance.

For first, as I have already observed, it would greatly lessen the number of Papists, with whom we are yearly over-run, being the principal breeders of the nation, as well as our most dangerous enemies, and who stay at home on purpose to deliver the kingdom to the Pretender, hoping to take their 160 advantage by the absence of so many good Protestants, who have chosen rather to leave their country, than stay at home, and pay tithes against their conscience, to an Episcopal curate.

Secondly, The poorer tenants will have something valuable of their own, which by law may be made liable to distress, and help to pay their landlord's rent, their corn and cattle being already seized, and *money a thing unknown*.

Thirdly, whereas the maintenance of an hundred thousand children, from two years old and upward, cannot be computed at less than ten shillings a piece per annum, the nation's stock 170 will be thereby increased fifty thousand pounds *per annum*, besides the profit of a new dish, introduced to the tables of all gentlemen of fortune in the kingdom who have any refinement in taste, and the money will circulate among ourselves, the good being entirely of our own growth and manufacture.

Fourthly, The constant breeders, beside the gain of eight shillings sterling *per annum*, by the sale of their children, will be rid of the charge of maintaining them after the first year.

---

[9]To nurse at the breast.
[10]On an average.
[11]François Rabelais (see chapter 18).
[12]Roman Catholics, especially those who ardently support the pope.

---

[13]Slaughterhouses.

Fifthly, This food would likewise bring great custom to taverns, where the vintners will certainly be so prudent as to **180** procure the best receipts for dressing it to perfection, and consequently have their houses frequented by all the fine gentlemen who justly value themselves upon their knowledge in good eating; and a skilful cook, who understands how to oblige his guests, will contrive to make it as expensive as they please.

Sixthly, This would be a great inducement to marriage, which all wise nations have either encouraged by rewards, or enforced by laws and penalties. It would increase the care and tenderness of mothers toward their children, when they were **190** sure of a settlement for life, to the poor babes, provided in some sort by the public, to their annual profit instead of expense. We should see an honest emulation among the married women, which of them could bring the fattest child to the market. Men would become as fond of their wives, during the time of their pregnancy, as they are now of their mares in foal, their cows in calf, their sows when they are ready to farrow, nor offer to beat or kick them (as is too frequent a practice) for fear of a miscarriage.

Many other advantages might be enumerated. For instance, **200** the addition of some thousand carcasses in our exportation of barrelled beef, the propagation of swine's flesh, and improvement in the art of making good bacon, so much wanted among us by the great destruction of pigs, too frequent at our table, which are no way comparable in taste, or magnificence, to a well-grown, fat yearling child, which roasted whole will make a considerable figure at a Lord Mayor's feast, or any other public entertainment. But this and many others I omit, being studious of brevity.

Supposing that one thousand families in this city would be **210** constant customers for infants' flesh, beside others who might have it at merry-meetings, particularly at weddings and christenings, I compute that Dublin would take off annually about twenty thousand carcasses; and the rest of the kingdom (where probably they will be sold somewhat cheaper) the remaining eighty thousand.

I can think of no one objection, that will possibly be raised against this proposal, unless it should be urged that the number of people will be thereby much lessened in the kingdom. This I freely own, and it was indeed one principal **220** design in offering it to the world. I desire the reader to observe, that I calculate my remedy *for this one individual kingdom of Ireland, and for no other that ever was, is, or I think, ever can be upon earth.* Therefore let no man talk to me of other expedients: *Of taxing our absentees at five shillings a pound: Of using neither clothes, nor household furniture, except what is of our own growth and manufacture: Of utterly rejecting the materials and instruments that promote foreign luxury: Of curing the expensiveness of pride, vanity, idleness, and gaming*[14] *in our women: Of introducing a vein of parsimony,* **230** *prudence and temperance: Of learning to love our Country, wherein we differ even from* Laplanders, *and the inhabitants of* Topinamboo[15]: *Of quitting our animosities and factions, nor act any longer like Jews, who were murdering one*

another at the very moment their city was taken: Of being a little cautious not to sell our country and conscience for nothing: Of teaching landlords to have at least one degree of mercy toward their tenants. Lastly of putting a spirit of honesty, industry, and skill into our shopkeepers, who, if a resolution could now be taken to buy only our native goods, **240** would immediately unite to cheat and exact upon us in the price, the measure, and the goodness, nor could ever yet be brought to make one fair proposal of just dealing, though often and earnestly invited to it.

Q What aspects of Swift's proposal contribute to its effectiveness as a tool for political reform?

Voltaire and *Candide*

Swift's satires were an inspiration to that most scintillating of French *philosophes* and leading intellectual of French society, François Marie Arouet (1694–1778), who used the pen name Voltaire (Figure **25.3**). Born into a rising Parisian middle-class family and educated by Jesuits, Voltaire rose to fame as poet, playwright, critic, and as the central figure of the French *salons*. In his numerous pamphlets and letters, he attacked bigotry as manmade evil and injustice as institutional evil. On two separate occasions, his controversial verse-satires led to his imprisonment in the Bastille (the French state prison). His visits to England instilled in him high regard for constitutional government, the principles of toleration, and the concepts of equality found in the writings of John Locke—all of which he championed in his writings.

More than any of the *philosophes*, Voltaire extolled the traditions of non-Western cultures: having read the works of Confucius in Jesuit translations, he esteemed the ancient teacher as a philosopher–sage. Voltaire was also the first modern intellectual to assess the role of Russia in world society. In his *Essay on Manners*, a universal history that examines the customs of nations around the world, Voltaire gave thoughtful attention to the history of the Russian state. His fascination with Russia as a curious blend of Asian and European traditions became the basis for a lifelong pursuit of things Russian, including a long correspondence with Catherine the Great, who ruled as Empress of Russia from 1762 to 1796.

Like most of the *philosophes*, Voltaire condemned organized religion and all forms of religious fanaticism. A declared deist, he compared human beings to mice who live in the recesses of an immense ship without knowing of its captain or its destination. Any confidence Voltaire might have had in beneficent Providence was dashed by the terrible Lisbon earthquake and tidal wave of 1755, which took the lives of more than 20,000 Portuguese. For Voltaire, the realities of natural disaster and human cruelty were not easily reconciled with the belief that a good God had created the universe or that humans were by nature rational—views basic to Enlightenment optimism. In the satirical tale *Candide* (subtitled *Optimism*), Voltaire

[14]Gambling (the most popular pastime of the upper class).
[15]A district in Brazil supposedly inhabited by savages.

Figure 25.3 JEAN-ANTOINE HOUDON, *Voltaire in Old Age*, 1781. Marble, height 20 in. Musée de Versailles. © Corbis/Bettmann, London.

addressed the age-old question of how evil could exist in a universe created and governed by the forces of good. More important, he leveled a major blow at the optimistic credo postulated by the German philosopher Gottfried Wilhelm Leibniz (see chapter 24) that this was "the best of all possible worlds." A parody of the adventure romances and travel tales (Equiano and Swift both come to mind) in vogue in Voltaire's time, *Candide* describes the exploits of a naive and unsophisticated young man whose blissful life is daunted by a series of terrible (and hilarious) experiences. Initially, the youthful Candide (literally, "candid" or "frank") approaches life with the glib optimism taught to him by Dr. Pangloss (meaning "all tongue"), Voltaire's embodiment of Leibniz. But Candide soon discovers the folly of believing that "all is for the best in this best of all possible worlds." He experiences the horrors of war (the consequences of two equally self-righteous opposing armies), the evils of religious fanaticism (as manifested by the Spanish Inquisition), the disasters of nature (the Lisbon earthquake), and the dire effects of human greed (an affliction especially prevalent among the aristocracy and derived, according to Voltaire, from boredom). Experience becomes the antidote to the comfortable fatalism of Pope's "Whatever is, is right." After a lifetime of sobering misadventures, Candide ends his days settled on a farm (in Turkey) in the company of his long-lost friends. (Not coincidentally, the aging Voltaire penned *Candide* while living on his farm retreat just outside Geneva.) "We must cultivate our garden," he concludes. This metaphor for achieving personal satisfaction in a hostile world relieves the otherwise devastating skepticism that underlies *Candide*. It is Voltaire's answer to blind optimism and to the foolish hope that human reason can allay evil.

Voltaire's genius, and the quality that separates his style from that of Swift, is his penetrating wit. Like the marksman's sword, Voltaire's satire is sharply pointed, precise in its aim, and devastating in its effect. With a sure hand, Voltaire manipulates the principal satirical devices: irony, understatement, and overstatement. Using irony—the contradiction between literal and intended meanings—he mocks serious matters and deflates lofty pretensions; he calls war, for instance, "heroic butchery" and refers to Paquetta's venereal disease as a "present" she received from "a very learned Franciscan." He exploits

understatement when he notes, for example, that Pangloss "only lost one eye and one ear" (as the result of syphilis). And he uses overstatement for moral effect: the 350-pound baroness of Westphalia is "greatly respected"; thus corpulence—actually an indication of self-indulgence—becomes a specious sign of dignity and importance.

Voltaire's mock optimism, dispatched by Candide's persistent claim that this is "the best of all possible worlds" (even as he encounters repeated horrors), underscores the contradiction between the ideal and the real that lies at the heart of all satire. Although it was censored in many parts of Europe, *Candide* was so popular that it went through forty editions in Voltaire's lifetime. A classic of Western satire, *Candide* has survived numerous adaptations, including a superb twentieth-century version as a comic operetta with lyrics by the American poet Richard Wilbur (b. 1921) and music by the American composer Leonard Bernstein (1918–1990). Approximately one-third of Voltaire's philosophical tale is included in the following excerpt.

READING 4.25 From Voltaire's *Candide, or Optimism* (1759)

Chapter 1

How Candide Was Brought Up in a Fine Castle, and How He Was Expelled From Thence

There lived in Westphalia,[1] in the castle of my Lord the Baron   1
of Thunder-ten-tronckh, a young man, on whom nature had
bestowed the most agreeable manners. His face was the index
to his mind. He had an upright heart, with an easy frankness;
which, I believe, was the reason he got the name of *Candide*.
He was suspected, by the old servants of the family, to be the
son of my Lord the Baron's sister, by a very honest gentleman
of the neighborhood, whom the young lady declined to marry,
because he could only produce seventy-one armorial
quarterings,[2] the rest of his genealogical tree having been   10
destroyed through the injuries of time.

The Baron was one of the most powerful lords in
Westphalia; his castle had both a gate and windows; and his
great hall was even adorned with tapestry. The dogs of his
outer yard composed his hunting pack upon occasion, his

---

[1] A province in Germany.

[2] Genealogical degrees of noble ancestry; since each quartering represents one generation, the family "tree" is over two thousand years old—an obvious impossibility.

grooms were his huntsmen, and the vicar of the parish was his chief almoner. He was called My Lord by everybody, and everyone laughed when he told his stories.

My Lady the Baroness, who weighed about three hundred and fifty pounds, attracted, by that means, very great attention, and did the honors of the house with a dignity that rendered her still more respectable. Her daughter Cunegonde, aged about seventeen years, was of a ruddy complexion, fresh, plump, and well calculated to excite the passions. The Baron's son appeared to be in every respect worthy of his father. The preceptor, Pangloss,[3] was the oracle of the house, and little Candide listened to his lectures with all the simplicity that was suitable to his age and character.

Pangloss taught metaphysico-theologo-cosmoloonigology.[4] He proved most admirably, that there could not be an effect without cause; that, in this best of possible worlds,[5] my Lord the Baron's castle was the most magnificent of castles, and my Lady the best of Baronesses that possibly could be.

"It is demonstrable," said he, "that things cannot be otherwise than they are: for things having been made for some end, they must necessarily be for the best end. Observe well, that the nose has been made for carrying spectacles; therefore we have spectacles. The legs are visibly designed for stockings, and therefore we have stockings. Stones have been formed to be hewn, and make castles; therefore my Lord has a very fine castle; the greatest baron of the province ought to be the best accommodated. Swine were made to be eaten; therefore we eat pork all the year round: consequently, those who have merely asserted that all is good, have said a very foolish thing; they should have said all is the best possible."

Candide listened attentively, and believed implicitly; for he thought Miss Cunegonde extremely handsome, though he never had the courage to tell her so. He concluded, that next to the good fortune of being Baron of Thunder-ten-tronckh, the second degree of happiness was that of being Miss Cunegonde, the third to see her every day, and the fourth to listen to the teachings of Master Pangloss, the greatest philosopher of the province, and consequently of the whole world.

One day Cunegonde having taken a walk in the environs of the castle, in a little wood, which they called a park, espied Doctor Pangloss giving a lesson in experimental philosophy to her mother's chambermaid; a little brown wench, very handsome, and very docile. As Miss Cunegonde had a strong inclination for the sciences, she observed, without making any noise, the reiterated experiments that were going on before her eyes; she saw very clearly the sufficient reason of the Doctor, the effects and the causes; and she returned greatly flurried, quite pensive, and full of desire to be learned; imagining that she might be a sufficient reason for young Candide, who also, might be the same to her.

On her return to the castle, she met Candide, and blushed; Candide also blushed; she wished him good morrow with a faltering voice, and Candide answered her, hardly knowing what

he said. The next day, after dinner, as they arose from table, Cunegonde and Candide happened to get behind the screen. Cunegonde dropped her handkerchief, and Candide picked it up; she, not thinking any harm, took hold of his hand; and the young man, not thinking any harm neither, kissed the hand of the young lady, with an eagerness, a sensibility, and grace, very particular; their lips met, their eyes sparkled, their knees trembled, their hands strayed.—The Baron of Thunder-ten-tronckh happening to pass close by the screen, and observing this cause and effect, thrust Candide out of the castle, with lusty kicks [to the behind]. Cunegonde fell into a swoon and as soon as she came to herself, was heartily cuffed on the ears by my Lady the Baroness. Thus all was thrown into confusion in the finest and most agreeable castle possible.

Chapter 2

What Became of Candide Among the Bulgarians[6]

Candide being expelled the terrestrial paradise, rambled a long while without knowing where, weeping, and lifting up his eyes to heaven, and sometimes turning them towards the finest of castles, which contained the handsomest of baronesses. He laid himself down, without his supper, in the open fields, between two furrows, while the snow fell in great flakes. Candide, almost frozen to death, crawled next morning to the neighboring village, which was called Waldber-ghoff-trarbk-dikdorff. Having no money, and almost dying with hunger and fatigue, he stopped in a dejected posture before the gate of an inn. Two men, dressed in blue,[7] observing him in such a situation, "Brother," says one of them to the other, "there is a young fellow well built, and of a proper height." They accosted Candide, and invited him very civilly to dinner.

"Gentlemen," replied Candide, with an agreeable modesty, "you do me much honor, but I have no money to pay my share."

"O sir," said one of the blues, "persons of your appearance and merit never pay anything; are you not five feet five inches high?"

"Yes, gentlemen, that is my height," returned he, making a bow.

"Come, sir, sit down at table; we will not only treat you, but we will never let such a man as you want money; men are made to assist one another."

"You are in the right," said Candide; "that is what Pangloss always told me, and I see plainly that everything is for the best."

They entreated him to take a few crowns, which he accepted, and would have given them his note; but they refused it, and sat down to table.

"Do not you tenderly love—"

"O yes," replied he, "I tenderly love Miss Cunegonde."

"No," said one of the gentlemen; "we ask you if you do tenderly love the King of the Bulgarians?"

"Not at all," said he, "for I never saw him."

---

[3]The tutor's name is (literally) "all-tongue."
[4]Note the French *nigaud* ("booby") included in the elaborate title of this pompous-sounding discipline.
[5]One of many allusions in *Candide* to the philosophic optimism systematized by Leibniz and popularized by Pope (see chapter 24).

[6]Voltaire's name for the troops of Frederick the Great, King of Prussia, who, like their king, were widely regarded as Sodomites; the association between the name and the French *bougre* ("to bugger") is patent.
[7]The color of the uniforms worn by the soldiers of Frederick the Great.

"How! he is the most charming of kings, and you must drink his health."

"O, with all my heart, gentlemen," and drinks.   **120**

"That is enough," said they to him; "you are now the bulwark, the support, the defender, the hero of the Bulgarians; your fortune is made, and you are certain of glory." Instantly they put him in irons, and carried him to the regiment. They made him turn to the right, to the left, draw the ramrod, return the ramrod, present, fire, step double; and they gave him thirty blows with a cudgel. The next day, he performed his exercises not quite so badly, and received but twenty blows; the third day the blows were restricted to ten, and he was looked upon by his fellow-soldiers, as a kind of prodigy.   **130**

Candide, quite stupefied, could not well conceive how he had become a hero. One fine Spring day he took it into his head to walk out, going straight forward, imagining that the human, as well as the animal species, were entitled to make whatever use they pleased of their limbs. He had not traveled two leagues, when four other heroes, six feet high, came up to him, bound him, and put him into a dungeon. He is asked by a Court-martial, whether he chooses to be whipped six and thirty times through the whole regiment, or receive at once twelve bullets through the forehead? He in vain argued that the will is free, and that **140** he chose neither the one nor the other; he was obliged to make a choice; he therefore resolved, in virtue of God's gift called *freewill*, to run the gauntlet six and thirty times. He underwent this discipline twice. The regiment being composed of two thousand men, he received four thousand lashes, which laid open all his muscles and nerves, from the nape of the neck to the back. As they were proceeding to a third course, Candide, being quite spent, begged as a favor that they would be so kind as to shoot him; he obtained his request; they hoodwinked him, and made him kneel; the King of the Bulgarians passing by, **150** inquired into the crime of the delinquent; and as this prince was a person of great penetration, he discovered from what he heard of Candide, that he was a young metaphysician, entirely ignorant of the things of this world; and he granted him his pardon, with a clemency which will be extolled in all histories, and throughout all ages. An experienced surgeon cured Candide in three weeks, with emollients prescribed by no less a master than Dioscorides.[8] His skin had already began to grow again, and he was able to walk, when the King of the Bulgarians gave battle to the King of the Abares.   **160**

Chapter 3

How Candide Made His Escape From the Bulgarians, and What Afterwards Befell Him

Nothing could be so fine, so neat, so brilliant, so well ordered, as the two armies.[9] The trumpets, fifes, hautboys, drums, and cannon, formed an harmony superior to what hell itself could invent. The cannon swept off at first about six thousand men on each side; afterwards, the musketry carried away from the best of worlds, about nine or ten thousand rascals that infected its surface. The bayonet was likewise the sufficient reason of the death of some thousands of men. The whole number might amount to about thirty thousand souls. Candide, who trembled like a philosopher, hid himself as well as he **170** could, during this heroic butchery.

At last, while each of the two kings were causing *Te Deum*—glory to God—to be sung in their respective camps, he resolved to go somewhere else, to reason upon the effects and causes. He walked over heaps of the dead and dying; he came at first to a neighboring village belonging to the Abares, but found it in ashes; for it had been burnt by the Bulgarians, according to the law of nations. Here were to be seen old men full of wounds, casting their eyes on their murdered wives, who were holding their infants to their bloody breasts. You might see in another **180** place, virgins outraged after they had satisfied the natural desires of some of those heroes, whilst breathing out their last sighs. Others, half-burnt, praying earnestly for instant death. The whole field was covered with brains, and with legs and arms lopped off.

Candide betook himself with all speed to another village. It belonged to the Bulgarians, and had met with the same treatment from the Abarian heroes. Candide, walking still forward over quivering limbs, or through rubbish of houses, got at last out of the theater of war, having some small quantity **190** of provisions in his knapsack, and never forgetting Miss Cunegonde. His provisions failed him when he arrived in Holland;[10] but having heard that every one was rich in that country, and that they were Christians, he did not doubt but he should be as well treated there as he had been in my Lord the Baron's castle, before he had been expelled thence on account of Miss Cunegonde's sparkling eyes.

He asked alms from several grave-looking persons, who all replied, that if he continued that trade, they would confine him in a house of correction, where he should learn to earn his **200** bread.

He applied afterwards to a man, who for a whole hour had been discoursing on the subject of charity, before a large assembly. This orator, looking at him askance, said to him:

"What are you doing here? are you for the good cause?"

"There is no effect without a cause," replied Candide, modestly; "all is necessarily linked, and ordered for the best. A necessity banished me from Miss Cunegonde; a necessity forced me to run the gauntlet; another necessity makes me beg my bread, till I can get into some business by which to earn it. **210** All this could not be otherwise."

"My friend," said the orator to him, "do you believe that the Anti-Christ is alive?"

"I never heard whether he is or not," replied Candide; "but whether he is, or is not, I want bread!"

"You do not deserve to eat any," said the other; "get you gone, you rogue; get you gone, you wretch; never in thy life come near me again!"

The orator's wife, having popped her head out of the chamber window, and seeing a man who doubted whether **220**

---

[8]A famous Greek physician of the first century C.E. whose book on medicine was for centuries a standard text.

[9]A mocking reference to the Seven Years' War (1756–1763) fought between the Prussians (Bulgars) and the French–Austrian coalition, to whom Voltaire gives the name Abares—a tribe of semicivilized Scythians.

[10]Holland, a mecca of religious freedom for over two centuries, had given asylum to the Anabaptists and other radical religious sects.

Anti-Christ was alive, poured on his head a full vessel of. . . . Oh heavens! to what excess does religious zeal transport the fair sex!

A man who had not been baptized, a good Anabaptist,[11] named *James*, saw the barbarous and ignominious manner with which they treated one of his brethren, a being with two feet, without feathers, and endowed with a rational soul.[12] He took him home with him, cleaned him, gave him bread and beer, made him a present of two florins,[13] and offered to teach him the method of working in his manufactories of Persian stuffs, which are fabricated in Holland. Candide, prostrating himself   230 almost to the ground, cried out, "Master Pangloss argued well when he said, that everything is for the best in this world; for I am infinitely more affected with your very great generosity, than by the hard-heartedness of that gentleman with the cloak, and the lady his wife."

Next day, as he was taking a walk, he met a beggar, all covered over with sores, his eyes half dead, the tip of his nose eaten off, his mouth turned to one side of his face, his teeth black, speaking through his throat, tormented with a violent cough, with gums so rotten, that his teeth came near falling   240 out every time he spit.

Chapter 4

How Candide Met His Old Master of Philosophy, Dr. Pangloss, and What Happened to Them

Candide, moved still more with compassion than with horror, gave this frightful mendicant the two florins which he had received of his honest Anabaptist James. The specter fixed his eyes attentively upon him, dropt some tears, and was going to fall upon his neck. Candide, affrighted, drew back.

"Alas!" said the one wretch to the other, "don't you know your dear Pangloss?"

"What do I hear! Is it you, my dear master! you in this dreadful condition! What misfortune has befallen you? Why   250 are you no longer in the most magnificent of castles? What has become of Miss Cunegonde, the nonpareil of the fair sex, the master-piece of nature?"

"I have no more strength," said Pangloss.

Candide immediately carried him to the Anabaptist's stable, where he gave him a little bread to eat. When Pangloss was refreshed a little, "Well," said Candide, "what has become of Cunegonde?"

"She is dead," replied the other.

Candide fainted away at this word; but his friend recovered   260 his senses, with a little bad vinegar which he found by chance in the stable.

Candide, opening his eyes, cried out, "Cunegonde is dead! Ah, best of worlds, where art thou now? But of what distemper did she die? Was not the cause, her seeing me driven out of the castle by my Lord, her father, with such hard kicks on the breech?"

"No," said Pangloss, "she was gutted by some Bulgarian soldiers, after having been barbarously ravished.[14] They knocked my Lord the Baron on the head, for attempting to protect her;   270 my Lady the Baroness was cut in pieces; my poor pupil was treated like his sister; and as for the castle, there is not one stone left upon another, nor a barn, nor a sheep, nor a duck, nor a tree. But we have been sufficiently revenged; for the Abarians have done the very same thing to a neighboring barony, which belonged to a Bulgarian Lord."

At this discourse, Candide fainted away a second time; but coming to himself, and having said all that he ought to say, he enquired into the cause and the effect, and into the sufficient reason that had reduced Pangloss to so deplorable a   280 condition. "Alas," said the other, "it was love; love, the comforter of the human race, the preserver of the universe, the soul of all sensible beings, tender love." "Alas!" said Candide, "I know this love, the sovereign of hearts, the soul of our soul; yet it never cost me more than a kiss, and twenty kicks. But how could this charming cause produce in you so abominable an effect?"

Pangloss made answer as follows: "Oh my dear Candide, you knew Paquetta, the pretty attendant on our noble Baroness; I tasted in her arms the delights of Paradise, which   290 produced those torments of hell with which you see me devoured. She was infected,[15] and perhaps she is dead. Paquetta received this present from a very learned Franciscan, who had it from an old countess, who received it from a captain of horse, who was indebted for it to a marchioness, who got it from one of the companions of Christopher Columbus. For my part, I shall give it to nobody, for I am dying."

"Oh Pangloss!" cried Candide, "what a strange genealogy! Was not the devil at the head of it?" "Not at all," replied the great man; "it was a thing indispensable; a necessary   300 ingredient in the best of worlds; for if Columbus had not caught, in an island of America, this disease, we should have had neither chocolate nor cochineal. It may also be observed, that to this day, upon our continent, this malady is as peculiar to us, as is religious controversy. The Turks, the Indians, the Persians, the Chinese, the Siamese, and the Japanese, know nothing of it yet. But there is sufficient reason why they, in their turn, should become acquainted with it, a few centuries hence. In the mean time, it has made marvellous progress among us, and especially in those great armies composed of honest hirelings, well   310 disciplined, who decide the fate of states; for we may rest assured, that when thirty thousand men in a pitched battle fight against troops equal to them in number, there are about twenty thousand of them on each side who have the pox.

"This is admirable," said Candide; "but you must be cured." "Ah! how can I?" said Pangloss; "I have not a penny, my friend; and throughout the whole extent of this globe, we cannot get any one to bleed us, or give us a glister, without paying for it, or getting some other person to pay for us."

---

[11]A Protestant sect (originating in Zürich in 1524) advocating the baptism of adult believers and the practice of simplicity, mutual help, the exercise of individual conscience, and the separation of Church and state.

[12]The minimalist definition of man ascribed to the philosopher Plato and used here to suggest James' sympathy with all humankind.

[13]Gold coins.

---

[14]Raped.

[15]With venereal disease; syphilis, which entered Europe in the late fifteenth century, was one of the most virulent legacies of the Euro–American exchange.

This last speech determined Candide. He went and threw himself at the feet of his charitable Anabaptist James, and gave him so touching a description of the state his friend was reduced to, that the good man did not hesitate to entertain Dr. Pangloss, and he had him cured at his own expense. During the cure, Pangloss lost only an eye and an ear. As he wrote well, and understood arithmetic perfectly, the Anabaptist made him his bookkeeper. At the end of two months, being obliged to go to Lisbon on account of his business, he took the two philosophers along with him, in his ship. Pangloss explained to him how every thing was such as it could not be better; but James was not of this opinion. "Mankind," said he, "must have somewhat corrupted their nature; for they were not born wolves, and yet they have become wolves; God has given them neither cannon of twenty-four pounds, nor bayonets; and yet they have made cannon and bayonets to destroy one another. I might throw into the account bankrupts; and the law which seizes on the effects of bankrupts only to bilk the creditors." "All this was indispensable," replied the one-eyed doctor, "and private misfortunes constitute the general good; so that the more private misfortunes there are, the whole is the better." While he was thus reasoning, the air grew dark, the winds blew from the four quarters of the world, and the ship was attacked by a dreadful storm, within sight of the harbor of Lisbon.

Chapter 5

Tempest, Shipwreck, Earthquake and What Became of Dr. Pangloss, Candide and James the Anabaptist

One half of the passengers being weakened, and ready to breathe their last, with the inconceivable anguish which the rolling of the ship conveyed through the nerves and all the humors of the body, which were quite disordered, were not capable of being alarmed at the danger they were in. The other half uttered cries and made prayers; the sails were rent, the masts broken, and the ship became leaky. Every one worked that was able, nobody cared for any thing, and no order was kept. The Anabaptist contributed his assistance to work the ship. As he was upon deck, a furious sailor rudely struck him, and laid him sprawling on the planks; but with the blow he gave him, he himself was so violently jolted, that he tumbled overboard with his head foremost, and remained suspended by a piece of broken mast. Honest James ran to his assistance, and helped him on deck again; but in the attempt, he fell into the sea, in the sight of the sailor, who suffered him to perish, without deigning to look upon him. Candide drew near and saw his benefactor, one moment emerging, and the next swallowed up for ever. He was just going to throw himself into the sea after him, when the philosopher Pangloss hindered him, by demonstrating to him, that the road to Lisbon had been made on purpose for this Anabaptist to be drowned in. While he was proving this, *a priori*, the vessel foundered, and all perished except Pangloss, Candide, and the brutal sailor, who drowned the virtuous Anabaptist. The villain luckily swam ashore, whither Pangloss and Candide were carried on a plank.

When they had recovered themselves a little, they walked towards Lisbon. They had some money left, with which they hoped to save themselves from hunger, after having escaped from the storm.

Scarce had they set foot in the city, bewailing the death of their benefactor, when they perceived the earth to tremble under their feet,[16] and saw the sea swell in the harbor, and dash to pieces the ships that were at anchor. The whirling flames and ashes covered the streets and public places, the houses tottered, and their roofs fell to the foundations, and the foundations were scattered; thirty thousand inhabitants of all ages and sexes were crushed to death in the ruins. The sailor, whistling and swearing, said "There is some booty to be got here." "What can be the sufficient reason of this phenomenon?" said Pangloss. "This is certainly the last day of the world," cried Candide. The sailor ran quickly into the midst of the ruins, encountered death to find money, found it, laid hold of it, got drunk, and having slept himself sober, purchased the favors of the first willing girl he met with, among the ruins of the demolished houses, and in the midst of the dying and the dead. While he was thus engaged, Pangloss pulled him by the sleeve; "My friend," said he, "this is not right; you trespass against universal reason, you choose your time badly." "Brains and blood!" answered the other; "I am a sailor, and was born at Batavia; . . . you have found the right man, this time, with your universal reason."

Some pieces of stone having wounded Candide, he lay sprawling in the street, and covered with rubbish. "Alas!" said he to Pangloss, "get me a little wine and oil; I am dying." "This trembling of the earth is no new thing," answered Pangloss. "The City of Lima, in America, experienced the same concussions last year; the same cause has the same effects; there is certainly a train of sulphur under the earth, from Lima to Lisbon." "Nothing is more probable," said Candide; "but, for God's sake, a little oil and wine." "How probable?" replied the philosopher; "I maintain that the thing is demonstrable." Candide lost all sense, and Pangloss brought him a little water from a neighboring fountain.

The day following, having found some provisions, in rummaging through the rubbish, they recruited their strength a little. Afterwards, they employed themselves like others, in administering relief to the inhabitants that had escaped from death. Some citizens that had been relieved by them, gave them as good a dinner as could be expected amidst such a disaster. It is true that the repast was mournful, and the guests watered their bread with their tears. But Pangloss consoled them by the assurance that things could not be otherwise; "For," said he, "all this must necessarily be for the best. As this volcano is at Lisbon, it could not be elsewhere; as it is impossible that things should not be what they are, as all is good."

A little man clad in black, who belonged to the Inquisition,[17] and sat at his side, took him up very politely, and said: "It seems, sir, you do not believe in original sin; for if all is for the best, then there has been neither fall nor punishment."

"I most humbly ask your excellency's pardon," answered Pangloss, still more politely; "for the fall of man and the curse necessarily entered into the best of worlds possible." "Then, sir, you do not believe there is liberty," said the inquisitor.

---

[16] The first Lisbon earthquake and fire took place on November 1, 1755. It destroyed much of the city and took over 20,000 lives.

[17] An officer of the Inquisition, a special church court designed to try heretics; the officer was empowered to arrest anyone he suspected of heresy.

"Your Excellency will excuse me," said Pangloss; "liberty can consist with absolute necessity; for it was necessary we should be free; because, in short, the determinate will—" **430**

Pangloss was in the middle of his proposition, when the inquisitor made a signal with his head to the tall armed footman in a cloak, who waited upon him, to bring him a glass of port wine.

Chapter 6

How a Fine *Auto-da-Fé*[18] Was Celebrated to Prevent Earthquakes, and How Candide Was Whipped

After the earthquake, which had destroyed three-fourths of Lisbon, the sages of the country could not find any means more effectual to prevent a total destruction, than to give the people a splendid *auto-da-fé*. It had been decided by the university of Coimbra, that the spectacle of some persons burnt to death by a slow fire, with great ceremony, was an infallible antidote for earthquakes.

In consequence of this resolution, they had seized a **440** Biscayan, convicted of having married his godmother,[19] and two Portuguese, who, in eating a pullet, had stripped off the bacon.[20] After dinner, they came and secured Dr. Pangloss, and his disciple Candide; the one for having spoke too freely, and the other for having heard with an air of approbation. They were both conducted to separate apartments, extremely damp, and never incommoded with the sun.[21] Eight days after, they were both clothed with a gown[22] and had their heads adorned with paper crowns. Candide's crown and gown were painted with inverted flames, and with devils that had neither tails nor **450** claws; but Pangloss' devils had claws and tails, and the flames were pointed upwards. Being thus dressed, they marched in procession, and heard a very pathetic speech followed by fine music on a squeaking organ. Candide was whipped on the back in cadence, while they were singing; the Biscayan, and the two men who would not eat lard, were burnt; and Pangloss, though it was contrary to custom, was hanged. The same day, the earth shook anew,[23] with a most dreadful noise.

Candide, affrighted, interdicted, astonished, all bloody, all panting, said to himself: "If this is the best of possible worlds, **460** what then are the rest? Supposing I had not been whipped now, I have been so, among the Bulgarians; but, Oh, my dear Pangloss; thou greatest of philosophers, that it should be my fate to see thee hanged without knowing for what! Oh! my dear Anabaptist! thou best of men, that it should be thy fate to be drowned in the harbor! Oh! Miss Cunegonde! the jewel of ladies, that it should be thy fate to have been outraged and slain!"

He returned, with difficulty, supporting himself, after being lectured, whipped, absolved, and blessed, when an old woman accosted him, and said: "Child, take courage, and follow me." **470**

---

[18]The public ceremony (literally, "act of faith") by which those found guilty of heresy were punished.

[19]A swipe at papal efforts to condemn as incestuous marriages in which the parties might be bound by family relation.

[20]Unwittingly revealing that they were secretly Jews—Jewish dietary laws prohibit the eating of pork. Under the pressure of the Spanish and Portuguese Inquisitions, many Iberian Jews had converted to Christianity.

[21]Prison cells.

[22]Yellow penitential garments worn by the confessed heretic.

[23]A second earthquake occurred in Lisbon on December 21, 1755.

Chapter 7

How an Old Woman Took Care of Candide, and How He Found the Object He Loved

Candide did not take courage, but he followed the old woman to a ruinated house. She gave him a pot of pomatum[24] to anoint himself, left him something to eat and drink, and showed him a very neat little bed, near which was a complete suit of clothes. "Eat, drink, and sleep," said she to him, "and may God take care of you. I will be back to-morrow." Candide, astonished at all he had seen, at all he had suffered, and still more at the charity of the old woman, offered to kiss her hand. "You must not kiss my hand," said the old woman, "I will be back to-morrow. Rub yourself with the pomatum, eat and take rest." **480**

Candide, notwithstanding so many misfortunes, ate, and went to sleep. Next morning, the old woman brought him his breakfast, looked at his back, and rubbed it herself with another ointment; she afterwards brought him his dinner; and she returned at night, and brought him his supper. The day following she performed the same ceremonies. "Who are you," would Candide always say to her; "Who has inspired you with so much goodness? What thanks can I render you?" The good woman made no answer; she returned in the evening, but brought him no supper. "Come along with me," said she, "and say not a **490** word." She took him by the arm, and walked with him into the country about a quarter of a mile; they arrived at a house that stood by itself, surrounded with gardens and canals. The old woman knocked at a little door, which being opened, she conducted Candide by a private stair-case into a gilded closet, and leaving him on a brocade couch, shut the door and went her way. Candide thought he was in a revery, and looked upon all his life as an unlucky dream, but at the present moment, a very agreeable vision.

The old woman returned very soon, supporting with **500** difficulty a woman trembling, of a majestic port, glittering with jewels, and covered with a veil. "Take off that veil," said the old woman to Candide. The young man approached and took off the veil with a trembling hand. What joy! what surprise! he thought he saw Miss Cunegonde; he saw her indeed! it was she herself. His strength failed him, he could not utter a word, but fell down at her feet. Cunegonde fell upon the carpet. The old woman applied aromatic waters; they recovered their senses, and spoke to one another. At first, their words were broken, their questions and answers crossed each other, **510** amidst sighs, tears and cries. The old woman recommended them to make less noise, and then left them to themselves. "How! is it you?" said Candide; "are you still alive? do I find you again in Portugal? You were not ravished then, nor disemboweled, as the philosopher Pangloss assured me?" "Yes, all this was so," said the lovely Cunegonde; "but death does not always follow from these two accidents." "But your father and mother! were they not killed?" "It is but too true," answered Cunegonde, weeping. "And your brother?" "My brother was killed too." "And why are you in Portugal? and how did you know that I **520** was here? and by what strange adventure did you contrive to bring me to this house?" "I will tell you all that, presently," replied the lady; "but first you must inform me of all that has

---

[24]Ointment.

happened to you, since the harmless kiss you gave me, and the rude kicking which you received for it."

Candide obeyed her with the most profound respect; and though he was forbidden to speak, though his voice was weak and faltering, and though his back still pained him, yet he related to her, in the most artless manner, every thing that had befallen him since the moment of their separation. Cunegonde lifted up her eyes to heaven; she shed tears at the death of the good Anabaptist, and of Pangloss; after which she thus related her adventures to Candide, who lost not a word, but looked on her, as if he would devour her with his eyes.

Chapter 8

The History of Cunegonde

"I was in my bed and fast asleep, when it pleased heaven to send the Bulgarians to our fine castle of Thunder-ten-tronckh; they murdered my father and my brother, and cut my mother to pieces. A huge Bulgarian, six feet high, perceiving the horrible sight had deprived me of my senses, set himself to ravish me. This abuse made me come to myself; I recovered my senses, I cried, I struggled, I bit, I scratched, I wanted to tear out the huge Bulgarian's eyes, not considering that what had happened in my father's castle, was a common thing in war. The brute gave me a cut with his knife, the mark of which I still bear about me." "Ah! I anxiously wish to see it," said the simple Candide. "You shall," answered Cunegonde; "but let me finish my story." "Do so," replied Candide.

She then resumed the thread of her story, as follows: "A Bulgarian captain came in, and saw me bleeding; but the soldier was not at all disconcerted. The Captain flew into a passion at the little respect the brute showed him, and killed him upon my body. He then caused me to be dressed, and carried me as a prisoner of war to his own quarters. I washed the scanty linen he had, and cooked his meals. He found me very pretty, I must say it; and I cannot deny but he was well shaped, and that he had a white, soft skin; but for the rest, he had little sense or philosophy; one could plainly see that he was not bred under Dr. Pangloss. At the end of three months, having lost all his money, and being grown out of conceit with me, he sold me to a Jew, named *Don Issachar*, who traded to Holland and Portugal, and had a most violent passion for women. This Jew laid close siege to my person, but could not triumph over me; I have resisted him better than I did the Bulgarian soldier. A woman of honor may be ravished once, but her virtue gathers strength from such rudeness. The Jew, in order to render me more tractable, brought me to this country-house that you see. I always imagined hitherto, that no place on earth was so fine as the castle of Thunder-ten-tronckh; but I am now undeceived.

"The grand inquisitor observing me one day ogled me very strongly, and sent me a note, saying he wanted to speak with me upon private business. Being conducted to his palace, I informed him of my birth; upon which he represented to me, how much it was below my family to belong to an Israelite. A proposal was then made by him to Don Issachar, to yield me up to my Lord. But Don Issachar, who is the court-banker, and a man of credit, would not come into his measures. The inquisitor threatened him. At last, my Jew, being affrighted,

concluded a bargain, by which the house and myself should belong to them both in common; the Jew to have possession Monday, Friday, and Saturday, and the inquisitor, the other days of the week. This agreement has now continued six months. It has not, however, been without quarrels; for it has been often disputed whether Saturday night or Sunday belonged to the old, or to the new law. For my part, I have hitherto disagreed with them both; and I believe that this is the reason I am still beloved by them.

"At length, to avert the scourge of earthquakes and to intimidate Don Issachar, it pleased his Lordship the inquisitor to celebrate. He did me the honor to invite me to it. I got a very fine seat, and the ladies were served with refreshments between the ceremonies. I was seized with horror at seeing them burn the two Jews, and the honest Biscayan who married his godmother; but how great was my surprise, my consternation, my anguish, when I saw in a sanbenito and mitre, a person that somewhat resembled Pangloss! I rubbed my eyes, I looked upon him very attentively, and I saw him hanged. I fell into a swoon, and scarce had I recovered my senses, when I saw you stripped stark naked; this was the height of horror, consternation, grief, and despair. I will frankly own to you, that your skin is still whiter, and of a better complexion than that of my Bulgarian captain. This sight increased all the sensations that oppressed and distracted my soul. I cried out, I was going to say stop, barbarians; but my voice failed me, and all my cries would have been to no purpose. When you had been severely whipped: How is it possible, said I, that the amiable Candide, and the sage Pangloss, should both be at Lisbon;—the one to receive a hundred lashes and the other to be hanged by order of my Lord the Inquisitor, by whom I am so greatly beloved? Pangloss certainly deceived me most cruelly, when he said that everything was for the best in this world.

"Agitated, astonished, sometimes beside myself, and sometimes ready to die with weakness; my head filled with the massacre of my father, my mother, and my brother, the insolence of the vile Bulgarian soldier, the stab he gave me with his hanger, my abject servitude, and my acting as a cook to the Bulgarian captain; the rascal Don Issachar, my abominable inquisitor; the execution of Dr. Pangloss, the grand music on the organ while you were whipped, and especially the kiss I gave you behind the screen, the last day I saw you. I praised the Lord for having restored you to me after so many trials. I charged my old woman to take care of you, and to bring you hither as soon as she could. She has executed her commission very well; I have tasted the inexpressible pleasure of seeing you, hearing you, and speaking to you. You must have a ravenous appetite, by this time; I am hungry myself, too; let us, therefore, sit down to supper."

On this, they both sat down to table; and after supper, they seated themselves on the fine couch before mentioned. They were there, then Signor Don Issachar, one of the masters of the house, came in. It was his Sabbath day, and he came to enjoy his right, and to express his tender love.

[Candide, Cunegonde, and the old woman travel to Cadiz. The old woman recounts her past misfortunes. They sail to America, where Candide finds a South American paradise, El Dorado,

filled with kind and reasonable people; however, he loses Cunegonde to a Spanish colonial nobleman. On his way back to Europe, Candide meets the disillusioned pessimist, Martin, who opens Candide's eyes to the evil in the world. Following various adventures in Europe, Candide travels to Turkey and encounters Pangloss, whom he had thought dead.]

Chapter 29

How Candide Found Cunegonde and the Old Woman Again

While Candide, the Baron, Pangloss, Martin, and Cacambo were relating their adventures to each other, and disputing about the contigent and non-contigent events of this world, and while they were arguing upon effects and causes, on moral and physical evil, on liberty and necessity, and on the consolations a person may experience in the galleys in Turkey, they arrived on the banks of the Propontis, at the house of the 640 Prince of Transylvania. The first objects which presented themselves were Cunegonde and the old woman, hanging out some table-linen on the line to dry.

The Baron grew pale at this sight. Even Candide, the affectionate lover, on seeing his fair Cunegonde awfully tanned, with her eye-lids reversed, her neck withered, her cheeks wrinkled, her arms red and rough, was seized with horror, jumped near three yards backwards, but afterwards advanced to her, but with more politeness than passion. She embraced Candide and her brother, who, each of them, 650 embraced the old woman, and Candide ransomed them both.

There was a little farm in the neighborhood, which the old woman advised Candide to hire, till they could meet with better accommodations for their whole company. As Cunegonde did not know that she had grown ugly, nobody having told her of it, she put Candide in mind of his promise to marry her, in so peremptory a manner, that he durst not refuse her. But when this thing was intimated to the Baron, "I will never suffer," said he, "such meanness on her part, nor such insolence on yours. With this infamy I will never be 660 reproached. The children of my sister shall never be enrolled in the chapters[25] of Germany. No; my sister shall never marry any but a Baron of the empire." Cunegonde threw herself at her brother's feet, and bathed them with her tears, but he remained inflexible. "You ungrateful puppy, you," said Candide to him, "I have delivered you from the galleys; I have paid your ransom; I have also paid that of your sister, who was a scullion here, and is very homely; I have the goodness, however, to make her my wife, and you are fool enough to oppose it; I have a good mind to kill you again, you make me so angry." "You 670 may indeed kill me again," said the Baron; "but you shall never marry my sister, while I have breath."

Chapter 30

Conclusion

Candide had no great desire, at the bottom of his heart, to marry Cunegonde. But the extreme impertinence of the Baron determined him to conclude the match, and Cunegonde pressed it so earnestly, that he could not retract. He advised with

Pangloss, Martin, and the trusty Cacambo. Pangloss drew up an excellent memoir, in which he proved, that the Baron had no right over his sister, and that she might, according to all the laws of the empire, espouse Candide with her left hand.[26] 640 Martin was for throwing the Baron into the sea: Cacambo was of opinion that it would be best to send him back again to the Levant captain, and make him work at the galleys. This advice was thought good; the old woman approved it, and nothing was said to his sister about it. The scheme was put in execution for a little money, and so they had the pleasure of punishing the pride of a German Baron.

It is natural to imagine that Candide, after so many disasters, married to his sweetheart, living with the philosopher Pangloss, the philosopher Martin, the discreet Cacambo, and the old 690 woman, and especially as he had brought so many diamonds from the country of the ancient Incas, must live the most agreeable life of any man in the whole world. But he had been so cheated by the Jews,[27] that he had nothing left but the small farm; and his wife, growing still more ugly, turned peevish and insupportable. The old woman was very infirm, and worse humored than Cunegonde herself. Cacambo, who worked in the garden, and went to Constantinople to sell its productions, was worn out with labor, and cursed his fate. Pangloss was ready to despair, because he did not shine at the head of some 700 university in Germany. As for Martin, as he was firmly persuaded that all was equally bad throughout, he bore things with patience. Candide, Martin, and Pangloss disputed sometimes about metaphysics and ethics. They often saw passing under the windows of the farmhouse boats full of effendis, bashaws, and cadis,[28] who were going into banishment to Lemnos, Mitylene, and Erzerum. They observed that other cadis, other bashaws, and other effendis succeeded in the posts of those who were exiled, only to be banished themselves in turn. They saw heads nicely impaled, to be 710 presented to the Sublime Porte. These spectacles increased the number of their disputations; and when they were not disputing, their *ennui* was so tiresome that the old woman would often say to them, "I want to know which is the worst;—to be ravished an hundred times by negro pirates, to run the gauntlet among the Bulgarians, to be whipped and hanged, to be dissected, to row in the galleys; in a word, to have suffered all the miseries we have undergone, or to stay here, without doing anything?" "That is a great question," said Candide. 720

This discourse gave rise to new reflections, and Martin concluded upon the whole, that mankind were born to live either in the distractions of inquietude, or in the lethargy of disgust. Candide did not agree with that opinion, but remained in a state of suspense. Pangloss confessed, that he had always suffered dreadfully; but having once maintained that all things went wonderfully well, he still kept firm to his hypothesis, though it was quite opposed to his real feelings.

What contributed to confirm Martin in his shocking principles, to make Candide stagger more than ever, and to 730

———

[25]Noble assemblies.

———

[26]A marriage that denies noble status to the party of the lower rank.
[27]Voltaire's anti-Semitism seems to have been the result of financial losses he suffered from the bankruptcies of Jewish moneylenders.
[28]Highranking members of the Turkish nobility.

embarrass Pangloss, was, that one day they saw Paquetta and Girofflee, who were in the greatest distress, at their farm. They had quickly squandered away their three thousand piastres,[29] had parted, were reconciled, quarrelled again, had been confined in prison, had made their escape, and Girofflee had at length turned Turk. Paquetta continued her trade wherever she went, but made nothing by it. "I could easily foresee," said Martin to Candide, "that your presents would soon be squandered away, and would render them more miserable. You and Cacambo have spent millions of piastres, and are not a bit happier than Girofflee and Paquetta." "Ha! ha!" said Pangloss to Paquetta, "has Providence then brought you amongst us again, my poor child? Know, then, that you have cost me the tip of my nose, one eye, and one of my ears, as you see. What a world this is!" This new adventure set them a philosophizing more than ever.

There lived in the neighborhood a very famous dervish, who passed for the greatest philosopher in Turkey. They went to consult him. Pangloss was chosen speaker, and said to him, "Master, we are come to desire you would tell us, why so strange an animal as man was created."

"What's that to you?" said the dervish; "is it any business of yours?" "But, my reverend father," said Candide, "there is a horrible amount of evil in the world." "What does it matter," said the dervish, "whether there be good or evil? When his Sublime Highness sends a vessel to Egypt, does it trouble him, whether the mice on board are at their ease or not?" "What would you have one do then?" said Pangloss. "Hold your tongue," said the dervish. "I promised myself the pleasure," said Pangloss, "of reasoning with you upon effects and causes, the best of possible worlds, the origin of evil, the nature of the soul, and the pre-established harmony."—The dervish, at these words, shut the door in their faces.

During this conference, news was brought that two viziers and a mufti were strangled at Constantinople, and a great many of their friends impaled. This catastrophe made a great noise for several hours. Pangloss, Candide, and Martin, on their way back to the little farm, met a good-looking old man, taking the air at his door, under an arbor of orange trees. Pangloss, who had as much curiosity as philosophy, asked him the name of the mufti who was lately strangled. "I know nothing at all about it," said the good man; "and what's more, I never knew the name of a single mufti, or a single vizier, in my life. I am an entire stranger to the story you mention; and presume that, generally speaking, they who trouble their heads with state affairs, sometimes die shocking deaths, not without deserving it. But I never trouble my head about what is doing at Constantinople; I content myself with sending my fruits thither, the produce of my garden, which I cultivate with my own hands!" Having said these words, he introduced the strangers into his house. His two daughters and two sons served them with several kinds of sherbet, which they made themselves, besides caymac, enriched with the peels of candied citrons, oranges, lemons, bananas, pistachio nuts, and Mocha coffee, unadulterated with the bad coffee of Batavia and the isles. After which, the two daughters of this good Muslim perfumed the beards of Candide, Pangloss, and Martin.

"You must certainly," said Candide to the Turk, "have a very large and very opulent estate!" "I have only twenty acres," said the Turk; "which I, with my children, cultivate. Labor keeps us free from three of the greatest evils; boredom, vice, and need."

As Candide returned to his farm, he made deep reflections on the discourse of the Turk. Said he to Pangloss and Martin, "The condition of this good old man seems to me preferable to that of the six kings with whom we had the honor to dine." "The grandeurs of royalty," said Pangloss, "are very precarious, in the opinion of all philosophers. For, in short, Eglon, king of the Moabites, was assassinated by Ehud; Absalom was hung by the hair of his head, and pierced through with three darts; King Nadab, the son of Jeroboam, was killed by Baasha; King Elah by Zimri; Ahaziah by Jehu; Athaliah by Jehoiadah; the kings Joachim, Jechonias, and Zedekias, were carried into captivity. You know the fates of Croesus, Astyages, Darius, Dionysius of Syracuse, Pyrrhus, Perseus, Hannibal, Jugurtha, Ariovistus, Caesar, Pompey, Nero, Otho, Vitellius, Domitian, Richard II, Edward II, Henry VI, Richard III, Mary Stuart, Charles I of England, the three Henrys of France, and the Emperor Henry IV.[30] You know—" "I know very well," said Candide, "that we ought to look after our garden." "You are in the right," said Pangloss, "for when man was placed in the garden of Eden, he was placed there, *ut operatur cum*, to cultivate it; which proves that mankind are not created to be idle." "Let us work," said Martin, "without disputing; it is the only way to render life supportable."

All their little society entered into this laudable design, according to their different abilities. Their little piece of ground produced a plentiful crop. Cunegonde was indeed very homely, but she became an excellent pastry cook. Paquetta worked at embroidery, and the old woman took care of the linen. There was no idle person in the company, not excepting even Girofflee; he made a very good carpenter, and became a very honest man.

As to Pangloss, he evidently had a lurking consciousness that his theory required unceasing exertions, and all his ingenuity, to sustain it. Yet he stuck to it to the last; his thinking and talking faculties could hardly be diverted from it for a moment. He seized every occasion to say to Candide, "All the events in this best of possible worlds are admirably connected. If a single link in the great chain were omitted, the harmony of the entire universe would be destroyed. If you had not been expelled from that beautiful castle, with those cruel kicks, for your love to Miss Cunegonde; if you had not been imprisoned by the inquisition; if you had not traveled over a great portion of America on foot; if you had not plunged your sword through the baron; if you had not lost all the sheep you brought from that fine country, Eldorado, together with the riches with which they were laden, you would not be here to-day, eating preserved citrons, and pistachio nuts."

"That's very well said, and may all be true," said Candide; "but let's cultivate our garden."

Q What attitudes, beliefs, and institutions does Voltaire attack in *Candide*?

Q How does Voltaire's *Candide* "reply" to Pope's *Essay on Man*?

---

[29]Spanish dollars; piece of eight

[30]All rulers who came to a bad end.

Satire in Chinese Literature

While literary satire drew enthusiastic audiences in the West, this genre also came into vogue elsewhere in the world. Following the Manchu conquest of China in the mid-seventeenth century, Chinese writers produced bitter fictional tales that satirized a wide variety of contemporary practices, including Buddhist rituals, commercial banditry, and homosexual unions. One of the cruelest satires of the eighteenth century consisted of a collection of stories attacking the absurdities of the examination system by which talented individuals were brought into China's civil service. *The Scholars*, as the novel is titled, written around 1750 by Wu Jingzi (1701–1754), reflects Wu's own failure to pass the highly competitive exams, which often brought pseudo-scholars to positions of great wealth and political power in China. The satire emphasized the unpopular and anti-Confucian truth that the morally unscrupulous often gain great prizes in the world, while the virtuous do not always flourish.

Chinese satire was also effective in attacking some of the more socially inhibiting practices of traditional Chinese culture, such as female footbinding. Beginning in the eleventh century, upper-class Chinese parents bound the feet of their young daughters (thus breaking the arch and stunting the feet to half the normal size) in order to exempt them from common labor, hence make them more physically attractive as marriage partners to wealthy men. Toward the end of the great age of Chinese prose fiction, the philologist Li Ruzhen (1763–1830) attacked this practice in a satire entitled *Flowers in the Mirror*. An adventure tale similar to *Gulliver's Travels* or *Candide*, *Flowers* is a series of loosely woven stories that recount the experiences of a voyager to many strange lands, including the Country of Two-Faced People, the Country of Long-Armed People, and the Country of Women. In the last of these fictional lands, the traditional roles of the sexes are reversed, and the ruling women of the country set upon the hero to prepare him as "royal concubine": they plait his hair, apply lipstick and powder to his face, pierce his ears, and, to his ultimate dismay, they bind his feet in the traditional Chinese manner. Li Ruzhen's blunt social criticism and his bold assertion of equal rights for women fell on deaf ears, for despite the fact that Manchu rulers censured footbinding, the custom continued in many parts of China until the early twentieth century.

READING 4.26 From Li Ruzhen's *Flowers in the Mirror* (1828)

When Tang Ao heard that they had arrived at the Country of Women, he thought that the country was populated entirely by women, and was afraid to go ashore. But Old Tuo said, "Not at all! There are men as well as women, only they call men women, and women men. The men wear the skirts and take care of the home, while the women wear hats and trousers and manage affairs outside. If it were a country populated solely by women, I doubt that even Brother Lin here would dare

to venture ashore, although he knows he always makes a good profit from sales here!"

"If the men dress like women, do they use cosmetics and bind their feet?" asked Tang Ao.

"Of course they do!" cried Lin, and took from his pocket a list of the merchandise he was going to sell, which consisted of huge quantities of rouge, face powder, combs and other women's notions. "Luckily I wasn't born in this country," he said. "Catch me mincing around on bound feet!"

When Tang Ao asked why he had not put down the price of the merchandise, Lin said, "The people here, no matter rich or poor, from the 'King' down to the simplest peasant, are all mad about cosmetics. I'll charge them what I can. I shall have no difficulty selling the whole consignment to rich families in two or three days."

Beaming at the prospect of making a good profit, Lin went on shore with his list.

Tang Ao and Old Tuo decided to go and see the city. The people walking on the streets were small of stature, and rather slim, and although dressed in men's clothes, were beardless and spoke with women's voices, and walked with willowy steps.

"Look at them!" said Old Tuo. "They are perfectly normal-looking women. Isn't it a shame for them to dress like men?"

"Wait a minute," said Tang Ao. "Maybe when they see us, they think, 'Look at them, isn't it a shame that they dress like women'?"

"You're right. 'Whatever one is accustomed to always seems natural,' as the ancients say. But I wonder what the men are like?"

[Invited to sell his wares at the court of the "King," Lin visits the Palace.]

In a little time, Merchant Lin was ushered to a room upstairs where victuals of many kinds awaited him. As he ate, however, he heard a great deal of noise downstairs. Several palace "maids" ran upstairs soon, and calling him "Your Highness," kowtowed to him and congratulated him. Before he knew what was happening, Merchant Lin was being stripped completely bare by the maids and led to a perfumed bath. Against the powerful arms of these maids, he could scarcely struggle. Soon he found himself being anointed, perfumed, powdered and rouged, and dressed in a skirt. His big feet were bound up in strips of cloth and socks, and his hair was combed into an elaborate braid over his head and decorated with pins. These male "maids" thrust bracelets on his arms and rings on his fingers, and put a phoenix headdress on his head. They tied a jade green sash around his waist and put an embroidered cape around his shoulders.

Then they led him to a bed, and asked him to sit down.

Merchant Lin thought that he must be drunk, or dreaming, and began to tremble. He asked the maids what was happening, and was told that he had been chosen by the "King" to be the Imperial Consort, and that a propitious day would be chosen for him to enter the "King's" chambers.

Before he could utter a word, another group of maids, all tall and strong and wearing beards, came in. One was holding a threaded needle. "We are ordered to pierce your ears," he said, as the other four "maids" grabbed Lin by the arms and

Line markers: 10, 20, 30, 40, 50, 60, 1

legs. The white-bearded one seized Lin's right ear, and after rubbing the lobe a little, drove the needle through it.

"Ooh!" Merchant Lin screamed.

The maid seized the other ear, and likewise drove the needle through it. As Lin screamed with pain, powdered lead was smeared on his earlobes and a pair of "eight-precious" earrings was hung from the holes. 70

Having finished what they came to do, the maids retreated, and a black-bearded fellow came in with a bolt of white silk. Kneeling down before him, the fellow said, "I am ordered to bind Your Highness's feet."

Two other maids seized Lin's feet as the black-bearded one sat down on a low stool, and began to rip the silk into ribbons. Seizing Lin's right foot, he set it upon his knee, and sprinkled white alum powder between the toes and the grooves of the foot. He squeezed the toes tightly together, bent them down 80 so that the whole foot was shaped like an arch, and took a length of white silk and bound it tightly around it twice. One of the others sewed the ribbon together in small stitches. Again the silk went around the foot, and again, it was sewn up.

Merchant Lin felt as though his feet were burning, and wave after wave of pain rose to his heart. When he could stand it no longer, he let out his voice and began to cry. The "maids" had hastily made a pair of soft-soled red shoes, and these they put on both his feet.

"Please, kind brothers, go and tell Her Majesty that I'm a 90 married man," Lin begged. "How can I become her Consort? As for my feet, please liberate them. They have enjoyed the kind of freedom which scholars who are not interested in official careers enjoy! How can you bind them? Please tell your 'King' to let me go. I shall be grateful, and my wife will be very grateful."

But the maids said, "The King said that you are to enter his chambers as soon as your feet are bound. It is no time for talk of this kind."

When it was dark, a table was laid for him with mountains 100 of meat and oceans of wine. But Merchant Lin only nibbled, and told the "maids" they could have the rest.

Still sitting on the bed, and with his feet aching terribly, he decided to lie down in his clothes for a rest.

At once a middle-aged "maid" came up to him and said, "Please, will you wash before you retire?"

No sooner was this said than a succession of maids came in with candles, basins of water and spittoon, dressing table, boxes of ointment, face powder, towels, silk handkerchiefs, and surrounded him. Lin had to submit to the motions of 110 washing in front of them all. But after he had washed his face, a maid wanted to put some cream on it again.

Merchant Lin stoutly refused.

"But night time is the best time to treat the skin," the white-bearded maid said. "This powder has a lot of musk in it. It will make your skin fragrant, although I dare say it is fair enough already. If you use it regularly your skin will not only seem like white jade, but will give off a natural fragrance of its own. And the more fragrant it is, the fairer it will become, and the more lovely to behold, and the more lovable you will be. You'll see 120 how good it is after you have used it regularly."

But Lin refused firmly, and the maids said, "If you are so stubborn, we will have to report this, and let Matron deal with you tomorrow."

Then they left him alone. But Lin's feet hurt so much that he could not sleep a wink. He tore at the ribbons with all his might, and after a great struggle succeeded in tearing them off. He stretched out his ten toes again, and luxuriating in their exquisite freedom, finally fell asleep.

The next morning, however, when the black-bearded maid 130 discovered that he had torn off his foot-bandages, he immediately reported it to the "King," who ordered that Lin should be punished by receiving twenty strokes of the bamboo from the "Matron." Accordingly, a white-bearded "Matron" came in with a stick of bamboo about eight feet long, and when the others had stripped him and held him down, raised the stick and began to strike Lin's bottom and legs.

Before five strokes had been delivered, Lin's tender skin was bleeding, and the Matron did not have the heart to go on. "Look at her skin! Have you ever seen such white and tender 140 and lovable skin? Why, I think indeed her looks are comparable to Pan An and Sung Yu!" the Matron thought to himself. "But what am I doing, comparing her bottom and not her face to them? Is that a compliment?"

The foot-binding maid came and asked Lin if he would behave from now on.

"Yes, I'll behave," Lin replied, and they stopped beating him. They wiped the blood from his wounds, and special ointment was sent by the "King" and ginseng soup was given him to drink. 150

Merchant Lin drank the soup, and fell on the bed for a rest. But the "King" had given orders that his feet must be bound again, and that he should be taught to walk on them. So with one maid supporting him on each side, Merchant Lin was marched up and down the room all day on his bound feet. When he lay down to sleep that night, he could not close his eyes for the excruciating pain.

But from now on, he was never left alone again. Maids took turns to sit with him. Merchant Lin knew that he was no longer in command of his destiny. . . . 160

 Q What indignities are described in this satire?

Q What broader issues are suggested by the motif of role reversal?

The Visual Satires of William Hogarth

 The visual counterpart of literary satire is found in the paintings and prints of the English artist William Hogarth (1697–1764). A master draftsman, Hogarth produced a telling visual record of the ills of eighteenth-century British society. He illustrated the novels of Defoe and Swift, including *Gulliver's Travels*, and executed a series of paintings based on John Gay's *Beggar's Opera*—a mock-heroic comedy that equated low-class crime with high-class corruption. Popular novels and plays provided inspiration for what Hogarth called his "modern moral subjects"; while the theater itself prompted many of the devices he used for pictorial representation: boxlike staging, lighting from below, and a wealth of

"props." "I have endeavored," he wrote, "to treat my subjects as a dramatic writer: my picture is my stage, and men and women my actors."

Hogarth made engraved versions of his paintings and sold them (just as the volumes of Diderot's *Encyclopédie* were vended) by subscription. So popular were Hogarth's prints that they were pirated and sold without his authorization (a practice that continued even after Parliament passed the first copyright law in 1735). Especially successful were two series of prints based on his paintings. The first ("The Harlot's Progress") illustrates the misfortunes of a young woman who becomes a London prostitute; the second ("The Rake's Progress") depicts the comic misadventures of an antihero and ne'er-do-well named Tom Rakewell. Following these, Hogarth published a series of six engravings entitled "Marriage à la Mode," which describes the tragic consequences of a marriage of convenience between the son of a poverty-stricken nobleman and the daughter of a wealthy and ambitious merchant. The first print in the series, *The Marriage Transaction*, shows the two families negotiating the terms of the matrimonial union (Figure **25.4**). The scene unfolds as if upon a stage: the corpulent Lord Squanderfield, victim of the gout (an ailment traditionally linked with rich food and drink), sits pompously in his ruffled velvet waistcoat, pointing to his family tree, which springs from the loins of William the Conqueror. Across the table, the wealthy merchant and father of the bride carefully peruses the financial terms of the marriage settlement. On a settee in the corner of the room, the pawns of this socially expedient match turn away from each other in attitudes of mutual dislike. The earl's son, young Squanderfield, sporting a beauty patch, opens his snuffbox and vainly gazes at himself in a mirror, while his bride-to-be idly dangles her betrothal ring on a kerchief. She leans forward to hear the honeyed words of her future seducer, a lawyer named Lord Silvertongue. A combination of **caricature** (exaggeration of peculiarities or defects), comic irony, and symbolic detail, Hogarth's "stylish marriage" is drawn with a stylus every bit as sharp as Voltaire's pen.

Like Voltaire's Paris, Hogarth's London was not yet an industrial city, but it was plagued by some of the worst urban conditions of the day. It lacked sewers, streetlights, and adequate law enforcement. A city of vast contrasts between rich and poor, it was crowded with thieves, drunks, and prostitutes, all of whom threatened the jealously guarded privileges of the rich. Hogarth represented mid-eighteenth-century London at its worst in the famous engraving *Gin Lane* (Figure **25.5**). This devastating attack on the combined evils of urban poverty and alcoholism portrays poor, ragged, and drunk men and women in various stages of depravity. Some pawn their possessions to support their expensive addictions (lower left); others commit suicide (upper right corner); and one pours gin down the throat of a babe-in-arms, following the common practice of using liquor and other drugs to quiet noisy infants (far right). In the center of the print is the figure of a besotted mother—her leg covered with syphilitic sores—who carelessly allows her child to fall over the edge of the stair rail. Hogarth's visual satirization of gin addiction was a heroic attack on the social conditions of his time and on drug abuse in general. But even Parliament's passage of the Gin Law in 1751, which more than doubled the gin tax, did little to reduce the widespread use of this popular alcoholic

Figure 25.4 WILLIAM HOGARTH, *The Marriage Transaction*, from the "Marriage à la Mode" series, 1742–1746. Engraving, 15 × 18 in. Reproduced by courtesy of the Trustees of the British Museum, London.

beverage in eighteenth-century England. While Hogarth's prints failed to reduce the ills and inequities of his society, they remain an enduring condemnation of human hypocrisy, cruelty, vanity, and greed.

Rousseau's Revolt Against Reason

Jean-Jacques Rousseau, introduced in chapter 24 as a contributor to Diderot's *Encyclopédie*, was one of the Enlightenment's most outspoken critics. A playwright, composer, and educator, Rousseau took issue with some of the basic precepts of Enlightenment thought, including the idea that the progress of the arts and sciences might improve human conduct. Human beings may be good by nature, argued Rousseau, but they are ultimately corrupted by society and its institutions. "God makes all things good," wrote Rousseau; "man meddles with them and they become evil." Rousseau condemned the artificiality of civilized life and, although he did not advocate that humankind should return to a "state of nature," he exalted the "noble savage" as the model of the uncorrupted individual. Rousseau's philosophy of the heart elevated the role of instinct over reason and encouraged a new appreciation of nature and the natural—principles that underlay the romantic movement of the early nineteenth century (see chapters 27 to 29). In the following excerpt from the *Discourse on the Origin of Inequality among Men* (1755), Rousseau gives an eloquent account of how, in his view, human beings came to lose their freedom and their innocence.

READING 4.27 From Rousseau's *Discourse on the Origin of Inequality among Men* (1755)

The first man who, having enclosed a piece of land, thought of saying "This is mine" and found people simple enough to believe him, was the true founder of civil society. How many crimes, wars, murders; how much misery and horror the human race would have been spared if someone had pulled up the stakes and filled in the ditch and cried out to his fellow men: "Beware of listening to this impostor. You are lost if you forget that the fruits of the earth belong to everyone and that the earth itself belongs to no one!" But it is highly probable that by this time things had reached a point beyond which they could not go on as they were; for the idea of property, depending on many prior ideas which could only have arisen in successive 1

                                                                      10

stages, was not formed all at once in the human mind. It was necessary for men to make much progress, to acquire much industry and knowledge, to transmit and increase it from age to age, before arriving at this final stage of the state of nature. Let us therefore look farther back, and try to review from a single perspective the slow succession of events and discoveries in their most natural order.

Man's first feeling was that of his existence, his first 20
concern was that of his preservation. The products of the earth furnished all the necessary aids; instinct prompted him to make use of them. While hunger and other appetites made him experience in turn different modes of existence, there was one appetite which urged him to perpetuate his own species; and this blind impulse, devoid of any sentiment of the heart, produced only a purely animal act. The need satisfied, the two sexes recognized each other no longer, and even the child meant nothing to the mother, as soon as he could do without her.

Such was the condition of nascent[1] man; such was the life 30
of an animal limited at first to mere sensation; and scarcely

---
[1] Early, developing.

profiting from the gifts bestowed on him by nature, let alone was he dreaming of wresting anything from her. But difficulties soon presented themselves and man had to learn to overcome them. The height of trees, which prevented him from reaching their fruits; the competition of animals seeking to nourish themselves on the same fruits; the ferocity of animals who threatened his life—all this obliged man to apply himself to bodily exercises; he had to make himself agile, fleet of foot, and vigorous in combat. Natural weapons—branches of trees **40** and stones—were soon found to be at hand. He learned to overcome the obstacles of nature, to fight when necessary against other animals, to struggle for his subsistence even against other men, or to indemnify[2] himself for what he was forced to yield to the stronger.

[Rousseau then describes how people devised a technology for hunting and fishing, invented fire, and developed superiority over other creatures.]

Instructed by experience that love of one's own wellbeing is the sole motive of human action, he found himself in a position to distinguish the rare occasions when common interest justified his relying on the aid of his fellows, and those even rarer occasions when competition should make him distrust them. **50** In the first case, he united with them in a herd, or at most in a sort of free association that committed no one and which lasted only as long as the passing need which had brought it into being. In the second case, each sought to grasp his own advantage, either by sheer force, if he believed he had the strength, or by cunning and subtlety if he felt himself to be the weaker. . . .

. . . the habit of living together generated the sweetest sentiments known to man, conjugal love and paternal love. Each family became a little society, all the better united because mutual affection and liberty were its only bonds; at this stage **60** also the first differences were established in the ways of life of the two sexes which had hitherto been identical. Women became more sedentary and accustomed themselves to looking after the hut and the children while men went out to seek their common subsistence. The two sexes began, in living a rather softer life, to lose something of their ferocity and their strength; but if each individual became separately less able to fight wild beasts, all, on the other hand, found it easier to group together to resist them jointly. . . .

To the extent that ideas and feelings succeeded one **70** another, and the heart and mind were exercised, the human race became more sociable, relationships became more extensive and bonds tightened. People grew used to gathering together in front of their huts or around a large tree; singing and dancing, true progeny[3] of love and leisure, became the amusement, or rather the occupation, of idle men and women thus assembled. Each began to look at the others and to want to be looked at himself; and public esteem came to be prized. He who sang or danced the best; he who was the most handsome, the strongest, the most adroit[4] or the most eloquent became the **80** most highly regarded, and this was the first step toward inequality and at the same time toward vice. From those first

preferences there arose, on the one side, vanity and scorn, on the other, shame and envy, and the fermentation produced by these new leavens[5] finally produced compounds fatal to happiness and innocence.

As soon as men learned to value one another and the idea of consideration was formed in their minds, everyone claimed a right to it, and it was no longer possible for anyone to be refused consideration without affront. This gave rise to the **90** first duties of civility, even among savages: and henceforth every intentional wrong became an outrage, because together with the hurt which might result from the injury, the offended party saw an insult to his person which was often more unbearable than the hurt itself. Thus, as everyone punished the contempt shown him by another in a manner proportionate to the esteem he accorded himself, revenge became terrible, and men grew bloodthirsty and cruel. This is precisely the stage reached by most of the savage peoples known to us; and it is for lack of having sufficiently distinguished between different **100** ideas and seen how far those peoples already are from the first state of nature that so many authors have hastened to conclude that man is naturally cruel and needs civil institutions to make him peaceable, whereas in truth nothing is more peaceable than man in his primitive state. Placed by nature at an equal distance from the stupidity of brutes[6] and the fatal enlightenment of civilized man, limited equally by reason and instinct to defending himself against evils which threaten him, he is restrained by natural pity from doing harm to anyone, even after receiving harm himself: for according to the wise **110** Locke: "Where there is no property, there is no injury."

But it must be noted that society's having come into existence and relations among individuals having been already established meant that men were required to have qualities different from those they possessed from their primitive constitution. . . .

As long as men were content with their rustic huts, as long as they confined themselves to sewing their garments of skin with thorns or fishbones, and adorning themselves with feathers or shells, to painting their bodies with various colors, **120** to improving or decorating their bows and arrows; and to using sharp stones to make a few fishing canoes or crude musical instruments; in a word, so long as they applied themselves only to work that one person could accomplish alone and to arts that did not require the collaboration of several hands, they lived as free, healthy, good and happy men. . . .

. . . but from the instant one man needed the help of another, and it was found to be useful for one man to have provisions enough for two, equality disappeared, property was introduced, work became necessary, and vast forests were **130** transformed into pleasant fields which had to be watered with the sweat of men, and where slavery and misery were soon seen to germinate and flourish with the crops. . . .

 Q What aspects of civilized life, according to Rousseau, weaken and corrupt society?

[2]Compensate.
[3]Offspring.
[4]Skillful.

[5]Significant changes.
[6]Beasts.

Rousseau was haunted by contradictions within the social order and within his own mind (he suffered acute attacks of paranoia during the last fifteen years of his life). The opening words of his treatise, *The Social Contract* (1762), "Man is born free, and everywhere he is in chains," reflect his apprehension concerning the inhibiting role of institutional authority. In order to safeguard individual liberty, said Rousseau, people should form a contract among themselves. Unlike Hobbes, whose social contract involved transferring absolute authority from the citizens to a sovereign ruler, or Locke, whose social contract gave limited power to the ruler, Rousseau defined the state as "the general will" of its citizens. "The general will alone," he explained, "can direct the State according to the object for which it was instituted, that is, the common good." Rousseau insisted, moreover, that whoever refused to obey the general will should be constrained to do so by the whole society; that is, all humans should "be forced to be free." "As nature gives each man absolute power over all his members," wrote Rousseau, "the social compact gives the body politic absolute power over all its members also." Such views might have contributed to newly developed theories of democracy, but they were equally effective in justifying totalitarian constraints leveled in the name of the people.

Rousseau's wish to preserve the natural also led him to propose revolutionary changes in education. If society is indeed hopelessly corrupt, then let children grow up in accord with nature, argued Rousseau. In *Emile* (1762), his treatise on education, Rousseau advanced the hypothesis—unheard of in his time—that the education of a child begins at birth. He divided childhood development into five stages over a twenty-five-year span and outlined the type of rearing desirable for each stage. "Hands-on" experience was essential to education, according to Rousseau, especially in the period just prior to the development of reason and intellect, which he placed between the ages of twelve and fifteen. "Nature provides for the child's growth in her own fashion, and this should never be thwarted. Do not make him sit still when he wants to run about, nor run when he wants to be quiet." Rousseau also made a clear distinction between the education of men and that of women. Arguing that a woman's place was in the home and beside the cradle, he proposed for her a domestic education that cultivated modesty, obedience, and other virtues agreeable to her mate. Describing Emile's ideal mate, Rousseau writes, "Her education is in no way exceptional. She has taste without study, talents without art, judgment without knowledge. Her mind is still vacant but has been trained to learn; it is a well-tilled land only waiting for the grain. What a pleasing ignorance! Happy is the man destined to instruct her." Thus Rousseau's views on female education were less "enlightened" (by the standards of Mary Wollstonecraft, for one) than those advanced by Castiglione some two hundred years earlier in *The Book of the Courtier* (see chapter 16). Nevertheless, *Emile* became a landmark in educational theory, and Rousseau's new approach to education—particularly his emphasis on the cultivation of natural inquisitiveness over and above rote learning—influenced modern teaching methods such as those developed by the Italian educator Maria Montessori (1870–1952). Ironically, however, Rousseau saw fit to put all five of his own children in a foundling hospital rather than raise them himself.

Kant's Mind/World Revolution

The German philosopher Immanuel Kant (1724–1804) was "awakened from his slumber," as he put it, when he read the treatises of the Scottish philosopher David Hume (1711–1776). Hume had maintained that genuine knowledge was limited to two sorts: statements of logical relationships ("Bachelors are unmarried") and statements of sense perception ("This chalk is yellow"); all other statements described belief, not true knowledge. Provoked by the arguments of "the gentle skeptic," as Hume was called, Kant offered his own analysis. He explained the mind *not* as a passive recipient of information (Locke's "blank slate") but, rather, as a participant in the knowledge process. As Kant put it, "though our knowledge begins *with* experience, it does not follow that [all knowledge] arises *out of* experience." Concepts such as time, space, and causality are not (as Hume had it) mere habits of the mind, but the innate conditions of experience itself. The forms of intuition (space and time) and the categories of thought (quantity, quality, relationship, and modality) exist in the mind from birth; they shape the data of the senses into a consistent picture of the world.

Kant's argument altered the relationship between mind and world as radically as Copernicus had changed the relationship between earth and sun. Shifting the focus of philosophic debate from the nature of objective reality to the question of cognition itself—the process by which the mind comprehends experience—Kant perceived the mind as not merely reflecting experience, but as organizing experience into a coherent pattern. Knowledge, argued Kant, is a synthetic product of the logical self. In 1781, in the *Critique of Pure Reason*, Kant unfolded his revolutionary view of mind and world. The preeminence Kant gave to the role of the mind in constructing our idea of the world laid the basis for transcendental **idealism**, the doctrine that holds that reality consists of the mind and its forms of perception and understanding.

A giant in the field of modern ethics, Kant assessed the limits of reason with regard to morality. In contrast to Descartes and Locke, who held that knowledge was the key to humanity's advancement, Kant viewed knowledge as a means to enlightenment of a moral nature. In *An Answer to the Question: What is Enlightenment*" (1784), he wrote, "Enlightenment is man's emergence from his self-imposed immaturity. Immaturity is the inability to use one's understanding without guidance from another." In other words, rules and formulas, along with traditional patterns of thoughts and beliefs, are "shackles" that inhibit people from thinking for themselves. "*Sapere Aude!*" ("Have courage to use your own reason!") was Kant's motto for enlightenment. At the same time, Kant exalted reason as the keystone for human conduct. Recognizing that notions of good and evil varied widely among different groups of people, Kant proposed an ethical system that transcended individual circumstances. In the *Critique of Practical Reason* (1788), he proposed a general moral law called the "categorical imperative": namely, that we should act as if we could will that the maxim of our actions should become the law for all humankind. The basis of this moral law is the recognition of our duty to act rationally, that is, to act in ways justified by reasons so universal that they are good for all people at all times. It is not enough that our acts have good effects; it is necessary that we *will* the good. Kant's notion of "good will" is not, however, identical with Christian charity. Nor is it the same as Jesus' commandment to "Do to others as you would wish them do to you," since for Kant ethical conduct is based not on love for humankind (which, after all, one may lack), but on respect for the imperative to act rationally, a condition essential to human dignity.

The Revolutions of the Late Eighteenth Century

The American and French revolutions drew inspiration from the Enlightenment faith in the reforming power of reason. Both, however, demonstrated the limits of reason in achieving social change. As early as 1776, North America's thirteen colonies had rebelled against the longstanding political control of the British government. In the Declaration of Independence (see chapter 24), Jefferson restated Locke's assertion that government must protect its citizens' rights to life, liberty, and property. The British government, however, in making unreasonable demands for revenues, threatened colonial liberty, igniting the passions of fervent populists who sought democratic reform. Following some seven years of armed conflict, several thousand battle deaths, and a war expense estimated at over $100 million, in 1783 the thirteen colonies achieved their independence. And, in 1789, they began to function under the Constitution of the United States of America. The British political theorist Thomas Paine (1737–1809) proclaimed that the Revolution had done more to enlighten the world and diffuse a spirit of freedom among humankind than any event that had preceded it.

The American Revolution did not go unnoticed in France. French intellectuals followed its every turn; the French government secretly aided the American cause and eventually joined in the war against Britain. However, the revolution that began on French soil in 1789 involved circumstances that were quite different from those in America. In France, the lower classes sought to overturn longstanding social and political institutions and end upper-class privilege. The French Revolution was, in the main, the product of two major problems: class inequality, and a serious financial crisis brought about by some five hundred years of costly wars and royal extravagances (see chapter 21). With his nation on the verge of bankruptcy, King Louis XVI (1774–1792) sought new measures for raising revenue.

Throughout French history, taxes had fallen exclusively on the shoulders of the lower and middle classes, the so-called Third Estate. Almost four-fifths of the average peasant's income went to pay taxes, which supported the privileged upper classes. In a population of some 25 million people, the First Estate (the clergy) and the Second Estate (the nobility)—a total of only two hundred thousand citizens—controlled nearly half the land in France; yet they were exempt from paying taxes. Peasant grievances were not confined to matters of taxation: population growth and rising prices led to severe shortages of bread, the principal food of the lower classes.

When, in an effort to obtain public support for new taxes, Louis XVI called a meeting of the Estates General—its first in 175 years—the Third Estate withdrew and, declaring itself representative of the general will of the people, formed a separate body claiming the right to approve or veto all taxation. This daring act set the Revolution in motion. No sooner had the Third Estate proclaimed itself a national assembly than great masses of peasants and laborers began to riot throughout France.

On July 14, 1789, crowds stormed the Bastille destroyed the visible symbol of the old French regime (Figure **25.6**). Less than one month later, on August 4, the National Assembly—as the new body established by the Third Estate called itself—issued decrees that abolished the last remnants of medieval feudalism, including manorial courts, feudal duties, and church tithes. It also made provisions for a limited monarchy and an elected legislative assembly. The decrees of the National Assembly became part of a constitution, prefaced by the Declaration of the Rights of Man and Citizen, modeled on the American Declaration of Independence. A Declaration of the Rights of Woman and Citizen, drafted in 1791 by a butcher's daughter, Olympe de Gouges (1748–1793), demanded equal rights for women, the sex de Gouges described as "superior in beauty and courage." (Indeed, in October of 1789, 6,000 courageous women had marched on Versailles to protest the lack of bread in Paris.) For the first time in history women constituted a collective revolutionary force, making demands for equal property rights, government employment for women, and equal educational opportunities—demands guaranteed by the Constitution of 1793 but lost less than two years later by the terms of a new Constitution.

Enlightenment idealism, summed up in Rousseau's slogan "Liberty, Equality, Fraternity," had inflamed popular

Science and Technology

1752 Benjamin Franklin proves that lightning is a form of electricity

1768 James Watt patents the steam engine

1783 the first parachute is used in France

1783 the French make the first manned hot-air balloon flight

1795 the Springfield flintlock musket is developed in the United States

Figure 25.6 BRIFFAULT DE LA CHARPRAIS and **MME. ESCLAPART**, *The Siege of the Bastille, July 14, 1789*, 1791–1796. Engraving, 12 × 18¼ in. Pierpont Morgan Library, New York. Bequest of Gordon N. Ray, GNR 78 (plate #16). Art Resource, New York.

passions and inspired armed revolt. Nevertheless, from the storming of the Bastille through the rural revolts and mass protests that followed, angry, unreasoning mobs controlled the course of the Revolution. Divisions among the revolutionaries themselves led to a more radical phase of the Revolution, called the Reign of Terror. This phase saw the failure of the existing government and sent Louis XVI and his queen to the guillotine. Between 1793 and 1794, over 40,000 people (including Olympe de Gouges) met their deaths at the guillotine. Finally, in 1794, a National Convention devised a system of government run by two legislative chambers and a five-man executive body of directors. One of these—Napoleon Bonaparte (1769–1821)—would turn France into a military dictatorship some five years later. If, indeed, the French Revolution defended the Enlightenment bastions of liberty and equality, its foundations of reason and rationality ultimately crumbled under the forces of extremism and violence. The radicals of this and many other world-historical revolutions to follow rewrote the words of the *philosophes* in blood.

SUMMARY

The Enlightenment faith in the promise of reason, the cornerstone of eighteenth-century optimism, was tempered by an equally enlightened examination of the limits of reason. Olaudah Equiano's autobiography protested the inhumane trade in African slaves that persisted throughout the eighteenth century. In England, the keenest critic of Enlightenment idealism was Jonathan Swift, while in France, the acerbic writings of Voltaire described human folly as a universal condition. The European masters of satire found their East Asian counterpart in Li Ruzhen, whose witty prose attacked longstanding Chinese traditions. Voltaire's *Candide* remains the classic statement of comic skepticism in Western literature. Voltaire's contemporary, William Hogarth, brought the bitter invective of the satirist to the visual arts. His engravings exposed the social ills and class discrepancies of British society, even as they mocked universal human vices.

Questioning the value of reason for the advancement of the human condition, Jean-Jacques Rousseau argued that society itself corrupted humankind. He rejected the artificiality of the wig-and-silk-stocking culture in which he lived and championed "man in his primitive state." Rousseau's treatises on social history, government, and education explored ways in which individuals might retain their natural goodness and remain free and self-determining. In Germany, the philosopher Immanuel Kant examined the limits of the mind in the process of knowing. He argued that human beings have knowledge of the world through certain innate capabilities of mind. Kant appealed to "good will" as the basis for moral action.

While Enlightenment ideals fueled armed revolt in both America and France, the revolutions themselves blazed with antirational sentiment. In France especially, the men and women who fired the cannons of revolt abandoned reason as inadequate to the task of effecting social and political reform. Operating according to the dictates of their passions and their will, they gave dramatic evidence of the limits of reason to create a heaven on earth. The shift away from reason and the rational was to have major repercussions in the centuries to follow.

GLOSSARY

caricature exaggeration of peculiarities or defects to produce comic or burlesque effects

idealism in philosophy, the theory that holds that reality consists of the mind and its ideas; transcendental (or critical) idealism is Kant's name for the doctrine that knowledge is a synthetic product of the logical self

CHAPTER 26

Eighteenth-Century Art, Music, and Society

"In the presence of this miracle of [ancient Greek] art, I forget the whole universe and my soul acquires a loftiness appropriate to its dignity."
Johann Joachim Winckelmann

The dynamics of class and culture had a shaping influence on the arts of eighteenth-century Europe. European aristocrats of the period between 1715 and 1750 found pleasure in an elegant and refined style known as the *rococo*. Toward the end of the century, middle-class bonds to Enlightenment idealism and revolutionary reform, along with a new archeological appreciation of ancient Greece and Rome, ushered in the *neoclassical* style. In music, too, the era witnessed notable turns: from the ponderous baroque to the more delicate and playful rococo, and then, in the 1780s, to the formal and measured sounds of the *classical* symphony and the string quartet. An increased demand for secular entertainment called forth new genres in instrumental music and a wide range of subject matter in the visual arts. Despite their stylistic diversity, the arts shared a spirit of buoyant optimism and vitality that ensured their endurance beyond the Age of the Enlightenment.

The Rococo Style

The rococo style was born in France among members of the leisured nobility who had outlived Louis XIV. At Versailles and in the elegant urban townhouses (or *hôtels*, as they were called) of Paris, where the wealthy gathered to enjoy the pleasures of dancing, dining, and conversing, the rococo provided an atmosphere of elegant refinement.

The word "rococo" derives from *rocaille*, French for the fancy rock- or shell-work that was commonly used to ornament aristocratic gardens and grottoes. Rococo interiors display the organic vitality of seashells, plants, and flowers. Rococo artists preserved the ornate and luxuriant features of the baroque style, but they favored elements of play and intimacy that were best realized in works of a small scale, such as porcelain figurines, furniture, and paintings suitable for domestic quarters.

The Salon de la Princesse in the Hôtel de Soubise in Paris typifies the rococo style (Figure **26.1**): its interior is airy and fragile by comparison with a Louis XIV salon (see Figure 21.9). Brilliant white walls accented with pastel tones of rose, pale blue, and lime replace the ruby reds and royal blues of the baroque *salon*. The geometric regularity of the baroque interior has given way to an organic medley of

Figure 26.1 GERMAIN BOFFRAND, Salon de la Princesse, Hôtel de Soubise, Paris, ca. 1740. Oval shaped, max. 33 × 26 ft. © 1990, Photo Scala, Florence.

Figure 26.2 MARTIN CARLIN (master 1766–1785), Lady's desk, ca. 1775. Decorated with Sèvres porcelain plaques; tulipwood, walnut, and hardwood veneered on oak, height 31⅛ in., width 25⅝ in., depth 16 in. The Metropolitan Museum of Art, New York. Gift of Samuel H. Kress Foundation, 1958 (58.75.49).

curves and countercurves, echoed in elegant mirrors and chandeliers. The walls, ornamented with gilded tendrils, playful cupids, and floral garlands, melt into sensuously painted ceiling vaults crowned with graceful moldings.

Rococo furnishings are generally more delicate than baroque furnishings, and chairs are often fully uphol-stered—an innovation of the eighteenth century. Bureaus and tables may be fitted with panels of porcelain (Figure 26.2)—a Chinese technique that Marie Antoinette, the consort of Louis XVI, introduced at Versailles. Aristocratic women, especially such notable females as Marie Antoinette in France, Catherine the Great in Russia, and Maria Theresa in Austria, eagerly embraced the rococo style. Indeed, the rococo may be said to reflect the dis-tinctive influence of eighteenth-century women of taste.

Beyond the *salon*, the garden was the favorite setting for the leisured elite. Unlike Versailles' geometrically ordered parks, rococo gardens imitated the calculated naturalism of Chinese gardens. They featured undulating paths that gave false impressions of scale and distance. They often included artificial lakes, small colonnaded temples, ornamental pagodas, and other architectural "follies." Both outdoors and in, the fascination with Chinese objects and motifs—which began as a fashion in Europe around 1720—promoted the cult of *chinoiserie* (see chapter 21).

Although the rococo style originated in France, it reached spectacular heights in the courts of secular princes elsewhere in Europe. In Austria and the German states, it became the favorite style for the ornamentation of rural pilgrimage churches. The walls of Bavaria's Benedictine Church of Ottobeuren, designed by the German architect

Johann Michael Fischer (1692–1766), seem to disappear beneath a riot of stucco "frosting" as rich and sumptuous as any wedding cake (Figure 26.3). The more restrained ele-gance of French rococo interiors here gives way to a dazzling array of organic forms that sprout from the moldings and cornices like unruly flora (Figure 26.4). Shimmering light floods into the white-walled interior through oval win-dows, and pastel-colored frescoes turn ceilings and walls into heavenly antechambers. Illusionism reigns: wooden columns and stucco cornices are painted to look like marble; angels and cherubs, tendrils and leaves, curtains and clouds—all made of wood and stucco that have been painted and gilded—come to life as props in a theater of miracles. At Ottobeuren, the somber majesty of the Roman baroque church has given way to a sublime vision of paradise that is also a feast for the senses.

Rococo Painting in France

The pursuit of pleasure—a major eighteenth-century theme—dominates the paintings of the rococo masters. The first of these, the Flemish-born Antoine Watteau (1684–1721) began his career by painting theatrical scenes. In 1717, he submitted to the French Academy his *Departure from the Island of Cythera* (Figure 26.5), a work that pays tribute to the fleeting nature of romantic love. The painting shows a group of fashionable men and women preparing to board a golden boat by which they will leave the island of Cythera, the legendary birthplace of Venus.

Figure 26.3 JOHAN MICHAEL FISCHER, (right) interior, Benedictine abbey, Ottobeuren, Bavaria, 1736–1766. Painted and gilded wood and stucco. Vanni/Art Resource, New York.

Figure 26.4 (above) Cherubs, Benedictine church, Ottobeuren, Bavaria, 1736–1766. Stucco. © Barbara Opitz, Bildarchiv Monheim.

Figure 26.5 (above) **ANTOINE WATTEAU**, *Departure from the Island of Cythera*, 1717. Oil on canvas, 4 ft. 3 in. × 6 ft. 4 in. Louvre, Paris. Photo: R.M.N., © Gérard Blot.

Figure 26.6 (left) **FRANÇOIS BOUCHER**, *Venus Consoling Love*, 1751. Oil on canvas, 3 ft. 6⅛ in. × 33⅜ in. © 1998 Board of Trustees. National Gallery of Art, Washington, D.C. Chester Dale Collection.

Figure 26.7 Sèvres porcelain potpourri vase, mid-eighteenth century. Gondola-shaped body, scrolled handles, 4-lobed cover, height 14⅛ in., length 14½ in., width 8 in. This vase, purchased by Madame de Pompadour, is one of the finest products of the Sèvres porcelain factory, which she sponsored and patronized. The Metropolitan Museum of Art, New York. Gift of Samuel H. Kress Foundation, 1958 (58.75.88 a, b, c).

They have made this outing—a *fête galante* (literally, "elegant entertainment")—to pay homage to the Goddess of Love, whose rose-bedecked shrine appears at the far right. Amidst fluttering cupids, the pilgrims of love linger in pairs as they wistfully take leave of their florid hideaway. Watteau repeats the serpentine line formed by the figures in the delicate arabesques of the trees and rolling hills. He bathes the entire panorama in a misty, golden light. Not since the sixteenth-century artists Giorgione and Titian had any painter indulged so deeply in the pleasures of nature or the voluptuous world of the senses.

Watteau's fragile forms and delicate colors, painted with feathery brushstrokes reminiscent of Rubens, evoke a mood of reverie and nostalgia. His doll-like men and women provide sharp contrast with Rubens' physically powerful figures (see Figure 21.15) or, for that matter, with Poussin's idealized heroes (see Figure 21.12). Watteau's art conveys no moral or heroic message; rather, it explores the world of familiar but transitory pleasures.

If Watteau's world was wistful and poetic, that of his contemporary François Boucher (1703–1770) was sensual and indulgent. Boucher, a specialist in designing mythological scenes, became head of the Gobelins tapestry factory in 1755 and director of the Royal Academy ten years later. He was First Painter to King Louis XV (1715–1774) and a good friend of the king's favorite mistress, Jeanne Antoinette Poisson, the Marquise de Pompadour (1721–1764). A woman of remarkable beauty and intellect— she owned two telescopes, a microscope, and a lathe that she installed in her apartments in order to carve cameos—Madame de Pompadour influenced state policy and dominated fashion and the arts at Versailles for almost twenty years. With the idyllic *Venus Consoling Love*, Boucher flattered his patron by portraying her as Goddess of Love (Figure **26.6**). Surrounded by attentive doves and cupids, the nubile Venus relaxes on a bed of sumptuous rose and blue satin robes nestled in a bower of leafy trees and windswept grasses. Boucher delighted in sensuous contrasts of flesh, fabric, feathers, and flowers. His girlish women, with their unnaturally tiny feet, rosebud-pink nipples, and wistful glances, were coy symbols of erotic pleasure.

Boucher also designed sets and costumes for the Royal Opera and motifs for tapestries and porcelains. From the Sèvres porcelain factory, located near Paris and founded by Madame de Pompadour, came magnificent porcelains ornamented with gilded wreaths, arabesque cartouches, and playful cupids floating on fleecy clouds (Figure **26.7**). Outside of France, in Germany and Austria, porcelain figurines of shepherds and shepherdesses advertised the eighteenth-century enthusiasm for the pastoral life.

Fashion and fashionableness—public expressions of self-conscious materialism—were major themes of rococo art. Marie-Louise Elisabeth Vigée-Lebrun (1775–1842), the most famous of a number of eighteenth-century female artists, produced refined portrait paintings for an almost exclusively female clientele. Vigée-Lebrun's travels in the Low Countries allowed her to study the works of Rubens and van Dyck, whose painterly style she admired. Her glamorous likeness of Marie Antoinette is a tribute to the European fashion industry (Figure **26.8**). Plumed head-dresses and low-cut gowns bedecked with lace, ribbons, and tassels turned the aristocratic female into a conspicuous ornament; the size of her billowing skirt required that she turn sideways to pass through open doors. In response to the upper-class infatuation with pastoral and idyllic themes, Vigée-Lebrun also painted portraits of more modestly

Figure 26.8 MARIE-LOUISE ELISABETH VIGÉE-LEBRUN, *Marie Antoinette*, 1788. Oil on canvas, 12 ft. 1½ in. × 6ft. 3½ in. Musée de Versailles. Lauros/Giraudon/Bridgeman Art Library, London.

The Swing depicts a frivolous encounter that takes place in a garden bower filled with frothy trees, classical statuary, and delicate light. The young woman, dressed in yards of satin and lace, kicks her tiny shoe into the air in the direction of a statue of Cupid, while her lover, hiding in the bushes below, peers delightedly beneath her billowing skirts (Figure **26.9**). Whether or not the young lady is aware of her lover's presence, her coy gesture and the irreverent behavior of the *ménage à trois* (lover, mistress, and cleric) create a mood of erotic intrigue similar to that found in the comic operas of this period, as well as in the pornographic novel, which developed as a genre in eighteenth-century France. Fragonard's deft brushstrokes caress the figures and render the surrounding foliage in delicate pastel tones. Although Fragonard immortalized the union of

Figure 26.9 JEAN-HONORÉ FRAGONARD, *The Swing*, 1768–1769. Oil on canvas, 32 × 25½ in. Reproduced by permission of the Trustees, the Wallace Collection, London.

Figure 26.10 (right) **CLODION** (Claude Michel), *The Intoxication of Wine*, ca. 1775. Terracotta, height 23¼ in. The Metropolitan Museum of Art, New York. Bequest of Benjamin Altman, 1913 (14.40.687).

dressed women in muslin skirts and straw hats. Unlike Boucher, Vigée-Lebrun did not cast her subjects as goddesses, but she imparted to them a chic sweetness and artless simplicity. These talents earned her the equivalent of over $200,000 a year and allowed her an independence uncommon among eighteenth-century women.

Jean-Honoré Fragonard (1732–1806), the last of the great rococo artists, was the undisputed master of translating the art of seduction into paint. Working shortly before the French Revolution, he captured the pastimes of a waning aristocracy, especially the pleasures of courtship and flirtation. In 1766, a wealthy aristocrat commissioned Fragonard to paint a scene that showed the patron's mistress seated on a swing being pushed by a friendly old clergyman.

wealth, privilege, and pleasure enjoyed by the upper classes of the eighteenth century, he captured a spirit of sensuous abandon that has easily outlived the particulars of time, place, and social class.

Rococo Sculpture

The finest examples of eighteenth-century sculpture are small in scale, intimate in mood, and almost entirely lacking in dramatic urgency and religious fervor. Intended for the boudoir or the drawing room, rococo sculpture usually depicted elegant dancers, wooing couples, or other lighthearted subjects. The French sculptor Claude Michel, known as Clodion (1738–1814), who worked almost exclusively for private patrons, was among the favorite rococo artists of the late eighteenth century. His *Intoxication of Wine* revived a classical theme—a celebration honoring Dionysus, the Greek god of wine and fertility (Figure **26.10**). Flushed with wine and revelry, the **satyr** (a semibestial woodland creature symbolic of Dionysus) wildly embraces a **bacchante**, an attendant of Dionysus. Clodion made the piece in terracotta, a clay medium that requires rapid modeling, thus inviting the artist to capture a sense of spontaneity. Rococo painters sought similar effects through the use of loose and rapid brushstrokes and by sketching with pastels. The expressive impact of *The Intoxication of Wine* belies its tiny size—it is just under 2 feet high.

Eighteenth-Century French Genre Painting

Many of the *philosophes* found the works of Boucher, Clodion, and other rococo artists trivial and morally degenerate. Diderot, for example, denounced rococo boudoir imagery and demanded an art that made "virtue attractive and vice odious." The French artists Jean-Baptiste Greuze (1725–1805) and Jean-Baptiste-Siméon Chardin (1699–1779) heeded the plea for art with a moral purpose. Abandoning the indulgent sensuality and frivolity of the rococo, they painted realistic scenes of everyday life among the middle and lower classes. This shift mirrored the transition from a society dominated by royal absolutism and religious dogma to one guided by the secular morality of the Enlightenment.

Greuze, Diderot's favorite artist, exalted the natural virtues of ordinary people. His genre paintings brought to life such moralizing subjects as *The Father Reading the Bible to His Children*, *The Well-Beloved Mother*, and *The Effects of Drunkenness*. In the manner of Hogarth (whose works Greuze admired), he chose engaging narratives that might require a series of canvases. Greuze's *Village Betrothal* (Figure **26.11**) of 1761 tells the story of an impending matrimony among hardworking, simple-living rustics: the father, who has just given over the dowry to the humble groom, blesses the couple; the mother laments losing a daughter; while

Figure 26.11 JEAN-BAPTISTE GREUZE, *Village Betrothal*, 1761. Oil on canvas, 3 ft. 10½ in. × 3 ft. Louvre, Paris. © Photo Josse, Paris.

Figure 26.12 JEAN-BAPTISTE-SIMÉON CHARDIN, *The Kitchen Maid*, 1738. Oil on canvas, 18⅛ × 14¾ in. © 1998 Board of Trustees, National Gallery of Art, Washington, D.C. Samuel H. Kress Collection.

Science and Technology

1775 the flush toilet is patented in Britain

1777 steam heat is used in France for the first time since the Roman era

1779 the first bicycles appear in Paris

the other members of the household, including the hen and chicks (possibly a symbol of the couple's prospective progeny), look on approvingly. Greuze's painting could easily have been an illustration of a scene from a popular eighteenth-century novel or play. Greuze shunned the intellectualism of Poussin, the sensuality of Fragonard, and the satirical acrimony of Hogarth. His melodramatic representations appealed to common emotion and sentiment. Understandably, they were among the most popular images of the eighteenth and nineteenth centuries.

The art of Greuze's contemporary Chardin was less overt in sentimentality. Chardin painted humble still lifes and genre scenes showing nurses, governesses, and kitchen maids at work (Figure **26.12**). Unlike Greuze, who illustrated his moral tales as literally as possible, Chardin avoided both explicit moralizing and anecdotal themes. Yet Chardin's paintings bear a deep concern for commonplace humanity, and they convey an implicit message—that of the ennobling dignity of work and the virtues of domesticity. The forthright qualities of Chardin's subjects are echoed in his style: his figures are simple and monumental, and his compositions reveal an uncanny sense of balance reminiscent of the works of de Hooch and Vermeer. Each object seems to assume its proper and predestined place in the composition. Executed in mellow, creamy tones, Chardin's paintings evoke a mood of gentility and gravity.

Greuze and Chardin brought painting out of the drawing room and into the kitchen. Their canvases were in such high demand that they were sold widely in engraved copies. Ironically, while Chardin's subjects were humble and commonplace, his patrons were often bankers, foreign ambassadors, and royalty itself—Louis XV owned at least two of Chardin's paintings.

Not all eighteenth-century genre paintings contained the unstated moral meanings found in Chardin's works. Some, like the study of a man scraping chocolate by an anonymous Spanish artist (Figure **26.13**) offer an unidealized record of common labor. Kneeling before a heated grinding stone (introduced into Spain from the Americas), a young man scrapes a large slab of chocolate, a luxury brought from the Americas to Europe in the sixteenth century. His efforts will produce patties of chocolate seen in the foreground, as well as a grated chocolate paste (contained in the large bowl) that was the main ingredient for a favorite drink among all social classes in Europe.

Figure 26.13 *A Man Scraping Chocolate*, Spain, ca. 1680–1780. Oil on canvas, 41 × 28 in. North Carolina Museum of Art, Raleigh. Gift of Mr and Mrs Benjamin Cone, 1969 (69.20.1)

Eighteenth-Century Neoclassicism

Neoclassicism—the self-conscious revival of Greco-Roman culture—belonged to a tradition that stretched at least from the early Renaissance through the age of Louis XIV. During the seventeenth century, Poussin and other artists of the European Academies (see chapter 21) had resurrected the classical ideals of clarity, simplicity, balance, and restraint, as configured in the Grand Style of Raphael and other High Renaissance masters. During the eighteenth century, however, the longstanding respect for Antiquity was infused by a new development: the scientific study of classical ruins. In 1738, the king of Naples sponsored the first archeological excavations at Herculaneum, one of the two Roman cities in southern Italy buried under volcanic ash by the eruption of Mount Vesuvius in 79 C.E. The excavations at Pompeii would follow in 1748. These enterprises, followed by European archeological expeditions to Greece and Asia Minor in 1750, inspired scholars to assemble vast collections of Greek and Roman artifacts (Figure **26.14**). Both the Louvre and the Vatican became museum repositories for the treasures of these expeditions, now available to artists, antiquarians, and the general public. For the first time in history, one was able to make clear distinctions between the artifacts of Greece and those of Rome. The result was a more archeologically correct neoclassicism than any that had previously existed.

Shortly after the first English expeditions to Athens, the German scholar Johann Joachim Winckelmann (1717–1768) began to study Greek and Roman antiquities. He published an eloquent assessment of these objects in his magnificently illustrated *History of Ancient Art* (1764). These and other of Winckelmann's widely circulated texts, which offered a critical analysis of art objects (rather than a biographical history of artists), established Winckelmann as the "father of modern art historical scholarship."

Although Winckelmann himself never visited Greece, he was infatuated with Hellenic and Hellenistic sculpture. He argued that artists of his time could become great only by imitating the ancient Greeks, whose best works, he insisted, betrayed "a noble simplicity and a quiet grandeur." Of his favorite ancient statue, the *Apollo Belvedere* (see Figures 5.30 and 26.18, left), Winckelmann proclaimed, "In the presence of this miracle of art, I forget the whole universe and my soul acquires a loftiness appropriate to its dignity." Winckelmann's reverence for antiquity typified the eighteenth-century attitude toward classicism as a vehicle for the elevation of human consciousness. Here, finally, was the ideal mode of expression for the Enlightenment program of reason, clarity, and order—a style that equated Beauty with Goodness, Virtue, and

Figure 26.14 GIOVANNI PAOLO PANINI (copy after), *Picture Gallery (Roma Antica)*, 1691–1765. Pen and black ink with brush and gray wash and watercolor over graphite on ivory laid paper, 17¼ × 27³⁄₁₆ in. © 1998 The Art Institute of Chicago. All Rights Reserved. Emily Crane Chadbourne Collection (1955.7.45).

Figure 26.15 GIOVANNI BATTISTA PIRANESI, *The Pantheon*, from *Views of Rome*, ca. 1748–1778. Etching. The towers flanking the portico, which were added in the seventeenth century when the Pantheon functioned as a church, have since been removed. Reproduced by Courtesy of the Trustees of the British Museum, London.

Truth. Winckelmann's publications became an inspiration for artists and aesthetes all over Europe. In Britain, Sir Joshua Reynolds (1723–1792), the painter and founder of the Royal Academy of Art in London, lectured on the Grand Manner; his *Discourses* were translated into French, German, and Italian. The lofty vision of a style that captured the nobility and dignity of the Greco-Roman past fired the imagination of intellectuals across Western Europe and America.

Since Renaissance times, Rome had been a favorite destination for well-educated tourists and artists. But during the eighteenth century, Rome and its monuments came under new scrutiny. Architects studied the monuments of antiquity, and artists made topographic sketches, often reproduced in copper engravings that were sold cheaply—in the manner of modern-day postcards. In 1740 the Venetian architect and engineer Giovanni Battista Piranesi (1720–1778) established himself in Rome as a printmaker. Piranesi's engravings of Rome were widely bought and appreciated (see Figure 9.9), while his studies of Roman monuments, with their precisely rendered technical details and inscriptions, exerted considerable influence on French and English architects of his time (Figure **26.15**). Piranesi's later works—nightmarish visions of dungeons inspired by the Roman sewer system—abandoned all classical canons of objectivity and emotional restraint. Nevertheless, with European artists more eager than ever

to rediscover antiquity through the careful study of its remains, the neoclassical revival was under way.

A major factor for the widespread interest in antiquity, and one that made eighteenth-century neoclassicism unique, was the scientific uncovering of ancient classical ruins.

Neoclassical Architecture

The classical revival of the eighteenth century was unique in its accuracy of detail and its purity of design. Neoclassical architects made careful distinctions between Greek and Roman buildings and between the various Renaissance and post-Renaissance styles modeled upon antiquity. They took inspiration from simple geometric shapes—spheres, cubes, and cylinders—to provide a new, more abstract and austere classicism. They rejected the illusionistic theatricality of the baroque style with its broken pediments, cartouches, and ornamental devices. They also turned their backs on the stucco foliage, cherubic angels, and "wedding-cake" fantasies of the rococo. The ideal neoclassical exterior was free of frivolous ornamentation, while its interior consisted of clean and rectilinear walls, soberly accented with engaged columns or pilasters, geometric motifs, and shallow niches that might house copies of antique statuary (see Figure 26.18).

In France, the leading architect of the eighteenth century was Jacques-Germain Soufflot (1713–1780). Soufflot's

Figure 26.16 (above) **JACQUES-GERMAIN SOUFFLOT**, Sainte Geneviève (renamed the "Panthéon" during the French Revolution), Paris, 1757–1792. Photo: A. F. Kersting, London.

Figure 26.17 (right) **JACQUES-GERMAIN SOUFFLOT**, interior of Sainte Geneviève ("Panthéon"), Paris, 1757–1792. Photo: A. F. Kersting, London.

Church of Sainte Geneviève (Figure **26.16**), the patron saint of Paris, follows a strict central plan with four shallow domes covering each of the arms. A massive central dome, supported entirely on pillars, rises over the crossing (compare Saint Paul's in London; Figure 22.2). The facade of Sainte Geneviève resembles the portico of the Pantheon in Rome (see chapter 6, and Figure 26.15), while the interior of the church (Figure **26.17**)—which entombs, among others, Voltaire and Rousseau—recalls the grandeur of Saint Peter's in Rome. As the "Panthéon" illustrates, Soufflot did not slavishly imitate any single classical structure; rather, he selected specific features from a variety of notable sources and combined them with clarity and reserve. In contrast with its baroque and rococo ancestors, the Church of Sainte Geneviève was no theater of miracles but rather a rationally ordered, this-worldly shrine.

Some of the purest examples of the classical revival are found in late eighteenth-century English country homes. The interiors of these sprawling symbols of wealth and prestige reflect close attention to archeological drawings of Greek and Roman antiquities. Kedleston Hall in Derbyshire, England, designed by the Scottish architect

Robert Adam (1728–1792), reflects a pristine taste for crisp contours and the refined synthesis of Greco-Roman motifs (Figure **26.18).** In such estates as this, the neoclassical spirit touched everything from sculpture (Figure **26.19)** and furniture to tea services and tableware. Among the most popular items of the day were the ceramics of the English potter Josiah Wedgwood (1730–1795). Wedgwood's wares were modeled on Greek and Roman vases and embellished with finely applied, molded white clay surface designs (Figure **26.20).**

The austerity and dignity of neoclassicism made it the ideal style for public monuments and offices of state. In Paris, Berlin, and Washington, D.C., neoclassical architects borrowed Greek and Roman temple designs for public and private buildings, especially for banks, where the modern-day gods of money and materialism replaced the ancient deities. In some instances, the spirit of revival produced daring architectural hybrids. In England, for instance, the Scottish architect James Gibbs (1682–1754) designed churches that combined a classical portico with a Gothic spire (Figure **26.21).** This scheme, which united the baroque love of dramatic contrast with the neoclassical rule of perfect symmetry, became extremely popular in America, primarily in the congregational churches built across New England.

Neoclassicism in America

A tour of the city of Washington in the District of Columbia will convince any student of the impact of neoclassicism on the architecture of the United States. The neoclassical movement in America did not originate, however, in the capital city, whose major buildings date

Figure 26.18 ROBERT ADAM, Marble Hall, Kedleston Hall, Derbyshire, England, 1763–1777. (Note copy of the *Apollo Belvedere* in niche at left.) 67 × 42 ft., height 40 ft. Photo: A. F. Kersting, London.

only from the nineteenth century, but rather among the Founding Fathers. One of the most passionate devotees of Greco-Roman art and life was the Virginia lawyer and statesman Thomas Jefferson (1743–1826), whose Declaration of Independence was discussed in chapter 24. Farmer, linguist, educator, inventor, architect, musician, and politician, the man who served as third president of the United States was an eighteenth-century *uomo universale* (see Figure 24.2). Jefferson was a student of ancient and Renaissance treatises on architecture and an impassioned apostle of neoclassicism. In 1786, he designed the Virginia State Capitol, using as his model the ancient Roman Maison Carrée (see Figure 26.32). For the design of his own country estate in Monticello and for the University of Virginia—America's first state university—he drew on the Pantheon, the most admired of all imperial Roman buildings (see Figure 26.15). Jefferson reconstructed this ancient temple at two-thirds its original size in the Rotunda, which housed the original library of the University of Virginia (Figure **26.22**). Considerably smaller than Soufflot's "Panthéon," the stripped-down Rotunda is also purer in form. Jefferson's tightly organized and geometrically correct plan for the campus of the University of Virginia reflects the basic sympathy between neoclassical design and the rationalist ideals of the Enlightenment. The "academical village," as Jefferson described it, was a community of the free-thinking elite—exclusively white, wealthy, and male, yet it provided both a physical and a spiritual model for nonsectarian education in the United States.

Figure 26.21 JAMES GIBBS, Saint Martin-in-the-Fields, London, 1721–1726. © Angelo Hornak, London.

The young American nation drew on the heritage of the ancients (and especially the history of the Roman Republic) to symbolize its newly forged commitment to the ideals of liberty and equality. The leaders of the American Revolution regarded themselves as descendants of ancient Roman heroes and some even adopted Latin names, much as the Italian Renaissance humanists had done. On the Great Seal of the United States, the Latin phrase "E pluribus unum" ("out of many, one") and the bundle of arrows in the grasp of the American eagle (suggesting the Roman fasces: a bundle of rods surrounding an ax—the ancient symbol for power and authority) identified America as heir to republican Rome (Figure **26.23**).

Figure 26.22 (left) **THOMAS JEFFERSON**, The Rotunda, University of Virginia, Charlottesville, Virginia, 1822–1826. Photo: Ralph Thompson. Albert and Shirley Small Special Collections Library, University of Virginia.

Figure 26.23 (above) Great Seal of the United States. Courtesy of the Bureau of Printing and Engraving, U.S. Treasury Department.

Neoclassical Sculpture

Neoclassical sculptors heeded the Enlightenment demand for an art that perpetuated the memory of illustrious men. Jean-Antoine Houdon (1741–1828), the leading portrait sculptor of Europe, immortalized in stone the features of his contemporaries. His portrait busts, which met the popular demand for achieving a familiar likeness, revived the realistic tradition in sculpture that had reached its high-water mark among the Romans. Houdon had a special talent for catching characteristic gestures and expressions: Diderot, shown without a wig, surveys his world with inquisitive candor (see Figure 24.4), while the aging Voltaire addresses us with a grim and knowing smile (see Figure 25.3). While visiting America, Houdon carved portraits of Jefferson (see Figure 24.2), Franklin, and other "virtuous men" of the republic. His life-sized statue of George Washington renders the first president of the United States as country gentleman and eminent statesman (Figure **26.24**). Resting his hand on a columnar *fasces*, the poised but slightly potbellied Washington recalls (however faintly) the monumental dignity of the Greek gods and the Roman emperors.

Figure 26.24 JEAN-ANTOINE HOUDON, *George Washington*, 1786–1796. Marble, height 6 ft. 2 in. State capitol, Richmond, Virginia. Credit: Cook Collection, Valentine Richmond History Center.

While Houdon invested neoclassicism with a strong taste for realism, most of his contemporaries followed the Hellenic impulse to idealize the human form. Such was the case with the Italian-born sculptor Antonio Canova (1757–1822). Canova's life-sized marble portrait of Napoleon Bonaparte's sister, Pauline Borghese, is a sublime example of neoclassical refinement and restraint (see Figure 26.19). Canova casts Pauline in the guise of a reclining Venus. Perfectly proportioned, she shares the flawless elegance of classical statuary and Wedgwood reliefs. In contrast to the vigorously carved surfaces of baroque sculpture (recall, for instance, Bernini's *Ecstasy of Saint Teresa*, Figure 20.2), Canova's figure is smooth and neutral—even stark. A comparison of Canova's *Pauline Borghese as Venus* with Clodion's *Intoxication of Wine* (see Figure 26.10) is also revealing: both depend on classical themes and models, but whereas Clodion's piece is intimate, sensuous, and spontaneous, Canova's seems remote, controlled, and calculated. Its aesthetic distance is intensified by the ghostlike whiteness of the figure and its "blank" eyes—eighteenth-century sculptors seem to have been unaware that classical artists painted parts of their statues to make them look more lifelike.

Neoclassical Painting and Politics: The Art of David

The last decades of the eighteenth century, as the tides of revolution began to engulf the indulgent lifestyles of the French aristocracy, the rococo style gave way to a sober new approach to picturemaking. The pioneer of this style was the French artist Jacques-Louis David (1748–1825). David's early canvases were executed in the rococo style of his teacher and distant cousin, Boucher. But after winning the coveted Prix de Rome, which sent him to study in the foremost city of antiquity, David found his place among the classicists. In 1784 he completed one of the most influential paintings of the late eighteenth century: *The Oath of the Horatii* (Figure **26.25**). The painting was commissioned by the French king some five years before the outbreak of the Revolution; ironically, however, it became a symbol of the very spirit that would topple the royal crown.

The Oath of the Horatii illustrates a dramatic event recorded by Livy in his *History of Rome*: the moment when the three sons of Horatius Proclus swear to oppose the treacherous Curiatii family in a win-or-die battle that is to determine the future of Rome. In France, Livy's story had become especially popular as the subject of a play by the French dramatist Pierre Corneille (1606–1684). David captured the spirit of the story in a single potent image: resolved to pursue their destiny as defenders of liberty, the Horatii lift their arms in a dramatic military salute. Bathed in golden light, the statuesque figures stand along the strict horizontal line of the picture plane. The body of the warrior on the far left forms a rigid triangular shape that is subtly repeated throughout the composition—in the arches of the colonnade, for instance, and in the group of grieving women (one of whom represents the fiancée of a Curiatius). According to the tale, her victorious brother, the sole survivor of the combat, returned home to find her mourning for her dead lover and, in a fit of rage, he murdered her.

Figure 26.25 JACQUES-LOUIS DAVID, *The Oath of the Horatii*, 1784. Oil on canvas, 10 ft. 10 in. × 14 ft. Louvre, Paris. Photo: © Photo Josse, Paris.

David's painting was an immediate success: people lined up to see it while it hung in the artist's studio in Rome, and the city of Paris received it enthusiastically when it arrived there in 1785. The huge canvas (over 10 by 14 feet) came to be perceived as a clear denunciation of aristocratic pastimes. His painting presented life as serious drama: it proclaimed the importance of reason and the intellect over and above feeling and sentiment, and it defended the ideals of male heroism and self-sacrifice in the interest of one's country. In place of the lace cuffs, silk suits, and powdered wigs of the rococo drawing room, David had detailed the trappings of war. Stylistically, too, the painting was revolutionary: David rejected the luxuriant sparkle of rococo art for sober simplicity. He replaced the pliant forms, sensuous textures, and pastel tones of the rococo with rectilinear shapes, hard-edged contours, and somber colors—features that recalled the art of Poussin (whom David deeply admired). His technique was austere, precise, and realistic—witness the archeologically correct Roman helmets, sandals, and swords.

Three years after painting *The Oath of the Horatii*, David conceived the smaller but equally popular *Death of*

Socrates (Figure **26.26**). The scene is a fifth-century B.C.E. Athenian prison. It is the moment before Socrates, the father of Greek philosophy, drinks the fatal hemlock. Surrounding Socrates are his students and friends, posed in various expressions of lament, while the apostle of reason himself—illuminated in the style of Caravaggio—rhetorically lifts his hand to heaven. Clarity and intellectual control dominate the composition: figures and objects are arranged as if plotted on a grid of lines horizontal and vertical to the picture plane. This ideal geometry, a metaphor for the ordering function of reason, complements the grave and noble message of the painting: reason guides human beings to live and, if need be, to die for their moral principles. In *The Death of Socrates*, as in *The Oath of the Horatii*, David put neoclassicism at the service of a morality based on Greco-Roman Stoicism, self-sacrifice, and stern patriotism.

Ingres and Academic Neoclassicism

David's most talented pupil was Jean-Auguste-Dominique Ingres (1780–1867). The son of an artist–craftsman, Ingres rose to fame with his polished depictions of classical history and mythology and with his accomplished portraits of middle- and upper-class patrons. He spent much of his career in Italy, where he came to prize (as he himself admitted), "Raphael, his century, the ancients, and above all the divine Greeks." Ingres shunned the weighty realism of David in favor of the purity of line he admired in Greek vase painting, in the published drawings of the newly unearthed classical artifacts, and in engraved book illustrations for the works of Homer and Hesiod.

Commissioned to paint a ceiling mural for the Louvre, Ingres produced a visual testament to Europe's infatuation with its classical heritage. The monumental *Apotheosis of Homer* shows the ancient Greek bard enthroned amidst forty-six notables of classical and modern times; he is "deified" with a laurel crown bestowed by a winged figure of Victory (Figure **26.27**). Surrounding Homer is an academic assembly that includes Plato, Dante, Raphael, Poussin, Racine, and other Western "luminaries" (thirty of whom are identified in Figure **26.28**). Ingres' iconic figure sits at the apex of the compositional pyramid; at his feet are the allegorical figures of his epics, the *Iliad* and the *Odyssey*, while behind him is a neoclassical temple façade, not unlike that of "La Madeleine," which was then under construction in Paris (see Figure 26.31).

Both in composition and in conception, the *Apotheosis* looks back to Raphael (see *The School of Athens*, Figure 17.29), but Ingres has brought self-conscious rigor to his application of the neoclassical principles of clarity and symmetry.

Late in his career, Ingres turned his nostalgia for the past to more exotic themes. Intrigued, for instance, by Turkish culture (publicized by Napoleon's campaigns in Syria and North Africa), he painted languorous harem slaves, such as *La Grande Odalisque* (Figure 26.29). A revisualization of both Titian's *Venus of Urbino* (see Figure 17.43) and Canova's *Pauline Borghese as Venus* (see Figure 26.19), Ingres' nude turns in a self-consciously seductive manner: both away from and toward the beholder. The firm contours and polished brushstrokes are typically neoclassical; but Ingres rejected neoclassical canons of proportion by elongating the limbs in the tradition of the Italian Mannerists (see, for instance, Figure 20.4). The "incorrect" anatomy of the figure drew strong criticism from Ingres' contemporaries, who claimed that his subject had three too many vertebrae. Nevertheless (or perhaps because of its bold departures from both real and ideal norms), *La Grande Odalisque* remains one of the most arresting images of womanhood in Western art.

Figure 26.26 JACQUES-LOUIS DAVID, *The Death of Socrates*, 1787. Oil on canvas, 4 ft. 3 in. × 6 ft. 5¼ in. The Metropolitan Museum of Art, New York. Catharine Lorillard Wolfe Collection. Wolfe Fund, 1931 (31.45).

Figure 26.27 JEAN-AUGUSTE-DOMINIQUE INGRES, *The Apotheosis of Homer*, 1827. Oil on canvas, 12 ft. 8 in. × 16 ft. 10¾ in. Louvre, Paris. Photo R.M.N. – © René-Gabriel Ojéda.

Figure 26.28 Plan of *The Apotheosis of Homer*, 1827. Following Emilio Radius, *L'opera complete di Ingres*, the following figures are identified:

1 Virgil	18 Dante
2 Raphael	19 Iliad
3 Sappho	20 Odyssey
4 Euripides	21 Aesop
5 Demosthenes	22 Shakespeare
6 Sophocles	23 La Fontaine
7 Herodotus	24 Tasso
8 Orpheus	25 Mozart
9 Pindar	26 Poussin
10 Hesiod	27 Corneille
11 Plato	28 Racine
12 Socrates	29 Molière
13 Pericles	30 Glück
14 Michelangelo	31 Apelles
15 Aristotle	32 Phidias
16 Aristarchus	
17 Alexander the Great	

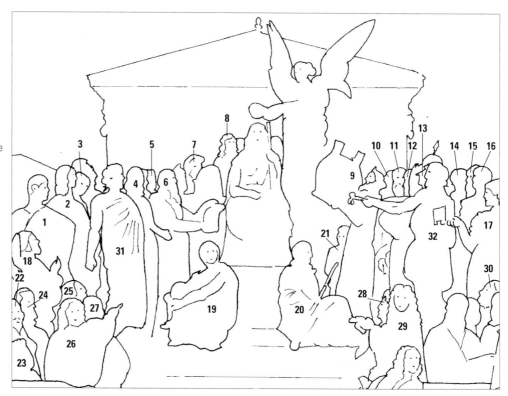

Figure 26.29 JEAN-AUGUSTE-DOMINIQUE INGRES, *La Grande Odalisque*, 1814. Oil on canvas, 2 ft. 11¼ in. × 5 ft. 3¾ in. Louvre, Paris. Photo: © 1990, Photo Scala, Florence.

Kauffmann and Academic Neoclassicism

Well into the eighteenth century, the painting of large-scale historical, mythological, and religious subjects was dominated by male artists. Talented females, such as Maria van Oosterwyck (see Figure 23.6) and Judith Leyster (see Figure 23.14), confined themselves to still-life subjects and portrait painting, genres considered of lesser importance among academicians. Nevertheless, the Italian-trained Angelica Kauffmann (1741–1807), like Artemisia Gentileschi (see Figure 20.10), established a glowing reputation as a skilled painter of historical subjects. Kauffmann, the daughter of a Swiss artist who schooled her in music, history, and the visual arts, was one of the founding members of England's Royal Academy of Arts, to which she contributed many critically successful paintings based on classical subjects. Commissioned to paint portrait likenesses of many of her contemporaries (including Johann Winckelmann) during her sojourns in Rome, Florence, and London, she also became one of the most sought-after and highly paid portrait painters of her day. Kauffmann's history subjects, many of which served as models for wall and ceiling designs in the neoclassical interiors of Robert Adam (see Figure 26.18), reveal her familiarity with the figure types found in the wall paintings of Pompeii and Herculaneum, her love of lyrical linear compositions, and her skillful, fluent brushwork. These features are especially apparent in the painting, *Zeuxis Selecting Models for His Painting of Helen of Troy* (Figure 26.30), in which the Greek artist is shown (as described by ancient historians) choosing the finest features of his various female models, so as to combine them in an idealized image of Helen of Troy. Kauffmann herself may have served as the model for the figure at the far right.

Neoclassicism under Napoleon

While neoclassicism was the "official" style of the French Revolution, it soon became the vehicle of French imperialism. Under the leadership of Napoleon Bonaparte (1769–1821), the imagery of classical Greece and republican Rome was abandoned for the more appropriate imagery of Augustan Rome. Like the Roman emperors, Napoleon used the arts to magnify his greatness. He appointed David to commemorate his military achievements, and he commissioned architects to redesign Paris in the spirit of ancient Rome. Paris became a city of straight, wide avenues and huge, impressive squares. Imaginary axes linked the various monuments raised to honor the emperor, and older buildings were remodeled in the new Empire style. Alexandre-Pierre Vignon (1763–1828) redesigned the Church of Saint Mary Magdalene (called "La Madeleine") as a Roman temple dedicated to the glory of the French army (Figure 26.31). Fifty-two Corinthian columns, each 66 feet tall, surround the temple, which rises on a 23-foot-high podium, like a gigantic version of the Maison Carrée in Nîmes (Figure 26.32). Vignon's gloomy interior—a nave crowned with three domes—falls short of reflecting the majesty of the exterior, despite his use of the Corinthian and Ionic orders in the decorative scheme.

Elsewhere, Napoleon's neoclassicism was more precise. The Arc du Carrousel, which stands adjacent to the Louvre, is faithful to its Roman model, the Arch of Constantine in Rome. And the grandest of Paris' triumphal

Figure 26.30 ANGELICA KAUFFMANN, *Zeuxis Selecting Models for His Painting of Helen of Troy*, ca. 1765. Oil on canvas, 32⅛ × 44⅛ in. The Annmary Brown Memorial, Brown University, Providence, Rhode Island.

Figure 26.31 (below, left) ALEXANDRE-PIERRE VIGNON, Church of Saint Mary Magdalene ("La Madeleine"), Paris, 1807–1842. Length 350 ft., width 147 ft., height of podium 23 ft. © Paul M. R. Maeyaert, El Tossal, Spain.

Figure 26.32 (above) Maison Carrée, Nîmes, France, 16 B.C.E. © Paul M. R. Maeyaert, El Tossal, Spain.

arches, which occupies the crossing of twelve avenues at the end of the famous Avenue des Champs-Elysées (Figure **26.33**), closely resembles the Arch of Titus in the Roman Forum (see Figure 6.20). The 164-foot-high commemorative monument—which was dedicated to the French army—was larger than any arch built in ancient times. Napoleon would become one of the nineteenth century's most celebrated romantic heroes (see chapter 28), but the monuments he commissioned for Paris were stamped unmistakably with the classical spirit.

Eighteenth-Century Western Music

The eighteenth century was as rich in music as it was in the visual arts. Music filled the courts and concert halls, the latter as a response to a rising popular demand for public recitals. The eighteenth-century concert hall was small by modern standards. Its lights were rarely dimmed during performances and audiences were not expected to wait until the end of each piece to applaud. Often they showed their enthusiasm by applauding after a movement, insisting that it be repeated—a practice that is very much out of favor in our own time. Religious compositions were still in demand, but church music was overshadowed by the vast amounts of music composed for secular entertainment. Composers sought the patronage of wealthy aristocrats, at whose courts they often served. At the same time, composers wrote music for amateur performance and for the concert hall. While opera remained the favorite vocal form, instrumental music began to free itself from religious and ceremonial functions.

During the eighteenth century certain distinctive characteristics came to dominate European music. These included the idea that harmony is proper and essential to music, that a piece of music should be thoughtfully (and individually) composed, and that it should be studiously rehearsed and performed in much the same manner each time it is played. Such standards, which emphasize control

Science and Technology

1680s the earliest form of the clarinet is invented in Germany

1700 the French coin the term acoustics to describe the science of sound

Figure 26.33 JEAN-FRANÇOIS THÉRÈSE CHALGRIN AND OTHERS, Arc de Triomphe, Paris, 1806–1836. Height 164 ft. © Paul M. R. Maeyaert, El Tossal, Spain.

and formality over spontaneity and improvisation, set Western musical culture apart from that of Africa, Asia, and the rest of the world.

Rococo Music

By the middle of the eighteenth century, the rococo (or *galant*) style began to challenge the popularity of Bach and Handel. Rococo composers abandoned the intricate counterpoint and dense textures of the baroque in favor of light and graceful melodies organized into short, distinct phrases. As with rococo art, rococo music was delicate in sound, thin in texture, and natural in feeling. These qualities graced the works of the French composer François Couperin (1668–1733).

Couperin, a contemporary of Bach, wrote in both the baroque and rococo styles, as did many composers of the early eighteenth century. In 1716, Couperin published one of the most important musical treatises of the period, *The Art of Playing the Clavecin*, which offers precise instructions for keyboard fingering and for the execution of musical ornaments known as *agréments*. The rococo preference for intimate forms of expression cast in miniature is reflected in Couperin's suites for harpsichord (in French, *clavecin*). The individual sections of these suites bear playful titles based on women's names, parlor games, or human attributes, such as Languor, Coquetry, and Jealousy. "Le Croc-en-jambe" ("*donner un croc-en-jambe*" means "to trip up" or "to play a dirty trick"), for example, is itself a tripping, lighthearted piece. Couperin's suites were written for solo instruments or for ensembles and accompanied such dances as the courante, the minuet, and the sarabande, all of which were performed in fashionable eighteenth-century *salons*. Embroidered with florid *agréments*, Couperin's music shares the lighthearted spirit and fragile elegance of the rococo style in the visual arts.

Classical Music

The word *classical*, when used in reference to music, has two principal meanings. In its broadest sense, it describes that which is enduring and authoritative (see "The Classical Legacy," in Book 1); hence "classical" is commonly used to distinguish serious (or "art") music from the more ephemeral "popular" (or "folk") music. "Classical" is also employed, however, to describe a specific musical style that prevailed in the West between approximately 1760 and 1820—one that shares the essential features of Greco-Roman art: symmetry, order, and formal restraint. Unlike neoclassical art and architecture, classical music had little to do with the heritage of Greece and Rome, for European composers had no surviving evidence of Greek and Roman music and, therefore, no antique musical models to imitate. Nevertheless, classical music would develop its own unique model for clarity of form and purity of design. Classical composers, most of whom came from Germany and Austria, completed the liberation of melody from baroque polyphony, a process clearly anticipated in rococo music. They wrote homophonic compositions with easy-to-grasp melodies, which are repeated or developed within a definitive formal structure.

Although classical composers retained the fast/slow/fast contrasts of baroque instrumental forms, they rid their compositions of many baroque features. They replaced, for instance, the abrupt changes from loud to soft with more gently graduated contrasts. They eliminated the unflagging rhythms and ornate embellishments of baroque polyphony in favor of clear-cut musical phrases. While counterpoint continued to play an important role in classical music, the intricate webs of sound (as heard in Bach's fugues) gave way to a new harmonic clarity. In short, classical music developed formal attributes that reflect the Enlightenment quest for reasoned clarity and the neoclassical artist's commitment to balance and purity of design.

The Birth of the Symphony Orchestra

Eighteenth-century instrumental music served as secular entertainment in public theaters and in the *salons* of courtly residences. The most important instrumental grouping to emerge at this time was the orchestra. The eighteenth-century Bohemian composer Johann Stamitz (1717–1757), who settled in the South German town of Mannheim in the 1740s, organized what is thought to have been one of the earliest forms of the classical orchestra. It consisted of groups of related instruments, each with its own character or personality. The **strings**, made up of violins, violas, cellos, and double basses, formed the nucleus of the orchestra, since they were the most melodious and lyrical of the instrumental families. The **woodwinds**, consisting of flutes, oboes, clarinets, and bassoons, specialized in mellow harmonies. The **brass** section, made up of trumpets and French horns (and, by the end of the century, trombones), added volume and resonance. Lastly the **percussion** section, using kettledrums (also known as timpani), functioned as rhythm markers (Figure **26.34**). Stamitz's orchestra was small by modern-day standards. It included some thirty-five pieces, many of which were still rudimentary: brass instruments lacked valves, and the clarinet was not perfected until roughly 1790. The piano, which was invented around 1720, remained until 1775 more closely related to the clavichord than to the modern grand piano. During the last quarter of the century, however, as the piano underwent technical refinement, it came to be the favorite solo instrument.

As musical instruments became more sophisticated, the orchestra, capable of an increasingly expressive and subtle range of sounds, grew in size and popularity. The eighteenth-century orchestra was led by a musician (often the composer himself) who played part of the composition on the clavier or keyboard instrument located at the place now occupied by the conductor's podium. The string section was seated to the right and left, while the other instruments were spread across the middle distance, in a pattern that has persisted to this day.

To facilitate the conductor's control over the music, the orchestra used a **score**, that is, a record of musical notation that indicates every sound to be played by each instrument. Each musical part appeared in groups of five-line

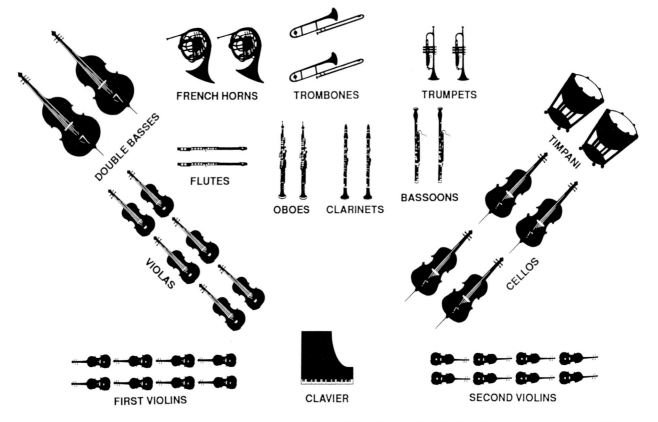

FRENCH HORNS

TROMBONES

TRUMPETS

DOUBLE BASSES

TIMPANI

FLUTES

OBOES   CLARINETS

BASSOONS

VIOLAS

CELLOS

FIRST VIOLINS

CLAVIER

SECOND VIOLINS

Figure 26.34 The classical symphony orchestra. From Carter Harmon, *A Popular History of Music*. Copyright © 1956 by Carter Harmon. Used by permission of Dell Books, a division of Bantam Doubleday Dell Publishing Group, Inc.

staffs that enabled the conductor to "view" the composition as a whole. Separate parts were written out for each instrument as well. In the eighteenth century, both instrumentation and methods of scoring became standardized. Scores included a time signature, which indicated the number of beats per measure; a key signature, which noted the number of sharps or flats in the specified key; and abbreviations of the Italian words that indicated the dynamics of specific passages: *f* for *forte* ("loud") and *p* for *piano* ("soft"). Interpretive directions, such as *scherzando* ("sprightly") and *affettuoso* ("with feeling"), signified the intentions of the composer as to how a musical passage should be performed. All these notational devices served the principle of formality that governed eighteenth-century music and Western musical composition in general.

Classical Instrumental Compositions

Classical composers wrote music for a variety of instrumental groupings. The largest of these was the orchestral form known as the **symphony**. The Italian word *sinfonia* was used during the seventeenth century to describe various kinds of instrumental pieces; but, by the mid-eighteenth century, the word came to mean an independent instrumental composition for full orchestra. In addition to the symphony, three other instrumental genres dominated the classical era: the **concerto**, a composition featuring one or more solo instruments and an orchestra; the **string quartet**, a piece for two violins, a viola, and a cello; and the **sonata**, a composition for an unaccompanied keyboard instrument or for another instrument with keyboard accompaniment.

Although the concerto and the sonata originated earlier (see chapter 23), they now took on a new formality. Indeed, all four instrumental forms—the symphony, the classical concerto, the string quartet, and the classical sonata—assumed the same formal structure: they were divided into three or four sections, or movements, each of which followed a specific tempo, or musical pace. The first movement was played *allegro* or in fast tempo; the second *andante* or *largo*, that is, in moderate or slow tempo; the third movement (usually omitted in concertos) was written in dance tempo (usually in three-quarter time); and the fourth was again *allegro*.

For the organization of the first and last movements, classical composers used a special form known as **sonata form** (or **sonata allegro** form; Figure **26.35**). This calls for the division of the movement into three parts: the exposition, the development, and the recapitulation. In the exposition, the composer "exposes," or introduces, a theme in the "home" key, then contrasts it with a second theme in a different key. Musical effect is based on the tension of two opposing key centers. In the development, the composer moves to further contrasting keys, expanding and altering the themes stated in the exposition. Finally, in the recapitulation, the themes from the exposition are restated, both now in the home key, resolving the earlier tension. A **coda** ("tail") is often added as a definitive end piece.

Classical composers frequently deviated from sonata form, but they looked to it to provide the "rules" of musical design—the architectural guidelines, so to speak, for musical composition. Just as neoclassical artists and writers favored clear definitions and an Aristotelian "beginning, middle, and end," so classical composers delighted in the threefold balance of the sonata form, the repetition of simple harmonies, and the crisp phrasing of bright, free-flowing melodies.

The Development of the Classical Style: Haydn

The classical style owes its development to the Austrian composer Franz Joseph Haydn (1732–1809). Of peasant birth, Haydn was recruited at the age of eight to sing in the choir of Saint Stephen's Cathedral in Vienna. As a young man, he taught music and struggled to make a living. In 1761, at the age of twenty-nine, he became musical director to the court of the powerful and wealthy Hungarian nobleman Prince Paul Anton Esterházy, who was also an accomplished musician. The magnificent Esterházy country estate (modeled on Versailles) included two theaters— one for opera and one for puppet plays—and two richly appointed concert halls. There, for almost thirty years, Haydn took charge of all aspects of musical entertainment: he composed music, trained choristers, oversaw the repair of instruments, and rehearsed and conducted an orchestra of some twenty-five musicians. At the princely court, Haydn produced music for various instrumental groups. Tailoring his creative talents to suit special occasions and the tastes of his wealthy patron, he wrote operas, oratorios, solo concertos, sonatas, overtures, and liturgical music. But his most original works were those whose forms he himself helped to develop: the classical symphony and the string quartet. The "father of the symphony," as Haydn is often called, wrote 104 symphonies and 84 string quartets. The string quartet, a concentrated instrumental form, met the need for elite entertainment in a small room or chamber—hence the term "chamber music." Unlike the symphony, the string quartet requires close attention to the fine points of musical discourse between the instruments. Unfortunately, such works are today often performed in huge music halls, rather than in the intimate surroundings for which they were intended.

After the death of Prince Esterházy in 1790, Haydn was invited to perform in London, where he composed his last twelve symphonies. In the London symphonies, which he wrote for an orchestra of some sixty players, he explored an expanded harmonic range and a wealth of dramatic effects. For some of the symphonies he used folk melodies as basic themes, inventively repeating key fragments in different parts of the piece. Among the most memorable of the London symphonies is No. 94, nicknamed "The Surprise" because Haydn introduced an unexpected *fortissimo* ("very loud") instrumental crash on a weak beat in the second movement of the piece. Tradition has it that the blaring chord was calculated to waken a drowsy audience— London concerts often lasted well past midnight—and entice them to anticipate the next "surprise," which never does occur. Haydn brought a lifetime of musical experience to his last works. Their witty phrasing and melodic effects made these symphonies enormously popular—so popular, in fact, that eighteenth-century music publishers often sold compositions that they falsely attributed to Haydn. A celebrity in his old age, "Papa Haydn" (as he was affectionately called) was one of the first musicians to attain the status of a culture hero during his own lifetime.

The Genius of Mozart

The foremost musical genius of the eighteenth century— and, some would say, of all time—was Haydn's younger contemporary and colleague, Wolfgang Amadeus Mozart (1756–1791). A child prodigy, Mozart wrote his first original composition at the age of six and his first symphony at the age of eight. His ability to sight read, improvise, and transpose music, to identify the pitch of any sound, and to transcribe flawlessly whole compositions that he had heard only once, remains unequaled in the history of music. During his brief life, Mozart produced a total of some 650 works, including 41 symphonies, 60 sonatas, 23 piano concertos, 70 string quartets, and 20 operas.

♪ See Music Listening Selections at end of chapter.

Figure 26.35 Sonata form.

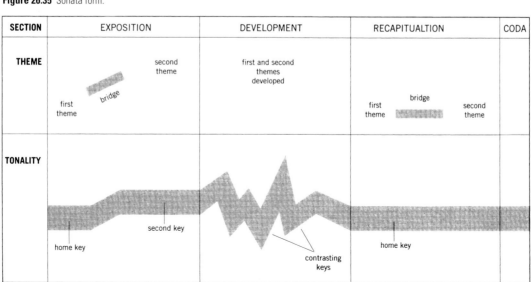

(These were catalogued and numbered in the late nineteenth century by Ludwig von Köchel, hence the "K." numbers used to identify Mozart's compositions.)

Wolfgang, the son of a prominent composer, was born in Salzburg, Austria. With his father, Leopold, and his sister Nannerl, he toured Europe, performing hundreds of public and private concerts before he was thirteen (Figure 26.36). He often performed his own pieces, particularly his piano concertos, which constitute some of his most important musical contributions. Unlike Haydn, Mozart did not invent any new forms. However, he brought to the instrumental genres of his time unparalleled melodic inventiveness. He borrowed melodies from popular dance tunes and transformed them into elegant compositions appropriate for garden parties, weddings, and balls. One such piece is the Serenade in G Major, K. 525, also known as "Eine kleine Nachtmusik" ("A Little Night Music"), a work for small string orchestra. He incorporated popular melodies into his symphonies as well, three of which (K. 543, K. 550, and K. 551) were written in a six-week period in 1788. These pieces remain among the most eloquent examples of the classical symphonic form.

After leaving the service of the Archbishop of Salzburg in 1781, Mozart sought appointments in the aristocratic courts of Europe, but he never received adequate patronage and had difficulty supporting himself and his family. Throughout his life, he was excessively concerned with money; when he died in Vienna at the age of thirty-six, he was buried in a pauper's grave.* During the last six years of his life, Mozart wrote four of his finest operas, receiving commissions for all but the first. These works are among the best loved in the Western operatic repertory: *Le nozze di Figaro* (*The Marriage of Figaro*, 1786), *Don Giovanni* (1787), *Così fan tutte* (*Thus Do All Women*, 1790), and *Die Zauberflöte* (*The Magic Flute*, 1791).

The *Marriage of Figaro* is an example of **opera buffa**, a type of comic opera that developed during the eighteenth century as a short, humorous entertainment. Formerly inserted between the acts of a serious play or opera, these intermezzos made use of stock, comic types such as the clever servant, the miser, and the fool. Like the playwright Molière (see chapter 21), Mozart transformed the stock characters of the Italian *opera buffa* into psychologically penetrating personalities. At the same time, he leveled a pointed attack on the decadence of the European aristocracy. Indeed, Mozart would have shared Molière's view that wealth and status are accidents of fortune, rather than marks of personal worth. The central intrigue of *Figaro* involves the maid Susanna and her fiancé, the valet Figaro, in a plot to outwit their master Count Almaviva, who seeks to seduce Susanna. In an era dominated by aristocratic privilege, and one that still honored the feudal claim to "first-night rights" over a female servant, The

Marriage of Figaro was unique: it championed the wit and ingenuity of the lower class (and especially the females of that class) over the self-serving arrogance of the nobility. And while such a theme might seem less than controversial today, it stirred heated debate in Mozart's time—Napoleon called the play by Pierre-Augustin Beaumarchais (1732–1799), on which the opera was based, "revolution already in action." Certainly Mozart was more interested in music than in political reform—he agreed to temper Beaumarchais' scolding satire by way of Lorenzo da Ponte's Italian libretto. But his scorn for the upper classes—perhaps stemming from his own personal difficulties with aristocratic patrons—is readily apparent in the piece.

Politics aside, the enduring beauty of *The Marriage of Figaro* lies in its lyrical force and its expressive ingenuity. Mozart had a special talent for shaping personalities by way of music. While the characters in the operas of Monteverdi and Lully were allegorical stick figures, Mozart's appeal to us as real human beings. They convey a wide range of human expression, from grief and despair to hope and joy. Mozart's vocal music is never sentimental; it retains the precision and clarity of the classical style and invests it with unparalleled melodic grace. Only by listening to Mozart's music can one appreciate the reason why Haydn called him "the greatest composer known to me either in person or by name."

Beethoven: The Early Years

Generally considered the third of the great classical composers, Ludwig van Beethoven (1770–1827) spanned the era between the classical and romantic styles in music. Born in Bonn, in northern Germany, Beethoven spent the greater part of his life in Vienna, where he studied briefly with Haydn. His earliest works, mainly keyboard pieces composed between 1782 and 1792, reveal his debt to Mozart, as well as his facility with classical form and style. Between 1793 and 1803, his first years in Vienna, Beethoven made his name as a virtuoso pianist, a composer of piano pieces, and a master of the string quartet. By 1799, however, he began to break with the more formal aspects of classical music. By the turn of the century, his compositions, which include the first two of his nine symphonies, would anticipate the tension and vigor, the emphasis on rhythm rather than melody, and the forceful instrumental language that would stretch classical form, and, ultimately, challenge the classical style (see chapter 29).

SUMMARY

Eighteenth-century European art and music reflected the changing character and tastes of its various social classes. The fashionable rococo style reflected the aristocratic affection for ornamental delicacy, intimacy, and playful elegance. This style dominated the salons of Paris and the courts and churches of Austria and Germany. In France, Watteau, Boucher, Vigée-Lebrun, Fragonard, and Clodion produced art that evoked a world of physical pleasure and sensuous delight.

♪ See Music Listening Selections at end of chapter.

*For a fascinating interpretation of Mozart's life, see the play *Amadeus* by Peter Shaffer (New York: Harper and Row, 1981) and the Academy Award-winning film version of the play produced in 1984.

Figure 26.36 LOUIS CARMONTELLE, *The Mozarts in Concert: Leopold, Wolfgang (age seven), and Nannerl*, 1764. Engraving. Reproduced by courtesy of the Trustees of the British Museum, London.

By mid-century, a reaction against the rococo style occurred among members of a growing middle class, who identified their interests with the rational ideals of the European Enlightenment. Encouraged by the *philosophes'* demand for an art of moral virtue, Greuze and Chardin produced genre paintings that gave dignity to the life and work of ordinary individuals. At the same time, archeological investigations in Greece and Southern Italy encouraged new interest in the classical past. Neoclassicism swept away the rococo in the same way that the French Revolution swept away the Old Regime. David's stirring pictorial recreations of Greek and Roman history invoked a message of self-sacrifice and moral purpose.

The neoclassical style symbolized the Enlightenment ideals of reason and liberty. In America neoclassicism was best expressed in the architectural achievements of Thomas Jefferson. In Europe, neoclassicism influenced all the arts, from Adam's English country houses and Soufflot's "Panthéon" to the portraits of Houdon and the ceramics of Wedgwood. During the reign of Napoleon, neoclassicists drew on the arts of imperial Rome to glorify Paris and the emperor himself.

The period between 1760 and approximately 1820 witnessed the birth of the orchestra and the development of the classical forms of Western instrumental music.

Classical music was characterized by order, symmetry, and intellectual control—features similar to those admired by neoclassical writers, painters, sculptors, and architects. Composers used the sonata form to govern the composition of the symphony, the string quartet, the sonata, and the concerto. Haydn shaped the character of the classical symphony and the string quartet; Mozart moved easily between rococo and classical styles, investing both with extraordinary melodic grace. In his operas, as well as in his symphonies, Mozart achieved a balance between lyrical invention and technical control that brought the classical style to its peak. In the decades to follow, the restrained formalism of the European Enlightenment would yield to the seductive embrace of the Romantic Era.

MUSIC LISTENING SELECTIONS

CD Two Selection 8   Couperin, "Le Croc-en-jambe" from Ordre No. 22, harpsichord, 1730.

CD Two Selection 9   Haydn, Symphony No. 94 in G Major, "Surprise," second movement, excerpt, 1791.

CD Two Selection 10   Mozart, Serenade No. 3 in G Major, K. 525, "Eine kleine Nachtmusik," first movement, excerpt, 1787.

CD Two Selection 11   Mozart, *Le nozze di Figaro*, "Dove sono" aria, 1786.

GLOSSARY

allegro   (Italian, "cheerful") a fast tempo in music

andante   (Italian, "going," i.e., a normal walking pace) a moderate tempo in music

bacchante   a female attendant or devotee of Dionysus

brass   a family of wind instruments that usually includes the French horn, trumpet, trombone, and tuba

coda   (Italian, "tail") passage added to the closing section of a movement or musical composition in order to create the sense of a definite ending

concerto   see Glossary, chapter 23; the classical concerto, which made use of *sonata form*, usually featured

one or more solo instruments and orchestra

fête galante   (French, "elegant entertainment") a festive diversion enjoyed by aristocrats, a favored subject in rococo art

fortissimo   (Italian, "very loud") a directive indicating that the music should be played very loud; its opposite is *pianissimo* ("very soft")

largo   (Italian, "broad") a very slow tempo; the slowest of the conventional tempos in music

opera buffa   a type of comic opera usually featuring stock characters

percussion   a group of instruments that are sounded by being struck or shaken, used especially for rhythm

satyr   a semi*bestial woodland creature symbolic of Dionysus

score   the musical notation for all of the instruments or voices in a particular composition; a composite from which the whole piece may be conducted or studied

sonata   a composition for an unaccompanied keyboard instrument or for another instrument with keyboard accompaniment; see also Glossary, chapter 23

sonata form (or **sonata allegro form**)   a structural form commonly used in the late eighteenth century for the first and fourth movements of symphonies and other instrumental compositions

string quartet   a composition for four stringed instruments, each of which plays its own part

strings   a family of instruments that usually includes the violin, viola, cello, and double bass (which are normally bowed); the harp, guitar, lute, and zither (which are normally plucked) can also be included, as can the viol, a bowed instrument common in the sixteenth and seventeenth centuries and a forerunner of the violin family

symphony   an independent instrumental composition for orchestra

woodwinds   a family of wind instruments, usually consisting of the flute, oboe, clarinet, and bassoon

Suggestions for Reading

CHAPTER 20

Bantel, Linda, and M. B. Burke. *Spain and New Spain: Mexican Colonial Arts in their European Context*. Corpus Christi, Tex.: Art Museum of South Texas, 1992.

Bianconi, Lorenzo. *Music in the Seventeenth Century*, translated by David Bryant. New York: Cambridge University Press, 1987.

Hammond, Frederick. *Music and Spectacle in Baroque Rome*. New Haven: Yale University Press, 1994.

Harbison, Robert. *Reflections on Baroque*. Chicago: University of Chicago, 2001.

Harris, Ann S. and K. P. Laurence. *Art and Architecture of the Seventeenth Century*. Upper Saddle River, N.J.: Prentice-Hall, 2004.

Marden, T. A. *Bernini and the Art of Architecture*. New York: Abbeville Press, 1999.

Martin, John Rupert. *Baroque*. New York: Harper, 1977.

Mullett, Michael A. *The Catholic Reformation*. New York: Routledge, 1999

Petersson, Robert T. *The Art of Ecstasy: Teresa, Bernini and Crashaw*. New York: Atheneum, 1970.

Puglisi, Catherine. *Caravaggio*. New York: Phaidon, 2003.

Sternfeld, F. W. *The Birth of Opera*. New York: Oxford University Press, 1995.

CHAPTER 21

Asher, Catherine B. *Architecture of Mughal India*. New York: Cambridge University Press, 1992.

Beguin, Giles and D. Morel. *Discoveries: The Forbidden City*. New York: Abrams, 1997.

De Montclos, Jean-Marie Perouse. *Versailles*. New York: Abbeville Press, 2005.

Delay, Nelly. *The Art and Culture of Japan*. New York: Abrams, 1998.

Howarth, W. D. *Molière: A Playwright and his Audience*. Cambridge: Cambridge University Press, 1982.

Lewis, W. H. *The Splendid Century: Life in the France of Louis XIV*. New York: Waveland Press, 1997.

Michell, George. *The Royal Palaces of India*. London: Thames and Hudson, 1994.

Mitford, Nancy. *The Sun King: Louis XIV at Versailles*. New York: Rpt. edn. Penguin USA, 1995. Harper and Row, 1966.

Scott, Virginia. *Molière: A Theatrical Life*. New York: Cambridge University Press, 2002.

Singer, Robert T. et al. *Edo: Art in Japan 1615–1868*. New Haven, Conn.: Yale University Press, 1999.

Spence, Jonathan D. *Emperor of China: Self-Portrait of K'ang Hsi*. New York: Vintage, 1988.

Vivier, Frederika. *Versailles: Its History, Its Splendor and Its Gardens*. New York: Moliere, 2002.

Wright, Christopher. *The French Painters of the Seventeenth Century*. New York: New York Graphic Society, 1986.

CHAPTER 22

Arnold, Denis. *Bach*. New York: Oxford University Press, 1984.

Clark, Kenneth. *An Introduction to Rembrandt*. New York: Harper, 1978.

Kahr, Madlyn M. *Dutch Painting in the Seventeenth Century*. New York: Harper, 1978.

McGrath, Alister. *In the Beginning: The Story of the King James Bible and How It Changed a Nation, a Language, and a Culture*. New York: Doubleday, 2001.

Palisca, C. V. *Baroque Music*, 3rd ed. Englewood Cliffs, N.J.: Prentice Hall, 1991.

Price, J. L. *Culture and Society in the Dutch Republic during the Seventeenth Century*. New York: Scribners, 1974.

Schama, Simon. *An Embarrassment of Riches: An Interpretation of Dutch Art*. New York: Knopf, 1987.

Schulenberg, David. *Music of the Baroque*. New York: Oxford University Press, 2001.

Schwendowlus, Barbara, and Wolfgang Dömling, eds. *Johann Sebastian Bach: Life, Times, Influence*. Basel: Bärenreiter Kassell, 1997.

Wolff, Christoph. *Johann Sebastian Bach: The Learned Musician*. New York: Norton, 2000.

CHAPTER 23

Alpers, Svetlana. *The Art of Describing: Dutch Art in the Seventeenth Century*. Chicago: University of Chicago Press, 1983.

——*Rembrandt's Enterprise: The Studio and the Market*. Chicago: University of Chicago Press, 1990.

Chapman, H. P. *Rembrandt's Self-Portraits: A Study in Seventeenth-Century Identity*. Princeton, N.J.: Princeton University Press, 1990.

Donington, Robert. *Baroque Music: Style and Performance*. New York: Norton, 1982.

Edgerton. Samuel Y. *The Heritage of Giotto's Geometry: Art and Science on the Eve of the Scientific Revolution*. Ithaca: Cornell University Press, 1994.

Hall, A. Rupert. *The Revolution in Science: 1500–1750*. New York: Longman, 1983.

Jacob, Margaret C. *The Cultural Meaning of the Scientific Revolution*. New York: Knopf, 1988.

Lloyd, Christopher. *Enchanting the Eye: Dutch Painting of the Golden Age*. London: Royal Collection, 2005.

Montias, John M. *Vermeer and His Milieu*. Princeton, N.J.: Princeton University Press, 1991.

Shapin, Steven. *The Scientific Revolution*. Chicago: University of Chicago Press, 1996.

Wheelock, Arthur K., Jr. *Vermeer and the Art of Painting*. New Haven: Yale University Press, 1995.

CHAPTER 24

Becker, Carl L. *The Heavenly City of the Eighteenth-Century Philosophers*. New Haven: Nota Bene, 2003. (reprint)

Gay, Peter. *The Enlightenment: The Science of Freedom*. New York: Norton, 1996.

Goodman, Dana. *The Republic of Letters: A Cultural History of the French Enlightenment*. Ithaca: Cornell University Press, 1996.

Gordon, Lyndall. *Vindication: A Life of Mary Wollstonecraft*. New York, HarperCollins, 2005.

Krieger, Leonard. *Kings and Philosophies 1689–1789*. Vol. 3 of *The Norton History of Modern Europe*. New York: Norton, 1970.

Outram, Dovinda. *The Enlightenment*. New York: Cambridge University Press, 1995.

Porter, Roy. *The Creation of the Modern World: The British Enlightenment*. New York: W. W. Norton, 2000.

Richard, Carl J. *The Founders and the Classics: Greece, Rome, and the American Enlightenment*. Cambridge, Mass.: Harvard University Press, 1994.

Sloan, Kim, ed. *Enlightenment: Discovering the World in Eighteenth Century*. London: The British Museum, 2003.

Vyverberg, Henry. *Human Nature, Cultural Diversity, and the French Enlightenment*. New York: Oxford University Press, 1989.

Watt, Ian. *The Rise of the Novel: Studies in Defoe, Richardson, and Fielding*. Berkeley, Calif.: University of California Press, 1957.

CHAPTER 25

Adams, F. D. and Barry Sanders, eds. *Three Black Writers in Eighteenth-Century England*. Belmont, Calif.: Wadsworth, 1971.

Babbitt, Irving. *Rousseau and Romanticism*. New York: Meridian, 1977.

Bernier, Olivier. *Words of Fire, Deeds of Blood: The Mob, the Monarchy, and the French Revolution*. Boston: Little, Brown, 1989.

Dunn, Susan. *Sister Revolutions: French Lightning, American Light*. New York: Faber & Faber, 1999.

Gershoy, Leo. *From Despotism to Revolution, 1763–1789*. Westport, Conn.: Greenwood Press, 1983.

Hallett, Mark. *The Spectacle of Difference: Graphic Satire in the Age of Hogarth*. New Haven, Conn.: Yale University Press, 1999.

Porter, Roy. *Flesh in the Age of Reason*. New York: Norton, 2004.

Richter, Peyton, and Ilona Ricardo. *Voltaire*. Boston: Twayne, 1980.

Sheriff, Mary D. *Moved by Love: Inspired Artists and Deviant Women in Eighteenth-Century France*. Chicago: University of Chicago, 2003.

Thomas, Hugh. *The Slave Trade: The Story of the Atlantic Slave Trade, 1440–1870*. New York: Simon & Schuster, 1997.

Uglow, Jennifer. *Hogarth: A Life and a World*. New York: Farrar Straus Giroux, 1997.

CHAPTER 26

Bernier, Olivier. *The Eighteenth-Century Woman*. New York: Doubleday, 1981.

Gutman, Robert W. *Mozart: A Cultural Biography*. New York: Harcourt Brace, 1999.

Harries, Karsten. *The Bavarian Rococo Church: Between Faith and Aestheticism*. New Haven: Yale University Press, 1983.

Irwin, David. *Neoclassicism*. London: Phaidon, 1997.

Jones, Stephen. *The Eighteenth Century*. Cambridge: Cambridge University Press, 1985.

Levey, Michael. *From Rococo to Revolution: Major Trends in Eighteenth-Century Painting*. New York: Norton, 1985.

Minor, Vernon Hyde. *Baroque and Rococo: Art and Culture*. Upper Saddle River, N. J.: Prentice-Hall, 2003.

Park, William. *The Idea of Rococo*. Cranbury, N.J.: University of Delaware Press, 1992.

Rosen, Charles. *The Classical Style: Haydn, Mozart, Beethoven*. New York: Norton, 1997.

Sheriff, Mary D. *The Exceptional Woman: Elizabeth Vigée-LeBrun and the Cultural Politics of Art*. Chicago: University of Chicago Press, 1996.

Solomon, Maynard. *Mozart*. New York: Harper, 1995.

Till, Nicolas, ed. *Mozart and the Enlightenment: Truth, Virtue, and Beauty in Mozart's Operas*. New York: Norton, 1993.

Wills, Garry. *Mr. Jefferson's University*. Washington, D.C.: National Geographic, 2003.

CREDITS

The author and publishers wish to thank the following for permission to use copyright material. Every effort has been made to trace or contact copyright holders, but if notified of any omissions, Laurence King Publishing would be pleased to insert the appropriate acknowledgement in any subsequent edition of this publication.

CHAPTER 20

READING 4.1 (p. 4): From *The Spiritual Exercises of St. Ignatius*, translated by Louis J. Puhl, S.J. (Loyola Press, 1951).Reprinted by permission of the publisher.

READING 4.2 (p. 7): From *The Complete Works of Saint Teresa of Jesus*, Vol. 1, translated by E. A. Peers, 1957. (Sheed & Ward, 1957), © 1957 Sheed & Ward Ltd., London. Reprinted by permission of Sheed & Ward, an Apostolate of the Priests of the Sacred Heart. 7373 South Lover's Lane Road, Franklin, Wisconsin 53132.

READING 4.3 (p. 7): From *The Poems of Richard Crashaw*, edited by L. C. Martin (Oxford University Press, 1957).

Boxed Insert (p. 14): From *New Revised Standard Version Bible with Apocryphal/Deuterocanonical Books* (HarperCollins Study Bible, 1991).

CHAPTER 21

READING 4.4 (p. 39): From *The Maxims of La Rochefoucauld*, translated by Louise Kronenberger (Random House, 1959), © 1959 Random House Inc., New York.

READING 4.5 (p. 40): From *Molière, Le Bourgeois Gentilhomme (The Tradesman Turned Gentleman)*, translated by Curtis Hidden Page (modernized by the author). (G. P. Putnam's Sons, 1908).

INSERT (p. 58): Matsuo Basho, five haikus from *An Introduction to Haiku* by Harold G. Henderson (Doubleday, 1958), © 1958 by Harold G. Henderson. Reprinted by permission of Doubleday, a division of Random House, Inc.

CHAPTER 22

READING 4.6 (p. 62): The "Twenty-Third Psalm" from *Douay Bible*, reprinted in *The College Survey of English Literature*, Shorter Edition by Alexander Witherspoon (Harcourt Brace Jovanovich, 1951). Reprinted by permission of the publisher; The "Twenty-Third Psalm" from *Authorised Version of the Bible (The King James Bible)* (Cambridge University Press).

READING 4.7 (p. 62), 4.8 (p. 64): From John Donne, *Devotions upon Emergent Occasions and Songs and Sonnets in The College Survey of English Literature*, Shorter Edition by Alexander Witherspoon (Harcourt Brace Jovanovich, 1951).

READING 4.9 (p. 65): From John Milton, *Paradise Lost: A Norton Critical Edition*. Second Edition, edited by Scott Elledge (Norton, 1975), © 1993, 1975 by W. W. Norton & Company, Inc. Reprinted by permission of the publisher. (footnotes).

CHAPTER 23

READING 4.10 (p. 78), 4.11 (p. 80): From Sir Francis Bacon, *Novum Organum* and *Of Studies* in *The Complete Works of Francis Bacon*, translated by James Spedding (modernized by the author). (Longman, 1960).

READING 4.12 (p. 81): From René Descartes, *Discourse on Method* in *Descartes Selections*, edited by Ralph M. Eaton. (Scribner, 1927), © 1927 Charles Scribner's Sons, © renewed 1955.

READING 4.13 (p. 82): From John Locke, *Essay Concerning Human Understanding* in *The Philosophic Works of John Locke*, edited by J. A. St. John (modernized by the author). (George Bell & Sons, 1892).

CHAPTER 24

READING 4.14 (p. 98): From Thomas Hobbes, *Leviathan*, edited by Herbert W. Schneider (Macmillan ,1958), © 1985, 1958 by Macmillan Publishing Company.

READING 4.15 (p. 100): From John Locke, *Of Civil Government in The Works of John Locke* (modernized by the author). (Thomas Tegg, 1823.)

READING 4.16 (p. 101): From T*homas Jefferson, The Declaration of Independence* (1776).

READING 4.17 (p. 103): From: *Adam Smith, An Inquiry into the Nature and Causes of the Wealth of Nations* (George Routledge and Sons, 1913).

READING 4.18 (p. 106): From Denis Diderot, *Encyclopédie in Diderot's Selected Writings*, edited by L. G. Crocker and D. Coltman (Macmillan, 1966), © 1966 by Macmillan Publishing Company. Reprinted by permission of Prentice Hall, Inc., Upper Saddle River, NJ.

READING 4.19 (p. 108): From Antoine Nicolas de Condorcet, *Sketch for a Historical Picture of the Progress of the Human Mind*, translated by June Barraclough (Weidenfeld & Nicolson, 1955), © 1955 George Weidenfeld & Nicolson Ltd. Reprinted-by permission of The Orion Publishing Group.

READING 4.20 (p. 109): From Mary Wollstonecraft, *A Vindication of the Rights of Woman* in *The Works of Mary Wollstonecraft*. Volume 5, edited by Jane Todd and Marilyn Butler (New York University Press, 1989).

READING 4.21 (p. 112): From Alexander Pope, *Essay on Man* in *Poetical Works of Alexander Pope* (Little Brown, 1854).

CHAPTER 25

READING 4.22 (p. 115): From Olaudah Equiano, *Travels*, edited by Paul Edwards (Heinemann Educational Books, 1970). Reprinted by permission of Reed Educational & Professional Publishing Ltd.

READING 4.23 (p. 118): Phillis Wheatley, 'On Being Brought from Africa to America' from *The Poems of Phillis Wheatley*, edited by Julian D. Mason (University of North Carolina Press, 1989).

READING 4.24 (p. 119): From Jonathan Swift, *A Modest Proposal*, from *The College Survey of English Literature*, edited by Alexander M. Witherspoon (Harcourt, Brace and Co, 1951).

READING 4.25 (p. 122): From Voltaire, *Candide* in *The Best Known Works of Voltaire* (Blue Ribbon Books, 1927). (with notes by G. K. Fiero; modernized and edited by G. K. Fiero).

READING 4.26 (p.131): From Li Ju-chen, *Flowers in the Mirror*, translated by Lin Tai-yi (University of California Press, 1965). Reprinted by permission of Peter Owen Ltd., London.

READING 4.27 (p.134): From Jean-Jacques Rousseau, *Discourse on the Origin of Inequality among Men*, translated by Maurice Cranston (Viking Penguin, 1984), translation © 1984 by Maurice Cranston. Reprinted by permission of Peters Fraser & Dunlop Group Ltd.

Index